Professional Reviews

"It's rare to find a book that truly captures the unique and sometimes brutal grandeur of Alaska. *Waiting to Deliver* is a must read for anyone who enjoys boats, fish, the ocean or Good Writing. Dixon has the experience and artistic chops to spin a winner."

– Bryan Willis, Artistic Director, Northwest Playwrights Alliance @ Seattle Repertory Theatre.

"Let me confess: I know Pat Dixon as a poet. I also knew that he was an excellent photographer; but I'm not sure I knew he was writing an account of his previous life—an epic journey—as a fisherman.

In *Waiting to Deliver*, we encounter both hardship on deck and success pulled from the sea, ingenious mechanical solutions and reckless navigating blunders. The book tells of shrimp, salmon and halibut, of rips, reds, and brailers and bibs.

Did I mention that the stunning black and white photos tell their own tale? And there's one more thing (which you might have guessed): the book gives us many fine poems. Dixon's ear for rhythmical language, for memorable details, for caring images of his companions (through words and the lens)— all of these make for a memorable read, for which the coda (from Dixon's poem *Farewell*) might read:

‘None of us
gets to choose
how it ends,
only how it goes'"

~ Tod Marshall, Washington State Poet Laureate, 2016-2018

Fan Reviews

"This book tells of a life that I never knew existed. Pat Dixon's prose grabbed me by the scruff and immersed me in his unimaginable adventures. He guided me through his apprenticeship in the fishing trade, making me feel like I was there on the pitching deck with him. As he transitions to becoming a seasoned ship captain, I felt like I got to know a bit of his soul too. He shares stories of survival, and stories of what a good day and a bad day look like. And in those situations, I got to see what he was thinking and why. I've never read anything like it."
— Ed, Bend, Oregon

"Like the salmon he sought, Pat's work explores the breadth of his fishing experiences and the depth of his consciousness. He weaves the immersive beauty of Alaskan waters with his thought-provoking artistic insights. You will enjoy exploring the world of this intelligent, reflective and talented fisher-poet."
— Doug, Lacey, Washington

"As a former Alaskan, I knew a little about commercial fishing and thought of it as a dangerous and tedious occupation. I learned it is indeed dangerous at times, but tedious? Dixon's accounts show it to be anything but. At times hilarious, other times tense or wacky, but always downright fascinating, his stories of life on and off Cook Inlet are great reading. His first-person accounts captivated me from the get-go and never let up. Great read!"
— Marc, Portland, Oregon

"When my friend Pat asked me to proof his memoir *Waiting to Deliver*, I jumped at the chance. My true motivation was to learn more about the 20+ years Pat lived in Alaska, when our contact was limited.

What I found was a "coming of age" story as it traces Pat's journey from a landlocked, greenhorn Hoosier to a respected Alaskan commercial fishing skipper.

An argument could also be made that Waiting to Deliver is a love story. Pat's poetry and photographs of the people in his life, the boats and cannery, as well as the beautiful shots of Alaska help the reader connect intimately."

— Jeremy, Zionsville, Indiana

"Got the book yesterday and read it all the way through immediately. It was fantastic! I even recognized a few boats' names because they're still around. Thank you for providing a window into the heyday of Cook Inlet fishing and an amazing reading experience. I'll be recommending it to all my friends."

— Dominick, Bozeman, Montana

"I have just finished reading *Waiting to Deliver*. It has taken my breath away. It is now my touchstone for all other memoirs. I am windswept with emotion, on a sea of sensory adventure-of the body, mind and soul."

— Donna, Whitehouse Station, NJ

and may you in your innocence
sail through this to that

from Blessing of the Boats
~ (at St. Mary's)

Lucille Clifton

WAITING TO DELIVER

– from greenhorn to skipper –

an Alaskan commercial fishing memoir

Patrick Dixon

ISBN: 978-1-0880261-3-7 (Paperback)
ISBN 978-0-9904960-5-2 (ebook)

Cover design by Toshiro Stang

FisherPoets Gathering Publishing
Olympia, Washington

Dixonphoto@comcast.net
www.patrickdixon.net
www.pdixonphotography.com

Previously Published

I greatly appreciate the editors and publishers of the following magazines, journals and anthologies who gave these pieces their first home.

Boat Puller	Cirque Literary Journal
Fat City	Alaska Fisherman's Journal
Flash in the Distance	FISH Anthology 2015
Mending Holes	North Pacific Focus
Middle Rip	*Like Fish in the Freezer*
Never Cross the Lines	National Fisherman
Overboard	*Anchored in Deep Water*
The Connection	Journal of Family Life

Acknowledgments

There's a long list of people to thank for their help and encouragement in writing this book but most especially my muse, mentor, critic, titler and unbelievably patient and wonderful wife, Veronica Kessler. My sons Kessler and Dylan have offered sound, honest advice on content and design, as has my generous nephew, Jeff.

Some of the best advice I received in revision was from Holly Hughes, a superb writer and coach. I also have several good friends (and a wonderful, talented writers' group) who volunteered as readers and provided excellent and honest feedback during the various draft stages of the manuscript, including 'My Marc' Berezin, Doug Ford, Ed LaChapelle and Jeremy Jones. I am immensely grateful to the gifted Toshiro Stang, who was extremely helpful in designing the book cover.

Without the characters in the stories, I would have no stories, so I am grateful to all the cannery employees and fisherfolk who appear in the book for giving me a rich history and twenty years of life led on and near the water.

My writing has been helped immeasurably by preparing many of the pieces in this volume for readings at the annual FisherPoets Gathering in Astoria, Oregon since 1998. My feelings of loss when I sold out of Cook Inlet were mitigated by my acceptance into that vibrant group of storytellers, poets and songsmiths who share a deep love of the sea and commercial fishing. I am honored to be a member of their community.

Finally, to Cook Inlet, thank you. I grew up on your waters, passed and failed the tests you handed out, but always was present for our love affair, including the rough waters. I still miss your harsh and perfect gifts. I still miss the beauty, the thrill and the adventure. I miss the fish…and the fishin'.

for

~~Dean and Don~~

Veronica

Contents

WAITING TO DELIVER

Cook Inlet, Alaska

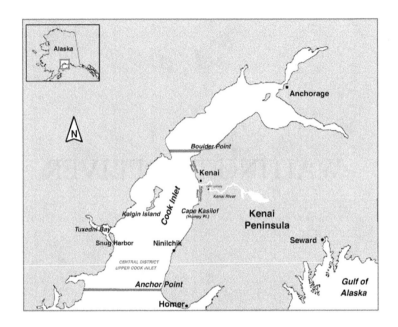

The Cook Inlet commercial drift gillnet fishery grounds extend from the southern border at Anchor Point 100 miles north to Boulder Point. The widest area within the district is approximately 60 miles. Salmon enter Cook Inlet from the Gulf of Alaska to the south, moving toward different river systems throughout the Inlet as they migrate north. The largest run (of sockeye, or red salmon) averages around 2.5 million fish, all bound for the Kenai River.

Introduction

Standing on the bow of the vintage paddle-wheeler *Delta Queen* with a fellow teacher in the humid June heat, I watch the city slide by as we head down the Ohio river. I'm 23 years old, and it's the end of my first year teaching in the inner city of Louisville, Kentucky. The staff of the school is celebrating the 1973-74 school year's end with a boat ride and dinner aboard. I sip a beer and discuss my impending trip to Alaska. After a successful year teaching – my first of what will become a 35-year career – I've pulled the plug to take the trip of a lifetime. Unsure of whether I want to stay in the Last Frontier, I haven't searched for jobs, but just as doubtful is the idea of returning to the Midwest, so I've resigned my position here.

"Why Alaska?" Debbie asks. While standing on a boat that has a rich history of plying the Ohio and Mississippi since the 1800's, I can't help but give her an honest answer.

"I think I was born 100 years too late," I say with a sigh. "I want to live somewhere still wild and untamed. Someplace where I might fit in better." She shakes her head. For her and most of my friends and family, leaving for Alaska is like going to the moon.

§

By the 16th of September, I am walking the shoreline in SE Alaska, near a small village named Wrangell. It's my 24th birthday, and the first sunny day in a week. My wife Cindy is walking the gravel beach with me, both of us wrapped in a fog of history. We have spent the past few hours finding and making rubbings of 3,000-year-old petroglyphs carved in boulders exposed by the low tide. We read about them in the premiere travel guide for Alaska, *The Milepost*, and on its advice, took crayons and butcher paper to create the rubbings. Seeing figures

1

and faces from such a distant past has us in an emotional mind-tune with something much bigger than ourselves. We're talking in subdued tones as we walk back to the van when we hear a noise like a rock falling into water behind and *above* us. We turn to see two ravens flying up the beach, maybe thirty feet in the air. One of them folds her wings and rolls onto her back, dropping out of the sky. Just when we think she's going to hit the ground in front of us, she rolls over, spreads her wings and stops her fall. She pumps them hard to climb up next to her mate. As they pass overhead, he makes the same sound, then folds his wings and executes the same maneuver, like it is a game they get to play because they have the gift of flight. The experience, brief as it is, stays with me. It feels like a greeting: a welcome to Alaska from one of its most iconic spiritual figures. I am immediately a huge fan of ravens.

Two days later we pull our 1966 Ford Falcon window van off the Alaska ferry into Haines, a small waterfront community where our first stop is a pullout overlooking the harbor. As Cindy and I relax and eat a sandwich, we notice the vessels docked at the piers. There are a few sailboats, but few yachts or pleasure craft. Most of the boats are streaked with rust, have indecipherable rigging and what looks like heavy equipment on deck. A man in a flannel shirt and rubber boots walks up the ramp from the harbor, and we ask him what those boats are all about. "That's the commercial fishing fleet," he answers. "They're in port for a few days until the next period starts."

I am an Indiana-born-and-raised Hoosier. I'm dimly aware that commercial fishing used to exist, but I'm surprised it's still a thing. I had assumed that line of work disappeared with the steam engine. I have been infatuated with boats, though, from an early age – particularly power boats. Every summer after I turned twelve, my dad took me to a series of lakes in the wilderness near Sioux Lookout, Ontario to fish for walleye. I was 13 when he asked me, "Wanna run the boat

2

today?" and once I opened up the 25-horse Evinrude, I was hooked. What did Toad say in *Wind in the Willows?* "There is nothing – absolutely nothing – half so much worth doing as simply messing about in boats." For me, truer words were never spoken.

Overlooking the Haines harbor, I feel a door open into exciting possibilities. I immediately begin walking the docks looking for work. Dressed in torn hippie coveralls, camera announcing my status as a tourist, my shoulder-length red hair and scraggly beard advertising my youth, drug preferences and political leanings, I never have a chance. Not one skipper looks twice at me, but I gather information. I learn that this harbor primarily hosts two different types of commercial fishing vessels: trollers that fish with hooks and lines dragged behind the boat; and gillnetters that catch fish with a net carried on a reel. It's enough to spawn a dream, even as Cindy and I continue our journey to the interior of Alaska.

We fall in love with the north country. Alaska charms us with magnificent mountain ranges, northern lights, and a summer sun that never sets. We try to make a go of staying, but Cindy can't find work, and though I get a job in Anchorage as a non-union laborer pounding nails and shoveling gravel on a construction project, Alaska is overcrowded with all the workers flooding the state to build the trans-Alaska pipeline. By October it's nine degrees, and we're living in our van in a campground on the edge of the city. We can't find an affordable place to live. We decide to head home before the snow flies and the temperature drops even more.

We return to Louisville for one more winter. I spend it applying to every school district in Alaska. The following July I get hired over the phone to teach at a Junior High in Kenai, three hours south of Anchorage at the mouth of the Kenai River. The river empties into Cook Inlet, an arm of water extending north from the Gulf of Alaska, and though I don't know it at the time,

Kenai has a thriving commercial fishing industry. *We'll stay for a little while*, we think, *just to check it out.*

Two years later, at the end of the summer of 1977, I am single and broke. Cindy and I split up during our first winter. She's back in Indiana attending grad school. I have weeks to go before teaching starts again, and a month after that before the first paycheck hits. When Thor Evenson, a friend and a commercial fisherman, calls me and asks if I'll be his deckhand for a few fishing periods while he scratches some silvers and dogs, whatever that means, I jump at the chance. His deckhand had to leave early, so the vacancy is mine for the taking. We fish together on his old wooden boat, the *Mabel E,* for four periods. The boat is slow and uncomfortable, rolls with the waves and smells of diesel, all of which make me queasy constantly. But Thor is a good fisherman, and we always seem to be catching fish. The work makes the seasickness fade, and I make enough to see me through until a regular teaching paycheck comes my way. I take to boat work and picking fish well enough that Thor recommends me to his dad Jim as a good prospect for crew the following summer.

Jim has already given the deckhand job to someone else, but with Thor's recommendation I climb to number two on his list. When his first choice injures his back at his oilfield job, Jim hires me for the next two summers. He and his wife Nedra happen to be my first neighbors in Alaska. They're homesteaders who have been in the area since the 1950's. He's an artist, a retired teacher and basketball coach, and he commercial fished in the days when all you had to help you get home was your compass, eyes, and instincts. They welcome me to fishing with a dinner at their home, and though Jim is a taciturn Norwegian, he's a savvy fisherman and a good human being. I can't believe my luck. I am 28 years old. I feel like I am starting a new journey – a new chapter in my life. Like going to Alaska, this feels like the beginning of an adventure.

Thor Evenson on the Mabel E, 1977.

Chapter One: Deckhand Days

The Cannery

As soon as school is out, I go to work for Jim to get ready for fishing. I drive to the cannery each day, often arriving well before I'm supposed to be there. Jim fishes for Columbia Wards Fisheries, a Seattle-based outfit that is one of the two biggest processors in the Kenai area. The plant is located near the mouth of the river, at the end of – where else? – Cannery Road. I use the extra time to wander the grounds, learn the layout of the plant, meet people and photograph. I photograph the buildings, the boats, the river, even the wildflowers growing everywhere. I frequent the cannery store where the ice cream bars compete with the fudgesicles. I quickly learn to never miss a mug-up, a cannery-wide coffee break. It's a great time to get to know who works on what boat, and to get acquainted with fishing crews and cannery workers. I meet skippers, machinists, boatwrights, other deckhands, and port engineers (mechanics) at mug-up.

Fishing is a semi-closed world for a greenhorn, and I find making friends isn't easy until you've earned your spot. Jim is pleasant, but he and most of his fishing friends are of a different generation, and aren't folks I would normally hang with. Or perhaps it's that I'm tremendously uncomfortable in my own skin as I confront a world I know nothing about. My first job in Indiana was at a local gas station, so I'm familiar with mechanics. I gravitate to the port engineers who work on the engines, hydraulics and other systems that keep the boats and cannery in working order. Jim frequently sends me to the PE shop to get fan belts, oil, oil filters and other supplies. While there I enjoy their easy banter and jokes. Jim Harrison is the head engineer, and he's a gentle man with a quick, impish smile. But my favorite cannery employee to visit is Benny, the carpenter. He is slight and wiry, twice my age, but sports a sense of humor I relate to and appreciate. The first day I meet him, he introduces himself with a smile and says, "Well you gotchyerself in it now, din'tcha?" He shakes my hand and nods his head at the far wall where several tools are hanging on pegs. "While yer here, might as well make yerself useful. Grab me that ten-inch left-handed crescent wrench over there." I start for the crescent wrenches, wondering how I'll know a ten-inch one, when it hits me. There's no such thing as a *left-handed* wrench. I turn around and give him a look. Benny is watching me with a wry smile, cigarette dangling from his lips. He raises his eyebrows and breaks into a grin. "Gotcha!" It's the start of a relationship I cherish until the day I visit him for the last time, in the hospital years later as he's dying of lung cancer. After spending a full minute coughing blood into his handkerchief and gasping for air, he looks up and asks, "Got a smoke?" I don't know what to say. He tilts his head, eyebrows up, and shrugs with a gallows smile. "Why quit now?"

CWF fisherman Jim Barr & Benny Lindgren in the carpenter's shop, 1978.

I learn to love errands that begin with Jim saying, "Run up to the carpenter shop and..." Benny and I share cigarettes, coffee and jokes while he deftly shapes a piece of wood on the giant bandsaw or roots through his lumber for a piece we need. He has a small barrel stove set up in the back that warms the far end of the shop on a chilly day and adds wood smoke to the aroma of the place, mixing with cedar scent of planks and fresh cut wood. I discover that during mug-up he has his own private coffee break with whomever might be around, relaxing on wood stools and a couple of old straight-backed chairs pulled near the stove. If I'm not huddled close to that stove on a rainy day, cradling a warm cup in my hand against the chill, I'm at the mess hall enjoying pastries. I develop the habit of wrapping a warm cinnamon roll in a napkin from the pastry table to drop off for him as I go back to the boat.

The 'Ways'

Our boat, the *North Sea*, is one of nearly a hundred vessels lined in rows parallel to the river. It sits in dry-dock, where it spent the winter. The hulls of our cannery fleet are wedged upright with wood blocks, keels resting on heavy beams fore and aft. The beams are coated with black grease, something I learn when ducking under them and put my hand in the thick goo. The beams stand five feet above the ground on top of wood pilings sunk deep into the clay of the boatyard like rows of short telephone poles.

The cannery has a special crew called the 'Beach Gang' that launches boats and hauls them back out of the water. They do a litany of hard and dangerous jobs near and on the water, from driving pilings that hold the floating dock before the season (and taking them out at the summer's end), to rescuing fishing boats that have broken down.

They also launch boats during high tide with a steam-powered winch and steel cables threaded through a series of

K Boats stored on the Ways, CWF, Kenai, 1977.

block-and-tackle pulleys. The cables are rigged to pull boats along the greased 'ways' until they line up with a launching ramp. The ramp looks like a railroad track angled down the riverbank to the water. The steam engine provides power to a large winch that pulls five-to-fifteen-ton vessels along the greased beams to the launch rail. The most dangerous part is at the beginning of the operation, when the steam engine whines as the winch in the 'donkey house' tugs on a large wooden block placed beside the cradle supporting the boat being moved. The boat is often stuck fast in the grease, a result of sitting in the same spot all winter. Before a boat can slide along the ways, the winch has to build enough force to free it. Each vessel takes a different amount of pressure, and when that amount has been reached, the boats break free, sometimes violently jerking several feet down the ways without warning. It's a surprisingly dangerous moment, and if someone were in the path of the suddenly moving, incredibly heavy projectile, they could be seriously injured or killed in an instant.

The scene is like watching an old documentary of a turn-of-the-century industry. When it's the *North Sea's* turn, Jim and I are waved off. We watch the beach gang from a distance as they set the rigging, moving under and around the boats. Dennis, with long hair and an easy smile, only has three fingers on his left hand, the result of an accident doing this work a few years ago. He and the rest of the crew move away. Little Mike eyeballs the cables, then circles a gloved index finger at the sky. The engine in the donkey house ramps up, screaming with the strain. Suddenly the *North Sea's* bow breaks free and slides to starboard. An instant later the stern follows. The boat stays upright, and everyone smiles and nods in relief, relaxing into the less dangerous phase of the operation.

We're headed toward the water. Jim and I walk alongside, watching as the winch pulls the boat sideways to a cradle waiting to launch us. After a few minutes waiting as they change the arrangement of the cables and tackle, we follow again as our boat and one other are lowered in tandem down the ramp toward the river. Once we reach a drawbridge-like gap in the boardwalk at the river's edge, the boats stop. A ladder is raised against the side of the *North Sea*, and we climb aboard. I hang on as we are jerked stern-first into the river. The boats float off the cradle as Jim and the other skipper start the engines. He puts it into reverse, moving us away from the other vessel and maneuvering into the current. The bow comes around. We motor to the dock, where I get an extended lesson in tying lines.

After weeks of working on the boat in dry-dock, suddenly the *North Sea* is 'wet'. No longer just another space on land where I go to work, she has come alive. She moves and behaves with a will of her own. If I don't secure a line properly, she will drift away from the dock into the river, or worse yet,

*CWF Beach Gang member George Showalter works on the
Ways with the steam-powered winch in the 'Donkey House'.*

dance unexpectedly on the surface as she rides the wakes of
passing boats. And she has a voice, a singsong bubbling that I
will come to know while lying in my bunk at anchor, as well as
a throbbing engine rumble that lulls me to sleep as we run. I
begin to understand how fishermen can love their boats. They

have personalities and characteristics that endear and frustrate. They are the recipients of a relationship that is dedicated, committed and deep. For their part, if well taken care of, they respond with strength and reliability.

The *North Sea* is a work vessel. She isn't a show horse known for her grace and beauty, neither is she a thoroughbred built for speed. She's more of a ranch horse that knows hard work and comes ready to get the job done. Even new, her best features were about how stout she was: how many fish she could pack and still be seaworthy. As long as her engine runs, there is no doubt she can haul the fish.

Our first cruise is to be a 'shakedown.' I'm not entirely certain what that means, but Jim says it's "not to catch fish as much as it is to work the bugs out." I hope the 'bugs' don't include me.

Fishing

2:00 am. I'm wide awake and filled with anxiety as I drive the 15 miles from my house to the cannery for my first fishing period in a light drizzle. I'm living in Soldotna with my fiancé Veronica, and we've had a restless night. We spent a long time talking about how dangerous this profession is, second only to mining in the number of deaths per year. Jim is an experienced skipper, with over twenty years on the Inlet. He's not lost a deckhand yet, and I'm determined not to be the first. "He knows what's safe and what's not," Veronica reassures me, but my concern doesn't disappear. Anxiety is something I'll deal with most of my career, especially when the wind blows before a fish day.

I arrive at the cannery from my home fifteen miles away. The scene before me is surreal. I expect a bustle of activity as the fleet readies itself for the first day. Instead, the place is dark and deserted. I wonder if I've gotten the day right. I see Jim's truck parked in the lot in his usual spot, so he's already here. A shadow walks between the carpenter's shop and the bunkhouse headed for the dock, and relief threads through me. I must be on time. I pull my jacket tight against the chilly rain and head to the boat. The cannery at night is a different creature. There's a hidden beauty revealed by orange sodium lights and green-hued fluorescent safety lamps. The boardwalks glisten with color, and the boats, pale and still, almost hover above the water as they wait next to the dock. The river doesn't flow as much as slide by. A lone black shadow slips downriver with the current, deckhand silhouetted on the bow, looping a tie-up line around his arm. From shore I can't even hear the engine. It's disappeared by the time I reach the floating dock.

I study the fleet as I walk down the ladder leading to the float. Not a cabin light on in any of the boats. No one seems to be interested in going out yet. I wonder why Jim wanted me here so early. I think of my warm bed at home and the woman snuggled there with a twinge of resentment. Maybe no one will go out today, and I can go home and climb back in with her. Just as I have that thought a diesel starts up with a throaty roar. *Ok then.* I climb aboard and wake Jim out of a sound sleep.

It's not easy to untie lines in the dusk of an Alaskan dawn. My hands feel soft and tender against the rough, scratchy manila hemp. I struggle at getting the knot around the cleat on the dock undone, and curse at myself for being so inept. Jim watches me from the cabin. I feel his gaze and wonder how long his patience will last. The line finally slackens and I slide it off the cleat and toss it into the stern. I hurry the 30 feet up the dock to the bow, hoping the line there is easier. It's not. It comes undone eventually, and I start to climb aboard but Jim waves me back. "Push the bow out!" he yells from the other side of the window. I lean against the heavy boat with all my weight, and it barely moves. Once it begins, though, it picks up speed. I wonder when to time it so I can get aboard without ending up in the water. Jim has warned me about the Kenai River. "The Kenai is fed by a glacier. If you fall in, the silt will fill your clothes and weigh you down. Last year a seventeen-year-old son

13

of a fisherman fell off their boat, and the river swept him between the boats tied at the dock." Jim vividly recalls the father's frantic yells as he ran his boat downstream in a panic. "They never found him." I grip the railing tight as I leap to the bow and scramble on board, one knee placed solidly in a puddle on deck. My pant leg soaks through with cold rainwater. *Shit.* I have to change clothes already, and we haven't even left the river. I remove the tie-up line from the bow cleat and replace it with end of the anchor line. The anchor is lashed down on the bow, but Jim has told me of 40-pound anchors working loose from their bindings in a rough sea and either coming through the windshield or going overboard. I assume anchors are expensive, and follow his instructions to be certain ours stays on the boat. I take the tie-up line and make my way to the back deck, where I secure it and the stern line to railings on either side of the top of the cabin, then stretch them to the stern cleats for hand-holds or 'safety lines' to use while we're at sea.

I tighten the lines as Jim steers the boat downriver. I look around and breathe in the cool salt air. The river is black, but reflections from the lights on shore fill the ripples with glistening, dancing colors. Large black buoys, shadowed balls floating in the river, come at us from out of the dark. Jim steers around them, following the channel. We slip past other boats with sleepy crews in skivvies sipping cups of coffee under the yellow glow of cabin lights, watching us cruise by. Jim keeps the throttle low so as not to create a wake and rock them off their feet. Before long they'll be under way too. A wider, taller boat – a tender – looms above us as we glide past, its arc lights throwing a pool of white on the river beside it. I can hear and feel the rumble from her large engines, but no one is visible and all her windows are dark. Tenders work to a different rhythm than the fleet. These guys will be up long after we're in the bunk on most nights, taking fish from the smaller boats and delivering them to the cannery dock well into the next day. They earn their sleep.

I finish tying the lines and duck into the cabin, chilly and ready to change pants. Jim doesn't believe in heating the cabin with the small diesel stove. "Seen too many boat fires from those things," is his explanation, so the chill remains with me even after I have on dry jeans. I try a cup of black instant coffee, water heated with the propane stove he has lashed to the top of the cold diesel one. It's hot and bitter, and the first cup is enough to steer me away from boat coffee for years. Jim throttles up as we near the river mouth. Our wake won't disturb anyone out here. The engine noise in the cabin is too loud for conversation, so we sit on stools in the tiny cramped cabin and bounce along as other boats roar by, creating wakes that cause us to heave and roll. He holds onto the wheel for balance while I wedge my shoulders into the corner of the cabin. Occasionally Jim points out a visual landmark: "See that dark stripe there?" I follow his pointing finger to the west to a deep gray pencil line on the horizon. "That's Kalgin Island." Or "See that funny-looking cloud up there against the flatter ones?" I look to the north, and spot wisps of lighter clouds stretching vertically against a gray blanket of sky. "That's steam from Collier's fertilizer plant. It's right next to the Tesoro refinery, what we call the 'Tank Farm.'" I wonder how he remembers all this. All day he points out Cook Inlet landmarks: Iliamna volcano, Chisik Island, Red Glacier, Humpy Point, the Clam Gulch tower, Anchor Point. To me, most of them are indistinguishable from one another, one graphite line on the horizon pretty much the same as another.

During the day's work, Jim tutors me as patiently as he would a child. "Now what's that over there?" he asks. Completely turned around, I glance frantically for any other visual help.

"Uh, Ninilchik?" I guess.

"No, Ninilchik is that way, he points nearly opposite of where I have been looking, "to the east. That's the south end of Kalgin."

"Oh." I shake my head and wonder how I'll ever know how to figure out these landmarks.

One calm day early in the season we are south of Kalgin Island running hard to the north on a fish call. I'm sitting on deck in the sun, with my back to the cabin, when I glance to port and see what appears to be people walking on the water a mile west of us. I stand up and look again, and sure enough, I see two people walking around! *That can't be right*, I think. I feel like I'm hallucinating. I hustle into the cabin and point them out to Jim, who grabs his binoculars.

"Looks like they ran aground on the south Kalgin bar," Jim says. "You can see the boat behind them." He hands me the glasses. There's a boat heeled over just north of the small figures. "This tide's pretty low. They're probably looking for clams. They're gonna be there awhile."

The sea rolls under my feet as we stand aft, in the picking well where the net is set and comes back aboard. Jim is teaching me to pick fish out of the webbing. The rollers are big but gentle, part of a sea swell that is coming into southern Cook Inlet from the Gulf of Alaska. Jim eyes them differently than I do, seeing them as a harbinger. "Those are pretty big. Probably a storm on the way." The boat lifts on large, sun-flecked waves of green. I eye two 10,000-foot volcanoes covered with snow towering above us only twenty miles to the west. I can make out glaciers on the mountains, and the occasional puffy cloud seems to fairly dance along the sky. I'm falling in love. This is why I was drawn to Alaska, to the water.

A fish comes on board, still kicking against the force of the net binding it. Jim shows me how to clear the layers of web from the body, then how to grab – not the fish but the web near its gills – and then use a one-two shake to pull the netting free. I am at a loss. I can see the fish through the web, but can't figure out how to know what to move to clear it. Just when I think I've got it, the fish kicks out of my grip with unexpected strength, falling back into the web. Jim shows me again, but more quickly this time. "Let me do the tough ones," he says, "especially when fishing is heavy. You learn on the easy ones first." I'm more relieved than insulted, and I eventually come to realize that this job involves teamwork. I learn how to spread the lines of the net for him as he reaches down to get a bagged fish, how to stretch web to help him clear the net away from a soft-bodied humpy, and how to anticipate and catch a fish that looks like it will drop out of the web before it comes on by pulling a line over to my side so the web will be under it as it falls.

We set the net out and pick it up several times as we look for fish to catch. We set with Jim in the cabin steering and me in the stern letting the net go. The net is spooled onto a large, hydraulic-powered reel bolted to the back deck of the boat. I release the brake on the reel, and as the net pays out, I bend down and use my hands like paddles to gather web hanging under the lines in a constant attempt to keep it from catching on itself and creating a backlash. A hang-up can tear a huge hole in the net that fish can swim through, and Jim has impressed upon me how much he hates them. Even so, I worry about my fingers getting caught in the nylon mesh as it flies over the stern. I shake my head as I find myself wondering if the web will rip off my finger or if I'll be pulled overboard. I push my fingers together harder and focus on the job. The reel hums as it spins. The lines peel off it and drop to the deck wiggling and dancing. When the lines drag and move toward the reel I reach in and paddle it away. Legs spread against the roll of the boat, moving side-to-side like a crab as I follow the net moving back-and-forth along the reel, one hand flying over the other, I become part of the dance. I stand up and stretch my back as the last of the line threads off the boat and the used fan belt at the end of the lead line drops off the stern with a splash. I holler to Jim over the engine noise. He puts the boat in neutral and looks out the door as the line tied from the corkline to the reel tightens and groans. It is a scene that will play out over and over all summer.

17

Deckhands yelling at the top of their lungs, "OKAY!!!" and skippers looking out cabin doors, microphones in hand, watching the net for hits and reporting what they see to their fishing group. For years I will look at silhouettes of men standing on hatch covers, hands in pockets or tucked inside their rain gear, watching the water behind their boats. Looking backwards, ever backwards. It is uniquely a fishing gesture, as if there is hope to be found from the past, even as they are immersed in the moment.

Once the net is in the water, we watch for fish hitting the gear. Hits come in an ocean of varieties: splashers, bobbers, cork-jerkers, pushers, jumpers, bunches, singles, small bunches, clatters. We catch five varieties of salmon: Kings (Chinook) are the biggest, often 50-60 pounds or more, but are the least common and tend to surface in shallow water, not out deep where we go. Pinks (Humpback or humpies) are the smallest and least desirable, fetching the lowest price. They are also very soft and difficult to pick out of the net. Dogs (Chum) hit harder, and silvers (Coho) fight longer than reds (Sockeye), the species we catch the most of, and that commands the highest price except for Kings. I learn that jumpers are indicators of schools of fish – "one in the air, ten down there". Jim informs me that rips – currents that are similar to rivers in the ocean – are places fish like, but are full of hazards. A nasty rip can suck your gear into it, ball up a net, fill a net with sticks and kelp, or pull two boats together unwillingly. Years later I am picking a set in a rip on my own boat when a strange buoy pops out from underneath my stern. I stare at it, wondering what is happening and where it came from. A net is attached to it, but my own buoy is still 50 yards off the stern. Then I realize the rip has pulled the boat just north of me down on us while we were picking. Our stern was facing south, so we never saw him coming. His net is under us. We yell back and forth, trying to figure out what we should do. I don't want to put the boat in gear, and he doesn't want to tow, both of us afraid I'll get 'web in the wheel', or the net caught in

18

my propeller. The rip finally slides me off his gear and he tows it away from us. We retell the story later over beers on shore, and he says, "If I can't be good, let me be lucky." There's a lot to learn.

The North Sea, 1978.

Each scheduled fishing period lasts twelve hours, but the work day is much longer for fishermen. They often leave hours early to get to the grounds, and it sometimes takes four or more hours just to get back to the river. Jim and I get caught toward the southern end of the district at closure one period, just after the tide starts to ebb against us while we head north to the river. I look out the starboard window at the Kenai Mountain range in the distance before taking a nap. Jim wakes me a couple of hours later so he can get some rest while I steer. I glance to starboard and notice in disbelief that the mountains haven't moved. Seeing my expression, Jim offers, "We're just holding our own against this tide. It'll ease up in an hour or so, and we'll start gaining on it." It's four more hours before we get to the river, and we still have to wait in line to unload, then clean up. It takes all summer to get used to the long days.

Boat Puller

~ for Jim

We are alone on the boat -
a green deckhand and a middle-aged Norwegian
riding emerald rollers sprinkled with drops of gold
in the late afternoon sun.
And though you are teaching me
how to get a salmon out of the bag
without popping the mesh,
　　I am somewhere else:

off the stern I see myself
neck deep in Indiana, floundering
in all those years of not knowing who I was,
or how to escape who I had become;
drowning in aching nights spent hoping
for the moment I might know a way to set my feet
　　upon a path of my own.

While I am picking fish with you,
stunned at the sight of the sea so near
and the mountains filling the western sky,
I think of dry Midwestern cornfields,
and of lost, empty days filled with a wish to leave
　　but nowhere to go.

You bend over a red to show me how to use a fish pick,
not realizing what is happening to me,
how you are stripping away the web of my past life,
　　pulling me through to solid ground.

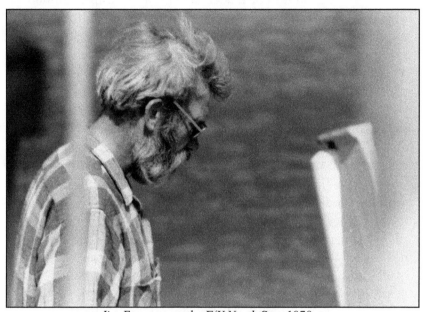

Jim Evenson on the F/V North Sea, 1978.

Chapter Two: Never Cross the Lines

So you want to be a deckhand on a Cook Inlet gillnetter? This is what you'll do: before the season starts, you'll drive to the cannery every day for weeks, park your car in a cloud of dust or a muddy drizzle and climb aboard the boat you're crewing on. Your skipper may or may not be there yet. The boat is in the yard, up on barrels, where it spent the winter. The ladder you will use to get on the boat may or may not be there either. You'll likely find it lashed to the cleat of another boat twenty yards away. This ladder will become an important element in your life for your first weeks of 'fishing.'

You'll go up and down it at least a dozen times each morning, and twice that in the afternoon. You'll go down it to go the carpenter's shop for wood to patch a hole in the cabin door, for galvanized screws or to borrow a coping saw from the boat next door. You'll go up it when you come back from the machine shop for engine oil, and you'll take the old oil back down it in a 5-gallon bucket, trying not to spill black goo all over yourself. You'll chase down coolant, hydraulic fluid, transmission fluid, Bondo to patch fiberglass, Splash-zone to patch over snags under the boat that might catch the net, 5200 silicone to stop leaks. You'll bring back zincs, bolts, nuts, washers, lock-washers, cotter pins, fan belts, duct tape, black tape, plumber's tape, stainless baling wire and more. You'll be sent back when the bolt is too short. You'll be sent back again when it's too long.

While you're doing all this, you'll be getting to know the carpenter, the port engineers, the beach gang and the machinists. There'll be at least one guy who will be outright unfriendly and mean. He'll be the one who'll ignore you when you need something from him, and he'll ridicule your ignorance of "the way things operate around here." He'll send you back to the boat empty-handed, asking the skipper to clarify whether he wants you to borrow the left-or-right-handed grease gun. You'll learn to hate going on errands where he works.

You'll go down the ladder on your way to the company store for your deckhand's license, soda to bring back to the boat, and an ice-cream sandwich on the single hot day without a cold wind that will have you remembering what summer used to be like. You'll go down the ladder to duct tape a hose to the sea-water intake valve so the pump doesn't burn up while the skipper runs the engine. You'll go back up again because you can't hear what the skipper is yelling from the engine room, then race back down to turn the water off. You'll run to the port engineers' shop to get electrical fittings, solder, butt-end connectors and silicone to seal them with to keep the salt air from corroding the wires. You'll haul tools up the ladder from your skipper's pick-up, sometimes carrying boxes in both hands as you climb, balancing on the rungs on the balls of your feet. You'll haul up sleeping bags, rain gear, boots and electronics until your feet and legs ache. You'll memorize where the missing rung on the ladder is, and you'll vow to fix it when you get time. You'll never get time.

You'll be sent to the skipper's locker in the old web loft to gather up buoys, survival suits, a worn block of paraffin wax, some black paint and old brushes wrapped in aluminum foil. You'll wax the survival suit zippers with the paraffin. You'll paint the boat name and license number on the buoys. You'll have to go to the carpenter's shop to get paint thinner to clean the brushes, and to the store again for more aluminum foil...and another ice-cream sandwich.

You'll be sent to town for the stainless screws and clips the cannery doesn't stock; while you're there, you'll be asked to pick up some beer, some burgers and fries, or maybe some pizza. When you come back, your skipper will be nowhere to be found. He'll be bullshitting with another fisherman who just came in that afternoon. You'll be expected to find something to do anyway, like picking up the trash accumulating under the boat. Cleaning the cabin is always a good idea. Don't put anything away – especially tools near an unfinished project. Just straighten. Clean the windows. Get some water in a bucket from a spigot nearby and wash the dishes piled in the sink. Avoid the skipper's coffee cup. He's the only one who washes that thing, and the last time was years ago. If you clean it, you'll destroy its 'unique' flavor.

You'll learn to budget your errands so you're near the mess hall when the mug-up whistle blows. Homemade cinnamon rolls and muffins in the morning, pies and cake in the afternoon. And always fresh-brewed coffee, hot chocolate and juice for the kids. Mug-up is a 15-minute cannery-wide break where you'll learn to keep your mouth shut and listen. The fishermen will talk about their boats, their nets, who's working with whom, the upcoming season, the price of fish. You'll hear terms like stuffing box, Grundens, Uroko, dog gear, hynautics and flying bridge. With any luck you'll start putting them in context and figuring out what they mean. But everyone agrees - mug-up always is too short.

You'll learn that gillnets in Cook Inlet are made of three twenty-foot deep 'shackles', clipped and sometimes sewn together. Each shackle is made of two 100-yard-long lines with web tied between them: the cork line floats on the water's surface, suspended by styrofoam corks threaded onto it and tied every three feet; and the leadline, literally rope wrapped around a core of lead that's designed to sink in the water and stretch the net like a wall for the fish to swim into, catching them by the gills. You'll load the shackles on a four-wheeled cart and pull them out of the warehouse, coiled in nylon or canvas net bags. You'll pull the heavy cart to the edge of the boardwalk where you'll heave them into your skipper's truck. You'll drive them to the back of the boat and open them one-by-one and clip the ends to a piece of line – not rope – never rope on a boat – a piece of line coming off the reel. You'll stand in the truck and feed the net out of the bag and up over the stern of the boat and onto the reel. The reel is powered by a bit of magic called hydraulics, and while the boat is running, your skipper can make the reel turn by stepping on a treadle board near it. As the net comes on board, he will guide the web, the corks and the heavy leadline onto the reel in a neat package, taking care not to cross the lines over each other. This is hugely important. Your skipper will likely impress upon you how important it is not to cross the lines. Remember this.

You'll start to wish you had a truck.

There'll be at least one guy, if you're lucky, who'll take to you. He'll joke with you and tell you what a garboard plank or corking is. He'll tell you who to avoid, and whom to seek out. He'll always be good for a cup of hot coffee and a rickety chair next to his wood stove on a wet, chilly spring day. Whenever you get the chance, take him a cinnamon roll if he's not at mug-up, or an extra burger and fries when you make that run to town. Better yet, before he closes the door at 5:00 o'clock show up with a bottle of Jack to drink with him out of dirty coffee mugs.

By now you've been 'fishing' for two, maybe three weeks. Your skipper will keep talking about "when we finally get wet." You haven't been paid a dime – remember, you're paid by the percentage of the fish you catch, and you haven't even seen a fish. You'll swear as you knock a Philips screwdriver off the cabin roof to land on the gravel below while you put up an antenna in a cold drizzle. One more trip down that fucking ladder and back up again. By the time the boat's launched, you'll hate that ladder.

Welcome to fishing.

Ransom
- Boat work in four parts

1

Balance on elbow in yoga-crab
pose, stretch under floorboards
in the engine room, between batteries
and the transducer post. Commit your weight
until the wrench pops free – punch of skin
and cartilage left on the starter motor –
another pre-season blood sacrifice.

The High Druid of Engines
chants obscenities as you rise and dance,
reciting lines from a waterborne play. Comedy?
Tragedy? You don't know the difference,
except the boat's not in the water.
That comes later, after your hands are
scabbed and tattooed in black grease.
Salt water will cleanse you. Until then,
bag balm stings the cuts, and the older
you are the more your knuckles ache.

2

Blood burns your eyes,
dripping off the gash in your forehead,
cracked on the prop blade under the boat.
Stunned, you drop to all fours in the gravel.
No dance when it hurts this bad. Just the swearing.
Blurred thick pearls slide off the end of your nose,
land black among stones, red on the back of your hand.

3

The one day you don't wear gloves,
your hand caresses a sheet of plywood.
The pressed wood puckers,
kisses a one-inch wooden sliver
into the meat of your palm. *That'll leave a mark,*
says the smart-ass shipwright.
If you weren't hopping around so
much,you'd crack him with the ball-
peen.

4

Stumble home through the woods –
2:00 am, drunk from the bar. Spruce
root flips you, drops you face-first
into a log peppered with broken branches.
Drag out of bed the next morning,
you don't recognize yourself in the mirror.

The season is around the next bend,
if you can just stay in the channel.
Scars fade in the waning light
of boat work. Cast off. Salt water
cools your hands on the mooring line,
your dreams no longer held ransom.

Chapter Three: The Six-Foot Journey, 1978

The rain is a kaleidoscope of white lines in the headlights. On high, the wipers hammer at it, tossing spray sideways with each frantic sweep across the windshield. The torrent pounds at the glass between strokes. Even at only 25 miles an hour, it's hard to see through the deluge, and my Fleetwood Mac cassette is barely audible through the drumming on the roof. I splash through pothole after pothole in the gravel of the cannery yard. A paper bag of groceries shifts in the seat next to me as I swerve to avoid a particularly large puddle. I slow and park in a sparse row of muddy trucks and beater cars facing the boardwalk. Even stopped, the wipers can't keep up with the downpour. It's two in the morning. I squint out at the river. Not one of the silhouettes of commercial fishing boats tied to the dock has a light on. I'm early. We are fishing today, but nobody is ready to leave in this storm. I scan the yard and boardwalk. Normally two or three people can be seen at this time of night making their way to their boats with groceries, duffels or other gear. Tonight, the yard is empty. The wind sprays rain on my side window. I'm not eager to go out there. I light a smoke, turn off the engine and crack the window while I consider whether or not to wait until the rain eases.

My cigarette is almost done when another gust whips cold water onto my cheek and neck. *Jesus,* I breathe. I lift the collar of my cannery jacket and zip it all the way up. I take a last drag before shoving the cigarette butt out the crack. It's soaked and sputtering before I let go, and the wind pins it to the window. I watch the last of the smoke die as it slides halfway down and stops. I roll up the window, grab my bag of groceries and open the door. After four fishing periods with my skipper, I have finally decided to bring my own food to the boat. His menu of bologna, ketchup and butter on white bread, along with bitter black instant coffee is all we eat when fishing, and I can't stand it anymore. I need better fare, so earlier this afternoon I loaded

28

the shopping cart with Oreos, deli chicken, chips, peanut butter, jelly, a six-pack of soda, peanut butter crackers, gum, a giant bag of peanut M & M's and a healthy handful of Snickers. *From now on I eat well while we fish!* I smile at the thought as the checker stuffs the bag.

I pull my ball cap tight and look down as I walk to the lower float – the floating dock that the fleet uses when there isn't room at the more convenient upper dock. The float itself is tethered to pilings stuck in the riverbed and is in good repair. Several boats tie off here between fishing periods, but where the upper float has an access ladder on wheels that raises and lowers with the huge Cook Inlet tides, the lower float is only accessible by a ramshackle walkway stretched from the riverbank to the float. It's a Rube Goldberg-looking affair made of slippery-looking planks, sheets of plywood and waterlogged pieces of 2x12's lashed together with makeshift lines and cables. I look up as I reach the walkway – or what's left of it. The enormous high tide that we've had in the night is racing out to sea, and the 4x8 piece of plywood I am supposed to walk across is tilted at a steep angle with a foot of water pouring over it like it's a half-exposed rock in the middle of a white-water rapids. A taut wire cable rises from deep below the surface of the river and stretches to a piling sunk in the muddy bank next to me. There's a gap in the ramp at least six feet long, not counting the half-submerged plywood. The cable vibrates from the force of the torrent rushing past. Halfway along its length a piece of kelp bounces and sways. There's no getting across this mess.

Standing in the downpour, I can see our boat tied to the outside of the float. My skipper is on board, asleep. I'd rather spend the night in my own bed and get up a little early before a fish day. I'm sure he would too, but he lives twenty-five miles out of town, so for him the boat is a better option. This is my first season, but in the past few weeks I've learned how every minute of sleep is to be savored during fishing. I'm not about to yell for help and wake everyone up. I look down the boardwalk toward the upper float and the cannery yard. Still no one in sight.

I put the groceries on the ground under the eave of the nearby gear shed and walk to the edge of the ramp. If I pull the line stretched between the 2x12 plank laying in the mud and the submerged plywood, I think, I might be able to lift the plywood back to the surface. At the edge of the river, the plank rests on the muddy bank at a 30-degree angle. I step onto it and ease my way to the water. The end of the plank is awash, and the eyebolt the line is tied to is barely above the surface. I lean out, grab the line and pull. It doesn't budge. Cold water surges up my arm and soaks my sleeve. I squat and pull hard using my legs, but the line doesn't move. My tennis shoes begin to slip on the wet wood, so I let go and step back. Raindrops, lit by the safety lights of the cannery, dance circles of colored light on the dark water. I consider going back to the truck to wait until the fleet wakes up, but Jim counts on me arriving early to wake him. He won't be happy if I don't show. I'm new at this, but I've already heard stories about skippers who go fishing without their crew if they're late.

I watch as rivulets of water pour from the brim of my cap. I'm staring at the inside of the float, where it's too shallow to tie up a 32-foot fishing boat like the *North Sea*. I'm looking at two *dories* tied off to it. *Wait a second.* I turn back to the gear shack. I'd set my groceries down ten feet from where someone leaned a new, ten-foot flat-bottomed plywood skiff. I tip the skiff over expecting to see oars inside, but they aren't there. I look from the skiff to the float. It's only thirty feet, but the current would sweep me downriver if I tried to push myself across from shore. The Kenai River is cold and tonight, swollen and angry – not a place to make a mistake. I step back under the eave and clean the rain off my glasses with the bandana from my pocket.

I give it a think. I can get within six feet of the float in the skiff if I pull hand-over-hand using the cable that's stretched between the piling and whatever it's tied to under the water. That will get me close enough that I should be able to push off and grab the float before the current can take me downriver. I drag the skiff to the edge of the water on the downstream side of the walkway. I put the groceries in the bottom, push the little boat out until it floats, and holding its small bow line with one hand and the line coming off the piling with the other, I step in.

The skiff reacts to my weight like a skateboard on ice, tipping and bucking left and right. I sit quickly on the stern, which is still firm in the mud. Squatting to keep my center of gravity low, I duck-walk to the middle seat while holding the cable. I try not to think about what will happen if I end up in the river. I drop the bow line and straddle the seat, facing the upriver side of the little boat. Pulling on the cable coming out of the water and using my weight, I scoot the skiff out into the current. Immediately the little boat tries to shoot downriver. My fingers are white as I clench the cable. The upriver side of the skiff dips low toward the water. Keeping a grip on the line, I stretch my arms and slide back on the seat toward the other side of the skiff, righting it. I slide my hands along the cable as it angles downward until my wrists are against the transom, my fingertips screaming with the strain. I have no more line and six feet to go. Breathing fast, I gain a little leverage by raising myself to a squat. I rock the skiff back, then pull hard and launch it toward the float and let go.

§

There are moments in life when your decisions couple with events and conspire to place you within the short reach of disaster. At those times – when the car rolls off the edge of the road, or your foot slips from the rung of the ladder and you begin the plunge – time slows and the seconds present themselves in brilliant slivers. Each detail – sunglasses sliding across the dash, a branch brushing against your cheek – is

31

painted in front of you and stretched with a clarity and sharpness that commands your detached attention as if you were only an observer and not participating in the affair itself. Until a resolution for better or worse is reached, and then time regains its normal progression and you either move on from there or you don't. The six-foot journey that the skiff travels with me straddling the seat but twisted, facing forward, arms spread and hands gripping both sides of the little boat, moves in time like a slide show – *click*: pouring rain lit by the arc lights of the cannery and boats anchored in the river, streaked by the drops on my glasses; *click:* the blur of silent black hulls of boats looming closer; *click*: the dirty cream and green stripes on the side of the floating dock growing larger as they near, almost within reach; *click*: the sensation of the river's surge underfoot as it pulls at the boat – all slide by in slow-motion until the bow of the skiff smacks the float, bounces off and swings back into the current. The skiff slips sideways, turns downstream, and as time regains its normal pace, I am caught in the flow, the float out of reach.

§

I am stunned. I was sure this would work! As I start to yell, the river swirls me a foot away from a dory, one of the fiberglass ones I saw earlier from shore, tied to the inside of the dock. Without thinking, I reach out and grab its oarlock. Already picking up momentum, my skiff swivels around and almost breaks my grip as it slams into the other vessel. I hang on with both hands. My little boat tips left, then right, then left again. I feel like I'm riding a surfboard with sides. I center my weight and pull backward, hand-over-hand against the river until I've worked around the dory and am next to the dock. Hanging on to the edge of the float with one hand, I grab the stern line and tie it off to a cleat.

The boat hangs at an angle as I duck-walk to the bow. I notice my soggy bag of groceries sitting in a puddle. I slide my hands underneath it and hug it to my chest. As I lean out and swing it toward the float, the soaked paper disintegrates and dumps all my food into the river. I watch my groceries sink or bob downstream and disappear into the dark. In my hand is a single pack of Oreos. I sigh, put them on the float and tie off the bow. Finally secure, I dig out my wet handkerchief and sit. For the first time since boarding the skiff, I feel the rain on my back. I listen to it hammer the float, ping off the metal rigging, splash on the surface of the river. My hands shake as I clean my glasses.

The side of the skiff barely reaches the top of the float. I try standing, but even tied up, the skiff acts squirrelly under me. I put my hands on the dock, lift myself and roll right into the middle of a large puddle. *Perfect.* Drenched, I clutch my cookies and climb aboard our fishing boat. It barely moves when I step aboard. I open the door to the cabin and drip my way inside. My skipper stops snoring and calls my name, his voice fuzzy with sleep. "Didn't you hear? Fish and Game shut us down. No fishing today. Go home. Get some rest."

Chapter Four: Fishing Gesture

I stand in the stern, holding a line and a bright orange buoy attached to the net spooled onto the reel next to me. My skipper is in the cabin on the radio. I can hear voices of other fishermen in our group, barking excited static from deck speakers: "Three in the air at once!" "Fish everywhere!" "…looks better a little south of me."

I watch for jumpers and wonder at this fishing enterprise I'm engaged in. In minutes, hundreds of us will cast our nets into the skin of the planet, fishing a surface sliver of deeper water to catch salmon swimming there. In their frenzy to return to the river of their birth and spawn, schools of them have risen from the depths under us and seem to want to fly the rest of the way home.

The boat idles in the choppy sea, drifting. I wait with building anxiety. What if they move past us? What if the tide takes us out of the school? What if another boat pulls in just south of us and corks us off? What if…

I notice the boat closest to us. We are far enough apart to not be in each other's way when we set the gear, but I see my counterpart on the other vessel, standing in the picking well, waiting like me, and my mind lifts…

§

I am above the fleet, seeing deckhand after deckhand, each holding a buoy, waiting for the surge of the throttle and the skipper's shout, "Let her go!"

The boats lurch forward, and together we toss the moment into the air; hundreds of bright orange buoys soar through morning light in fluid motion, like salmon leap to return to water, weightless, fishing air for the sea. The noise of engines recedes as the fishing gesture echoes its way into the past, connecting all these tossed nets to all other nets ever thrown into the ocean. We have done this before, not always like this, but always *like this*, with an arc of net and line lacing its way through the sky to the water, to the fish, to the planet.

Fishing the corridor, Cook Inlet, Alaska.

Chapter Five: The Bucket

All the years I been on a boat,
commercial fishin' on the ocean afloat,
I always seem to find a way to be
what you might call hygienic –
and never use a bucket at sea.

Now let me explain – my first job is as a crew
on a Cook Inlet gillnetter – and I'm new,
so I work hard and keep my mouth shut
when given all the crappiest jobs, but
all this business with work boats and fish,
the hardest thing to stomach is the dish
my skipper feeds me when he says with a smile,
like he knows just how I'll react all the while:
There ain't no toilet on a boat, it's called a 'head'.
We ain't got one here, so use that there bucket instead.

The container he points to is black and thin,
tucked behind the ladder, it barely has a rim.
I find out later some guys have a toilet seat
they put on their bucket to make it complete.
But the sketchiest thing is – I mean, what the hell?
I have to use it outside, on the back deck,
in the fish-picking well?

Everywhere we fish there are always other boats around;
seems to me the only privacy is back on solid ground,
or in the head of another boat that might tie up for a while –
where I can close a door and do my business in solitary style.
I'm convinced, but don't show it or say it out loud,
there is no way I'm performing in front of a crowd!

So I hold it – sometimes for days
and I refuse to relinquish my restricted ways.

While we're at sea or even anchored up –
doesn't matter for how long – I'm a bound-up pup!
With a nod toward the bucket, my skipper says,
Do you EVER take a shit?
Not on THIS boat! I shoot back, and turn my head and spit.
Well how do you go about that when we're fishin' for days?
he asks, and shakes his head at my unnatural ways.
I have a strong sphincter, I begin... *Ya see...I... ah, fuck it!*
I'm telling you, I'll never, ever use that stinkin' ol' bucket!
I won't have my turds slosh 'round when the weather gets rough
and slap my port and starboard as the boat rolls in the trough!
And what if that flimsy fucker collapses under me
when I'm sittin' out there emptyin' my scuppers at sea?
I'm tellin' you, skip, I have a fish hold full of motivation
for me to maintain this extensive constipation!
And I intend on holdin' it 'til the season's over and done,
when I can pull down my rain gear and rest my bum
on a nice, white toilet seat above a clean porcelain bowl –
where I can properly deposit... a civilized roll!"

That said, we go back to work,
and though I am full of it, I try to not be a jerk.
But whenever a boat with a head ties alongside
I start to feel the surge of an outgoing, ebbing tide.
And when we hit the dock, it's always a lively chase
as off the boat I fly and to the cannery john I race!
I know my skipper, on more than one occasion
has wagered a bet or two against me, but the rising sensation
inside me of impending jet propulsion
always seems to result in a positive conclusion.
I always make it. I'm really not sure how;
but my sphincter and legs make sure
my stern stays clean somehow.

I'll fly my flag high: I'm proud to say I've always ducked it,
and never, ever used that old black bucket!

Chapter Six: The First Big Day

The *North Sea* races north as fast as Jim can push her. The Cummins diesel roars inside the cabin, but back in the stern where I stand, the noise is muted. I feel the vibration of the propeller cavitating the water through the soles of my boots. We are running hard on a fish call, and he wants me back here, ready to set the net on his command. In anticipation, I have pulled the first several feet of gear off the reel, holding the line attached to the large orange buoy in my hands while I lean against the roller mounted to the transom at the back of the boat. The reel, brake off, rocks back and forth as if it's as anxious as I am to get this day under way.

My fishing career begins with two unexpected struggles. The first is my reaction to harvesting the fish. When I chose to become a fisherman, in my naiveté I didn't realize that meant killing hundreds, even thousands of fish. I have been an environmentalist all my adult life. The contrast between my beliefs about stewarding the planet collide with my love for fishing and being on the water. The first few fishing periods overwhelm me as I judge myself partly responsible for all the death I witness. But the salmon are near the end of their life cycle – they die after they spawn – and they are a valuable source of protein for thousands of people. I place my trust in the biologists who study fish behavior and make every attempt to preserve the species even as they manage the fishery and oversee the harvest of millions of individual fish. I come to grips with what I am doing slowly, but through conversations with Veronica and friends who know biology better than me, I arrive at a solution to my dilemma: as long as I can see a justification in what I do on the water – as long as it feeds people and actually helps the run survive by not allowing too many fish up the river, I can do this. Jim adds to my conviction that what we do is well-intentioned by honoring the first fish of

38

the season with a kiss, then releasing it. It's a ritual many fishermen have, and one I adopt. A small gesture, full of meaning.

The second challenge is an incredibly persistent seasickness. As I struggle my way through the early part of the season dreading the nausea but loving the sea, I try every available remedy, from Bonine to Pilot Bread to Dramamine – with no luck. More than once I sneak out on deck during a fish run and heave over the side. If we're not working, I rest outside in the chilly air and lean against the back of the cabin. I'm cold, but the fresh air keeps the seasickness at bay. It's a battle I'll fight most of my career, especially on slow days with a choppy sea, and I absolutely hate the sensation. Once the nausea starts, the idea of it is like a pit bull in my head refusing to let go. It makes me weak and shaky, and the very thought of food turns saliva into paste. I spend hours of fishing days trying to avoid vomiting. It's exhausting, yet I approach each period with the hope that my sea legs will soon develop. It takes more time than I like, but I eventually learn to tie lines, stow gear, keep the boat clean and pick fish as my stomach settles in to working on the water. I learn that the busier I am, the more I can push it away. By the time the big day arrives, I'm starting to think I almost belong on a boat.

Each year the commercial fishing season is scheduled to fish every Monday and Friday through the entire month of July and half of August. The fishing periods or 'openings' run from 6:00 am until 6:00 pm. The state of Alaska gives our local Department of Fish and Game jurisdiction over fishing time and area, including allowing extra periods or cancelling openings altogether. ADF&G makes those decisions, for the most part, based upon marine biology. Their top priority is to preserve and build the run by allowing an optimum number of returning sockeye salmon to spawn up the two major river systems in Cook Inlet, the Kenai and the smaller Kasilof. That optimum number is based upon estimates of how many salmon the river system can support. Throughout the season the biologists use the drift fleet to provide them with data about the strength of the run and to harvest enough fish to prevent an over-escapement. Too many fish up a river is just as bad for salmon survival as too few. With our information added to test fishing, aerial and shore-based surveys of fish moving into the river, including sonar counts of fish entering the river mouths, the team of ADF&G biologists dictate when and where the fish are harvested.

1978 is a normal year until the second week of July. Beginning on Monday that week, all commercial fishing is postponed due to a lack of fish up the river. We know there are fish in the inlet, and the feeling of losing a period during what is traditionally the peak of the run weighs heavily on many fishermen. According to everyone on the dock, it is an all-too-common experience to be shut down by Fish and Game until enough fish have made it into the river to satisfy their escapement needs, then to be turned loose on an inlet empty of fish. The big question on everyone's mind is whether Fish and Game will let us go in time to catch some of this run or not. The fishermen hold their collective breath as deckhands scrub and paint boats, run errands and listen to skippers talk. Missing those fish can mean the difference between paying your bills or taking a second job in the winter. For a deckhand working for 10% of the catch, it means even more.

The word finally comes at the end of the week. An unusual special opening is announced for Saturday, July 16 from noon to 6:00 pm. Six hours. Sockeye salmon have been trickling into the Kenai River for days, and the escapement is steadily nearing its optimum, with a large concentration of fish reported to be milling around outside the river mouth. Fish and Game decides on Friday evening to let us go on short notice. The fleet breathes a collective sigh of relief tempered with the hope that it isn't too late. Skippers strategize and scramble to get last-minute preparations completed. The tension is an electric current of energy that buzzes through everything we do.

Most skippers make quick trips to the store for groceries and head out the river Saturday morning. Word is that the biggest school of fish is just outside the river, meaning we don't need to leave early. We pull away from the dock around 10:00 am. Jim listens to the group radio intently as we head out with the last part of the fleet. Chatter indicates lots of jumpers on the east rip, just three miles straight out of the river mouth, and most of the boats are already there. As we arrive and slow down to look, another report comes in from five miles northwest of us. Jim figures we have just enough time to make it before opening. I'm not sure why he makes the choice to run, but that's not my call. Maybe he thinks it'll be less crowded. Maybe the report up there comes from a more reliable source. I just know he isn't interested in my opinion, if I actually had one. To him it sounds better than staying here. We make a dash for the second school with what appears to be barely enough time to spare.

At 12:05 I'm in the stern with buoy and lines in hand. Jim is coiled tight. He keeps poking his head out of the cabin as we near the body of nearly 200 boats already setting their gear. No one is on the radio. I'm as nervous as Jim. I know this isn't the time to screw up. A mistake now could cost us a lot of fish and might even cost me my job. Jim runs close to the boats on the eastern edge of the fleet. When he turns hard to starboard and yells, "Let her GO!" I toss the buoy and leadline into the water. I pull on the net with all my might, and the reel slowly starts turning. Once the water grabs the net, the reel freewheels with a low-pitched hum as the gear races off the stern. For a few seconds I flail at loose web, but Jim is setting so fast I stand aside and stay out of the way. I keep my hand on the brake in case we have a hangup and watch the web fly by, styrofoam corks hammering on the roller as they leave the boat in a rush.

As the last of the net rolls off the stern, Jim turns our bow south and puts the *North Sea* in neutral. I put the reel in

41

gear, then scramble out of the picking well, joining him on the hatch covers just aft of the cabin. He leans over and grabs both sides of the reel with his hands, staring at the net. I spread my legs wide to keep from being knocked off-balance by the small chop or a stray bigger wave and follow his gaze. White splashes appear up and down the gear. "There's a bunch!" Jim yells, excited. "And another!"

Watching fish hit the net.

I am seeing large splashes, what I'll later come to recognize as groups of twenty or thirty fish, hitting along the length of the net, but I'm totally not understanding what it means. The fish are running so hard with the tide that when they hit near the corkline they come completely out of the water. *Is this normal?* I wonder. A huge splash hits just off the stern, and we both let out a *WHOOP!* "Two bunches right here," I yell. In the excitement it's hard not to point, but Jim's trained me well. "Never point at hits," he warned me early in the season. "Other boats might see you and cork us off." But on this set, there is so much to point at!

Jim is not a man who smiles a lot. His normal demeanor is reserved and serious, so when he breaks into a jig on the hatch covers, I start to realize that this is an exceptional day. The radio chatter starts again and he disappears into the cabin. I keep calling out the hits as he exchanges information with our radio group of twenty boats. Everyone is seeing the same thing, including boats in the other fleet by the river mouth. When he comes out of the cabin, he stares for a short minute as bunch after bunch – maybe twenty or thirty fish each – plow into the net. No longer celebrating, he clenches and unclenches his jaw. "We'd better get to picking," he says grimly. "This keeps up much longer, we'll sink the net."

We both pull on white picking gloves and hop into the stern. Jim is on the port side where the controls are for steering and running the boat. I'm to starboard. Jim bumps the throttle a touch for power, then steps on the treadle at his feet to activate the hydraulic motor that turns the reel. With a high-pitched whine, the reel begins to move, winding the net on and pulling the boat backward along the gear. When the first few feet of net come over the roller, twenty-five seven-pound red salmon fall to the deck at our feet, wet and slapping. Some of the fish are still alive and kicking. We look at each other. "Good start!" he says, raising his eyebrows. Most of the fish are piled in a tangle at our feet, with a few hanging in the web near the lines stretching taut from roller to reel. One of us spreads lines so the other can lift out a fish draped in web. We try to pick fish without jerking web from each other's hands, and we pitch the fish that fall at our feet over the reel and into the hold. The only conversation is each of us keeping count of how many we've picked. When we get to 51, Jim recites his mantra, "51. The name of my old boat." It's a ritual I adopt for the rest of the years I fish: "51. The number of Jim's old boat."

By the time we pick a quarter of a shackle (75 feet) of net, we've passed 200. The corkline that's supposed to float on the surface of the water has disappeared. The entire net, except for the orange buoy that marks the end, 300 yards away, is completely sunk by the weight of the fish. The net vanishes straight down behind the boat, while the buoy floats some 50 yards from us. Jim leans out to look. "If we could tow it, we might be able to raise it up so it's easier to pull on board," he says, thinking out loud, "but the force and the weight of the fish might rip the web right off the lines. We could lose 'em all." His glasses and beard are already covered with fish scales, slime and blood. "We're gonna be here a while." It's 12:45. We haven't even been out here an hour.

The brake on the *North Sea's* reel is too old and weak to hold the weight of the net. The reel keeps slipping backward, sliding fish and web over the stern and back into the water. To prevent that, the boat has a short block of wood screwed to the deck under the reel, and Jim keeps a length of 2x4 cut the proper length to use as a wedge between the block of wood and the outside braces of the reel, locking it in place. Jim is worried that even that might not hold, so he cinches a length of line around the port stern cleat, loops it around the net just as it comes onto the boat, then passes it to me to tie off on the starboard side. Now we have a backup to hold the net in case the brace on the reel slips free or breaks.

We fall into a routine for the next five hours, Jim bumping the boat in reverse just enough to slacken the lines, then barking, "Now!" At his command, I loosen the line from the starboard cleat and undo the loop. He then puts the boat into neutral and steps on the treadle to turn the reel. We help it by pulling on the net until a new wad of fish comes aboard. As soon as they hit the deck, Jim releases the treadle and wedges the brace under the reel while I rewrap the loop of line next to the roller, pull it tight and tie it off on the cleat again. We pick the fish, toss them over the reel into the hold, then do it all again.

44

It's slow, laborious work, and it isn't long before both our backs are aching.

The radio is completely silent. We glance at the boats around us and see crews picking furiously on every back deck. We're lucky we're on the edge of the fleet. We notice several boats with their gear tangled in their neighbor's nets, two or three boats caught in someone else's gear. To salvage the day, more than one skipper has to cut his net free and let it be picked by another crew or lose it altogether. With luck, the other crew is someone they know, who'll pay them back later. Meanwhile, the clock is running. If our nets aren't out of the water by 6:00, we can be ticketed by Fish and Game, which can result in a loss of our catch for the day, confiscation of our gear and the impoundment of our vessel, not to mention a hefty fine.

By 4:00 we barely have half the net on board, almost a thousand fish in the hold, and know we're in trouble. We reel on another large wad of fish. Jim cleans his glasses and looks around with a frown, his jaw working again. Boats around us are loaded up and starting to leave, heading to the river. Without a word, he leaves me to pick while he goes to the cabin to call for help. Just before 5:00, two boats arrive, their fish already delivered. One is Gene Kempf, a member of our group who comes alongside and drops his deckhand, Craig, off with us. The other is Thor, Jim's son, on the *Cheryl Lynne*, named for his deckhand and girlfriend, Cheryl Amundsen, a local teacher and a friend. Cheryl has never run the boat until Thor gives her the helm and tells her to get close enough to us so he can step off the bow onto the *North Sea*. She tells me later she is terrified, but she handles the maneuver like a seasoned veteran, then moves the boat away and waits.

Thor and Jim hold a short, intense discussion as to what to do. They know we can't pick fast enough to be done by 6:00, so they decide to pull the net and fish onto the boat before we're out of time. We're already low in the water with the weight of all the fish, so we can't put the net in the stern without fear of

45

swamping. After talking it over, Jim looks at us. "Let's pull it over the reel and into the fish hold. Pat and Thor, you're the biggest, so you're in the stern, Craig and I'll get in the hold." It's a good plan, but we don't have anywhere near the manpower we need to lift all the weight of the loaded net. With the reel helping get fish into the stern, even all four of us can't muscle the weight of all those fish over it. After struggling and failing for several tries, we stop and talk it over. "Let's try pulling it up from the side of the boat," Thor suggests. "It's a shorter lift."

On either side of the roller are "fairleads," three-to four-foot-tall upright steel rollers that help guide the net onto the reel. It takes all four of us to lift a cleared section of the net over the three-foot-tall starboard fairlead. With the net still attached to the locked and braced reel, we slide the gear around the starboard side of the boat next to the fish hold, now almost half-full of salmon. Jim and Craig stand in the hold, nearly knee-deep in dead salmon while Thor and I kneel on the 12-inch combing between the open hold and the edge of the boat. As the boat rolls with the chop that the afternoon winds have stirred up, we bend over and reach as far down as we can to grab lines and web. We hold it as the boat pauses, then rolls back to port, lifting the gear and fish out of the water. We pass the net back to Jim and Craig. They hold it while Thor and I turn, lean over and grab another length. If the chop wasn't there to help us pull, we could never get any of the fish on board.

Two hours after they join us, Craig and Thor are back on their respective boats and running to the river. Unloaded and light, they disappear long before we make the mouth. The *North Sea's* speed over the ground is normally seven-knots, or eight miles an hour. We've drifted south with the tide most of the afternoon, and with the weight we're carrying – even with the tide behind us – we're barely doing three. Low in the water, we have a foot of freeboard to spare as we wallow our way up the Inlet. When we pull into the river it's after midnight. The sky is moonless and dark, but the cannery and the river in front of it is a bright beehive of activity. The dock is awash in white arc lights. Three different tenders bathed in orange sodium deck lights each have two lines of ten or more boats waiting to deliver. Black shadows of boats and skiffs ferrying fishermen to shore are moving up and down river. On the dock, workers shovel flake ice onto fish in plastic totes. Headlights glow and flash from forklifts moving totes from the dock to a staging area outside the cannery where they wait to be loaded onto flatbed trucks. Those trucks will ferry fish to canneries for processing a hundred miles away in Seward. No one, including the processors, expected such a harvest. Canneries up and down the river are all overwhelmed by the immense volume of fish.

We have our own problems. On the way in, I stand on the chaos of fish and lines in the hold and pick fish out of the gear until it gets too dark to see. I grab an hour in the bunk that feels like five minutes. Jim wakes me as we enter the river. We can't even think of getting in line to deliver until we can untangle the mess in the hold. We tie up next to the *St. Christina*, skippered by Frankie DeScala, a first-generation Italian and an old friend of Jim's. Frankie, short, stocky and boisterous, runs out of his cabin, enthusiastically pumps Jim's hand, asking questions about our day and telling us about his. As Jim rigs a trouble light for us to work by, I begin pulling the net out of the hold and over the reel where we can stand, pick and pile the lines as we clear the gear. Frankie invites us to dinner. Looking at all the work we have to do, neither of us feel like taking the time to eat, though the smell of authentic Italian spaghetti drifting out of the *St. Christina's* cabin is killing us. I haven't eaten since breakfast, at 8:00 am this morning. "It's really a two-person job," Jim apologizes. "We'd love to, but we need to get this straightened out, and it looks like it'll take most of the night." Obviously disappointed, Frankie nods and goes down the steps into his cabin with a wave. "He loves to talk," Jim whispers with a shrug.

We are just getting to work when Frankie comes out of the cabin again, this time with his deckhand in tow, a nephew he's brought over from the old country for the fishing season. Frankie insists one of us come eat while his nephew helps out. The nephew doesn't speak any English, but he knows what needs to be done. He joins me in the stern while Jim disappears with Frankie for a plate of spaghetti. My stomach rumbles for the next half hour. I can hear them talking and Frankie laughing while they eat and have a cigarette. Jim finally returns and sends me in for the best spaghetti meal I've ever tasted in that hot, cramped cabin. I return to our boat full, sweaty and refreshed. Jim, on the other hand, looks spent. "Hit the bunk," I tell him. "We got this. I'll wake you when we're done." It's 2:00 am.

By 5:00 the sky is just beginning to brighten when the nephew heads to the bunk, and I finish the last of the picking. We have the leadline coiled on one side of the picking well, and the corkline on the other with a mound of very raggedy-looking green web in between. I figure we have somewhere around 2,000 fish in the hold. I wake Jim up, and he makes us some welcome, though bitter, hot coffee. There are still two boats behind each of the tenders, so there's no rush. We start the *North Sea's* engine and use the reel to help us thread the net back onto the drum, then untie and get in line to deliver. The official tally is just over 2,200 fish, or 15,000 pounds. The price is $1.25 a pound.

At 10:00 am Sunday morning, after pitching all the fish into a brailer at the tender, I pull into our driveway – a full 24 hours after I left the river. Veronica is still in bed, awake and reading. Already sore and stiffening up, I shuffle into the bedroom smelling like fish, covered in blood and slime and peppered with scales. Her eyes widen. "How'd it go? Are you okay?" she asks. In answer I raise my arms. All day and night I picked fish with cotton gloves on my hands and my flannel

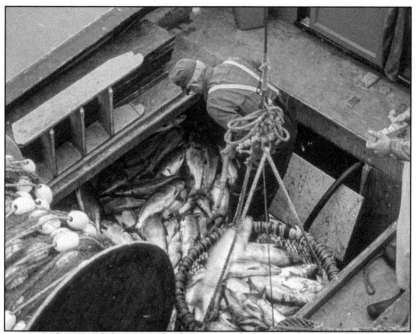
Delivering fish to a tender by tossing them into a brailer, 1976.

sleeves rolled. No skin is visible from my elbows to my wrists.
My forearms are completely covered with fish scales. She gets
up and gives me a kiss, but not before she picks a fish scale out
of my beard. "We have to get into this business!" I exclaim.

Chapter Seven: Transitions

I'm sitting on a painted, beat-up wooden stool next to Jim as we motor out the river for our first period of 1979. It's 2:00 am, and the sun is brushing a pale yellow under the clouds on the northeastern horizon. There's a chill in the air. Jim steers around the last bend where we are greeted with four-foot rollers as the incoming tide meets the outgoing river. The rollers don't last long, and soon we are leaving them behind on a southwest heading toward the red buoy marking the southernmost tip of the sand bar below Kalgin Island. It's a spot that regularly produces decent amounts of fish on the flood, and is a promising drift to start the period. The plan is to fish the southern part of our district today, then spend the weekend in an anchorage known on the charts as Tuxedni Bay, but more commonly known to the fishermen of the fleet as Snug Harbor, on the southwest side of the Inlet. We spent a weekend there last year too, rafted to other boats at anchor and skiffing to the small Snug Harbor cannery for showers, groceries and basketball on the boardwalk. Snug is strikingly beautiful, surrounded by 3,000-foot snow-tipped mountains rising out of the water, with all-white Mt. Iliamna, a 10,000-foot active volcano dominating the view behind them. I'm looking forward to the visit.

If we're not talking about boat work or fishing, Jim and I don't converse much. Though we have a lot in common – both of us are teachers, he's an artist and I'm a photographer, we both play basketball in the Kenai city league – we just have a difficult time relating. I am uncomfortable with his discomfort, and when I try and sort out the why of it, I think that even though he hired me, he disapproves of the way I handled the split with Cindy and the resulting relationship with my new wife. This is only my theory, and I'm on board for a second year, so I must've done something right. Or maybe he just doesn't want to train someone new again so soon. The uncertainty of it keeps my mouth shut.

The beauty of the morning, the salt smell in the air, and the anticipation of a fresh season wells up within me as he opens the throttle to the wide sea glistening in front of us, and I can't help myself when I blurt out, "This gets into your blood, doesn't it?" Jim turns abruptly and gives me a piercing look. He doesn't answer, and I never know whether I struck a chord with him or a nerve.

The first week of June, before I had to help out with boat work, Veronica and I take a trip to California. I'm on my way to attend the Ansel Adams Photography Workshop in Yosemite, but we land in San Francisco for a few days together before I have to leave. One particularly beautiful evening we are in Mill Valley for dinner, discussing whether or not to buy a boat and permit. We both have been asking friends and family what they think, and the reviews are mixed. We walk the sunset and worry we'll over-extend ourselves. Permits sell for $80,000 or more, and that doesn't include gear or a boat. I'm hoping to get a decent used cannery boat for $20,000, but 100 grand is an overwhelming amount of money to borrow. We both have jobs, but I'm not tenured yet, and she's just started working for Phillips Petroleum as a lab assistant. Then Veronica remembers what Spence DeVito, one of our most financially successful friends told me during a poker game: "When you're between 25 and 55, you're in the peak earning years of your life. That's the time to use other people's money as much as you can to get where you want. Don't be afraid to go into debt. Just pay it off before you retire." That tips the scales. We decide to buy in and fish together, maybe even raise a family of fishermen. Spence's advice is some of the best counsel I ever receive, and it only costs me the $40 I lose to him when his aces beat my queens.

1979 turns out to be as lousy a season as '78 was spectacular. We spend most days chasing fish that aren't there.

51

Reports on the radio go bust before we can make a move to them, and even the best fishermen in our group are returning to port with dismal catches. To make matters worse, Veronica and I are in the midst of a first-year rough patch, and are walking the edge of splitting up. Most of the summer, when I'm on land I'm wishing I was on the boat, and most of my time on the boat is spent wanting to be back on land. When Fish and Game shuts us down for the season at the end of July, I am both relieved and disappointed.

The slow days at the end of the season do have a silver lining, though. Jim asks me if I'm coming back for another year. "The job is yours if you want it," he remarks over a sandwich as we sit on a set watching the occasional single salmon plunk into the net.

"I've been considering buying my own permit," I answer. "What do you think?"

He actually smiles. "You'd make six."

"Huh?"

"I've had five crew end up skippers," he says, puffing up. "You'd be number six. I think you'll do fine. You're a better crew than some of those guys."

That conversation marks a sea change in our relationship. From that moment on, I have a mentor, a sensei to go to for advice, something I'll do for years when faced with decisions about fishing. Jim becomes a conduit of good sense who helps me navigate more than one difficult decision over the next several years. The first one is sooner than I expect.

Chapter Eight: Strike One

Launching the Skookum Too down the Ways for the first time, 1980.
Photo by Panoramio Don

Six of us, Veronica, myself and four friends ride our 'new' boat down the ways toward the river for the first time. It's the third week of June, 1980, and after weeks of boat work, this feels like a carnival ride. In between the whoops and hollers of excitement, Chris, my fishing partner and I are scrambling around checking for leaks, making sure the bilge pumps are working, taking the tin coffee can off the stack (it's been there all winter, keeping rain and snow out), checking and rechecking the screwdriver jammed into the empty side of the battery knife switch so both batteries will engage to start the engine, and generally making everyone else nervous. This short ride to the river is symbolic to us: it is the culmination of a journey that's taken a year of effort to complete. We've been moving down this ramp toward fishing since last fall, and now we're putting our boat in the water! If only she doesn't sink.

During the winter of 1979-80, Veronica and I partner up with Chris Banas and his wife Gigi, two close friends and fellow teachers, to buy a permit, boat and gear. They have no experience fishing, but love the idea of being on the water every bit as much as we do. The purchase takes creative financial scrambling. We find a permit and three shackles of used gear for $70,000. I negotiate a deal with the cannery to buy a boat for $16,000. For our half of the payment, Veronica and I scrape together all the money we can. I borrow $2,000 from my brother Mike, and she tosses in her Chevy Blazer as part of the deal. The boat we purchase from the cannery is an old company boat with a wooden hull. We are so excited that we show up at the cannery before anyone else is there. The winter watchman shakes his head at us as we clamber up the boat carrying power tools and supplies. "You know there's no electricity to the yard yet, right?" We wave him off with a smile and open the hatch covers to see how big the hold is. We stand in the stern, imagining what it'll be like to set the net and pull it on full of fish. We don't have a clue how much we don't yet know, but our enthusiasm is boundless. Chris and I spend every available minute of time crawling around inside her as the port engineers install a newly rebuilt engine. We ask questions about the fuel system, the electrical system, the exhaust, the cooling system, the hydraulics, the water tanks, the fuel tanks, the reel, the electronics. It's a crash course in how boats work, and we drink it all in until we have just enough knowledge to be dangerous rather than effective when we break down.

Our boat, the *F/V* (Fishing Vessel) *Skookum Too* was never designed to actually fish. It was a plug – a template – for making a fiberglass mold used to lay up hulls of 'real' boats. The planks have no corking, or cotton batting between them to keep seawater out like most wooden boats do. I notice this as I climb aboard her in the spring and see daylight between the planks of the hull. When I ask Cliff, the head of the Beach Gang what to do, he replies in his raspy, Minnesotan lisp, "You gotta water down the hull. Get some soaker hoses and put 'em in the hold and stern compartment. Run 'em for a week or so, and she should swell right up." I've never heard of such a thing. My mouth hangs open, but Cliff isn't Benny, so I don't think he's messing with me. I thank him and make a mental note to pick up some hoses at the hardware store in town. "Check out the *Kon Tiki*," Cliff adds as I turn to go. "She's the same hull as yours, and Chartan waters her every spring." As I head back to the boat, I swing by the *Kon Tiki* to find soaker hoses snaked over the pilings under her, spraying the length of the hull. *I'll be damned.*

Two weeks later, I'm looking for Cliff again. We've been watering the hull every day, and amazingly the planks have swollen some, but not enough. There are still some serious gaps between the planks of the hull. We now know why the *Skookum* has five – five! – bilge pumps. But even they won't be enough if we don't figure out a way to seal the hull better. I find Cliff sitting sidesaddle on his four-wheeler in front of the can shop. It's a pose I'll see him strike for the next 18 years. "Hey, Cliff." I explain our problem and he nods.

"When are you going in the water?"

"Tomorrow."

"Ok. Go up the stairs at the back of the warehouse. At the top, against the far wall you'll see some five-gallon buckets of Crisco and an old pair of leather gloves. Take the gloves and one of the cans, and grease up the seams between the planks tonight. The grease'll hold the water off until the planks swell up tight."

I laugh at him. "What? You're shitting me."

He gives me a patient smile. "Nope. Trust me. It'll work."

Cliff Oeren, Beach Gang foreman, 1982.

I still don't believe it, but sure enough the Crisco and gloves are exactly where he said they'd be. Chris and I grease the seams with generous wads of vegetable fat and worry that our boat will go down like a rock as soon as she hits the water.

She doesn't. We slide into the river, the engine fires right up, and we make our maiden voyage all of 100 feet to the float without a mishap. Now we really are fishermen. We must be. We have a boat. As we approached this day, I realized that over the past two years Jim taught me how to be *on* a boat, but not how to *run* one.

The next day Chris and I enlist Harold Holten, the skipper of the 61-foot cannery tender *Beaver* to show us how to dock the boat in the river. We pull away and return to the float dozens of times – against the current, with the current, and at slack tide, when the river stops flowing altogether. We learn to use the lines to help us steer away from the float when the wind or current is pushing against us. We learn how to use a midship 'spring line' to tie off quickly alongside another boat. We learn the subtlety of 'walking' the boat into or out of a tight spot, not by using engine power but by bumping it gently from forward to neutral and back again with the throttle at idle. We also begin to understand how different steering a boat is from driving a car. Boats are slower to respond to the wheel and have no brakes. A good skipper anticipates an action well in advance.

Harold is generous with his time, patient, and a good teacher. We've only known him a few short weeks, but we cement the friendship by drinking a half-rack of Budweiser with him afterward in the galley of the *Beaver*. We go out of our way to deliver our fish to him the rest of the season and treat his crew to ice-cold beers from our cooler each time we pull alongside.

One day, after we've had a good catch and are feeling particularly frisky, we're yelling over the noise and laughing as Harold works the hydraulics to raise a brailer full of salmon out of our fish hold. Brailers are large canvas bags lowered into the holds of the fishing boats that deckhands pitch fish into. Once they are filled with 100 or so fish, they are lifted out of the boat and deposited on the deck of the tender by releasing a catch-chain that opens a hole in the bottom of the bag. But this time the chain comes loose from its catch. None of us are paying attention, and when the end of the chain snags on the side cleat of the *Skookum*, it releases the load of fish between the two vessels, dumping almost 800 pounds of dead salmon into the river.

Everything – all motion, conversation, the whine of the hydraulics – stops. I stare at the river, then at Harold, who looks back at me with a shrug. "It's okay, Pat," he says with a sheepish grin. "We'll credit you the fish. But we'd probably better tone it down a little."

A few days after launching her, we plan a trip to take the *Skookum* out on the Inlet for a 'shakedown' cruise, where we can open up the engine and run her at full throttle. It's a few

57

The CWF tender Beaver, 1980.

days until the first period, so most guys are taking it easy, and half of them aren't even around the cannery at all. A good portion of the fleet is local, and those skippers and crew are most likely at home enjoying their families before the season starts. We untie from the outside of a raft of five boats and head downriver with beer in the cooler and a pizza on the table. We get 50 yards from the float when the engine dies. The tide is going out, and we're floating downriver with the current.

Before we left the dock, I noticed Eric, one of our group, was on his boat in the string in front of me. I call him on the CB. "Yeah, *Dancing Sky*, *Skookum Too*. You pick me up?" Eric considers himself to be the best fisherman in the Inlet, and though he's definitely good, his arrogance is off-putting. I'm a newbie and not worth his time. So far, we don't like each other much.

"*Dancing Sky* back." "Yeah, Eric. We're broken down and drifting downriver. Could you give us a tow back to the dock?"

"Uh, I'm pinned in by boats outside me. Don't think so. Why don't you call the cannery?"

"Ah, I guess I can. Since you're part of our fishing group, I called you first."

"Yeah, hang on." A minute later he comes back on. "Yeah, the *Cheechako's* on its way. He was outside me and heard the radio."

"Great! Thanks. *Skookum Too* out."

"I'm out."

Seconds later the *Cheechako*, a small, sleek brown boat pulls alongside. "You guys need a lift?" says the skipper with a wide bearded grin. I immediately like this guy.

"We'd love to stay here - it's a great view," I shoot back. "But yes, we could use a tow."

"I'm Dean and this is Danny," he laughs. "Let's tie off and I'll take you to a buoy. The cannery'll send a skiff out to haul you back. They can dock you way better than I can."

Dean pulls closer. We put buoys in between the two boats, then he and Danny teach us how to tie the side and stern cleats together and stretch a line between our bows. As we move upriver, we discuss why the engine stopped. "Check your fuel filter first," Dean advises. The floorboards are already open to the engine, and we discover the filter is clogged with what looks like clear jelly. "That's bacteria from your fuel tanks," Dean offers. "If you don't kill that stuff and treat your tanks every year, that'll happen."

"Wait," I say. "You mean bacteria GROWS in diesel?"

"Yep. Hard to believe anything lives in that shit, but it does." Dean puts our bow next to the buoy, where Chris grabs a line hanging off it with our boathook and loops the line around our bow cleat. We thank them as Danny unties and Dean heads back to the float with a wave. "The cannery office is on the VHF – channel 23. Shouldn't take them long to get to you."

Once we're back on land, I run to town and buy some diesel treatment at an auto parts store. I also swing by the liquor store and grab a half-case of Budweiser. Danny's told me it's Dean's favorite beer. I take it down to the *Cheechako* that evening, and Dean insists I not leave until we drink it together. Danny sips coffee and joins the fun. It's the beginning of two long, enjoyable friendships, and the best breakdown I ever have.

CWF Port Engineer Jim Harrison directing the lowering of the Skookum Too's rebuilt engine to the boat from the dock, 1980.

The biggest selling point for the *Skookum* is the rebuilt Caterpillar 3160 diesel that the cannery paid to install. The port engineers call it a "school-bus engine". It seems fitting for a schoolteacher-fisherman to use – a term I slowly realize is used to denigrate fishermen who aren't full-timers, and supposedly can't be as good at the job. When I hear the term "teacher-fisherman" stage-whispered at mug-up about me, I silently vow to become a better fisherman than the guy who mutters it loud enough for me to hear. I know him. On land, he's a blowhard. I doubt he's much different at sea.

Finally, after months of preparation, when the engine finally starts, after all the web is mended by Veronica's inexperienced hands, after all the groceries and gear are bought (on credit) and stowed, we meet Chris and Gigi at the cannery the evening before the first period and leave the river with the fleet.

Early in the season, the few fish in the district are only found near the southern boundary. It's a six-hour run for slow boats like ours, so we leave early on a fish day. The river mouth can go dry with a large ebb tide, and when that coincides with a fishing period, all but the fastest boats leave the river the night before. The bight on the east side of Kalgin Island is a popular anchorage when it blows from the southwest. Chris and I have done some homework about anchoring, but we've never attempted it. Word is that the Kalgin bight has a rocky bottom, making it difficult for an anchor to hold when the wind blows. It's dusk when we drop ours in a small space just north of most of the 30 or so boats already there, their single white anchor lights gleaming at the tops of their masts. I make a note to replace the burnt-out bulb in ours.

Dropping the anchor involves holding the boat in place until the anchor touches bottom, laying out twenty or more feet of line so the anchor has some 'scope', or room to swing the boat when the tide changes, then we bump the boat in reverse to 'set' the anchor, digging it into the bottom. Having never tried it, we take an embarrassingly long time to get it right. But it seems good when the four of us climb into the bunks for our first night on the boat. We go to bed full of ourselves. We feel like real fishermen, at least until sleep doesn't come. The boat rocks with the waves that are stirred up by the wind, and everything on the boat that can move, does. Dishes clank in the sink. Silverware shifts in the drawer. Tools clunk in the cubbies. The rigging clangs against the mast and outriggers. Something rolls back and forth and thuds in a drawer with each rock of the boat. Waves splash against the hull. Against all odds, Chris falls asleep and snores. *Jesus.*

Somehow, I drift off. When a boat roars by and wakes us, I feel like I haven't slept at all. We roll out of the bunks and look out the windows. "Where are we?" asks Gigi. Kalgin Island is over a mile west of us.

"We dragged anchor!" I'm astonished that we didn't hit any other boats or tangle anchors as we drifted out of the fleet in the night. We slept through the whole thing. I imagine our anchor fathoms deep, hanging in the water off our bow. We pull it and spend the day making set after set, getting waterhaul after waterhaul, the nickname for a set with no fish. Another realization about my lack of education with Jim hits me: after two seasons he taught me *how* to fish, but not how to *catch* fish. By the time we pull the last set on board and point the boat at the entrance to Snug Harbor, we have fourteen fish for twelve hours work.

Snug Harbor is the common name for Tuxedni Bay, a strikingly beautiful body of water between the 3,000-foot mountains of the Alaska Peninsula and the sheer cliffs and dense willow of Chisik Island. Originally built in the early 1900's to can the abundant clams harvested nearby, it was taken over by the cannery foreman, Eric Fribrock, who transformed it into a salmon cannery, complete with a dock, fueling station, mess hall, bunkhouses for workers and fishermen, a winter watchman's house and a giant warehouse housing a canning operation on the shores of the island. He also supervised the building of a small fleet of stout wooden 'Snug' boats, and ran the cannery successfully until his son Joe took over the operation in 1952 until he died in 1976.

The view from the cannery across the bay is staggering, with the snow-capped Iliamna volcano peaking over the smaller mountains rising from the sea and a fog bank rising near the far shore.

We spend the weekend in Snug. Saturday is filled with boat work and maintenance. We pull anchor and run to the cannery for ice for the cooler, water and fuel, then anchor up a little closer to shore near a waterfall cascading hundreds of feet off a shale cliff dotted with lush green willow. By day's end, we

Snug Harbor Cannery, Chisik Island, Alaska.

are ready for a relaxing evening of cards and beer. The sun sets after 11:00 pm in June, and the pink glow of the clouds reflects on the glassy water as a fog forms across the bay. The mountains to the west turn purple in the dusk. We all sleepily agree this is one of the most beautiful places we've ever seen. The last one to climb in the bunk, I take one more look around. A big fiberglass boat has pulled in behind us, and I hear his anchor chain rattle off the bow. I make a mental note of our position relative to a buoy just off shore. Satisfied the anchor is holding, I slide in next to Veronica and listen to the water gurgle past the hull as I drift off.

It's early Sunday morning when I awaken with the thought, *Something is different.* The sound of the water has changed. Trying not to wake anyone, I slide out of the bunk for

Veronica in the stern of the Skookum Too, Snug Harbor.

a look around. The buoy by the shore and the boat behind us seem to be in the same place. My eyes are dry, so I dab some water on them, towel them off and look again. The buoy has moved further up the shore. I look back at the boat behind us. It's bigger than it was, closer, bow looming toward our stern. I shout "WAKE UP! We're dragging anchor!" as I jump to the helm and grab the key, "We're drifting down on a boat behind us!" Chris is the first one out of the bunk. I turn the key on the dash, but the engine only groans. I look at the battery switch, and the long screwdriver we use to connect the second battery is gone. "Where's the fucking screwdriver!?!"

Veronica and Gigi scramble to open the toolbox. Barefoot, Chris jumps up the steps and out the door, yelling, "It's in the stern!" He runs aft while I move to the door. We are 50 feet from the other boat, our stern aiming dead-center for its tall bow. If we hit, the much bigger boat could ride right over us, sinking us in seconds. Chris grabs the screwdriver and lobs it over the reel in a perfect softball pitch. It skitters to a stop against the doorstep. I jam it in the knife switch and turn the key. The *Skookum's* engine fires up, and I move the gearshift and throttle forward as far as I can. She leaps forward, and looking out the door I see Chris standing in our stern, hand high on the other boat's bow, pushing it away. Aware of anchor lines from both boats in the water near us, I throttle back and we move off. We reset the anchor well clear of other boats and brew coffee to calm our nerves while we consider how close to disaster we were. We make a vow to always put the screwdriver back in the switch when we finish using it. I make a pledge to buy a new battery switch as soon as we get home.

The rest of Sunday is uneventful. We get a lift to the cannery in a skiff, take walks and enjoy poking around the old buildings until our ride heads back to the boats. After a good night's sleep, we wake up early to a beautiful dawn, enthusiastic and ready for another day's fishing. We eat store-bought muffins for breakfast, pull the anchor and start for the mouth of the bay. To add to our enthusiasm, we look around and realize we've got a jump on the rest of the fleet. We're the first ones up. As we idle through all the other boats still at anchor, Chris is on deck, yelling, "Let's go FISHING! WAKE UP!" when I get a radio call from Eric on the *Dancing Sky*.

"Uh, yeah, *Skookum Too*, where you going?"

Still caught up in the delirium of the moment, I eagerly key the microphone and half-shout, "We're going fishing! Better wake up and join us, or you'll miss out!" Veronica, Gigi and I all laugh.

"You must not have gotten the word. We're on strike. No fishing today."

Our bubble pops. I slow the boat down and turn back. Shit. "What? Really?'

"Yep. Price is too low. There's a meeting in town tomorrow about it. Everyone's heading back today. I'm out."

We are stunned, disappointed, embarrassed, then angry. "What does that mean?" we ask each other as we set the anchor one more time. "Who is on strike? Everyone? Why didn't we hear about this?" We find it hard to believe that every boat in the Inlet, over 700 of them, are all in agreement about this. We are educators, for Chrissakes! We've never seen a group of schoolteachers ever agree on anything, let alone a strike. They can't make a decision on what makes a student tardy rather than absent! Shitshitshit! When the tide is right, we head back to the river with the rest of the fleet.

On the way, we discuss what's happening. WHY are we striking? For a better price? What's wrong with the price we have? We don't understand fish markets yet, or expenses vs earnings, price-fixing or what's fair. All we've known since we decided to get into fishing is the incessant boat work of getting ready. Now we have to deal with politics? "Bullshit. Let's just go fishing," we argue among ourselves, "Let these other guys work out this crap. We need to figure out how to catch fish." Plus, we've got a ton of debt to recover. "We can't afford to sit at the dock and wait for the processors to come to us. We need to start making money."

I know that strike-breaking is the wrong thing to do. We all do. It's always been a no-brainer to me that if a teacher strike were to happen, to be an effective tool everyone needs to participate. My confusion isn't about supporting a strike. The problem is that I don't yet see myself as a fisherman. Sure, I have a permit and a boat; I work as hard as anyone else to get ready for the season; but I still haven't fished but one day in my life other than as a deckhand; I haven't earned the right to be a card-carrying member of the club. I suppose I'll merit it eventually, but until then, I'm just a "teacher who fishes." The concerns of fishermen aren't my problem, are they? If I go fishing while the rest of the guys sit on the beach, how can my small effort create a problem for all these other professionals?

The other fishermen around the cannery who see us as green and dumb make it a point to talk about strikebreakers when we're around. As the next scheduled fishing period looms, they mention guys who had gone fishing during the last strike in less than complimentary terms. Though the stories aren't clear or complete, we start listening more attentively. They are speaking about us, to us, without ever mentioning our names.

After listening frustrated on the dock all that first day, we meet back at Chris's house to hash things out. We decide that as much as we want to fish, we won't go until we get a straight answer from someone who knows what that means. We agree that Jim is the best person to ask. He has experience and perspective, and he'll be honest. I'll ask him the next day if it looks like the strike will continue.

I find him at mug-up the next morning. The canneries haven't budged on the price. There's a growing tension and an angry tone to the fishermen's talk around us as I ask him if we can have a private conversation on his boat after coffee. Tight-lipped, he agrees with a short nod of his head. I don't want to embarrass him by asking naive, perhaps sensitive questions of him in public, so I leave him in the mug-up room with the old-timers, and walk out to the boardwalk and listen to the fishermen complain:

"Fuckin' canneries. They can settle this in a heartbeat if they want to."

"No reason for us to sit on the beach, goddammit."

"This is a waste of time. I swear I'm leavin'. I'm sellin' downriver if this doesn't end soon."

"We're always getting' the lowest fuckin' price. Fuck these guys."

It's the beginning of a long education. I join Jim half-an-hour later in the cabin of the *North Sea*. I sit in the doorway as he works on a windshield-wiper motor. His actions are slow and deliberate. So is his speech. "You don't want to go fishing, Pat. Not during a strike. I know how bad you want to go, but you risk losing a lot more than a few dollars if you do." He tells me a story of a guy who had done just that, years ago. He fished while everyone else was on the beach striking, and for that he was blackballed by his friends and competitors alike. Other fishermen quit talking to him, even the cannery workers lost respect for him, and as a result he always had trouble getting the services he needed, couldn't count on help if he got in trouble at sea, and lost the friendships and support he had taken for granted when he decided to make money at someone else's expense. No one ever forgot what he did. After years of diminished support, he sold out, but his reputation followed him. When he moved to Bristol Bay, the same thing happened. He eventually got out of fishing altogether. "You don't want that." Jim looked as serious as I'd ever seen him as he tightened a screw on the wiper motor and looked over his glasses at me. "That's not the way to start your fishing career."

I sit on the step and nod. "I get it. Thanks, Jim." I make the long walk up the ramp to meet Chris, Gigi and Veronica. "What'd he say?"

We stay off the grounds with the rest of the fleet, go to meetings and chew our nails until the canneries up their price a week later. Wrapped in that decision is the realization that I really *am* a fisherman. I may be new, but I'm part of this world – not an outsider looking in. In the meantime, we can't stand not using this boat we'd spent so long getting ready to fish. During the closure, we load her up with sport fishing rods and a case of beer and go trolling for salmon in the river mouth. The other fishermen think we're crazy – and of course we are.

A week later, the canneries come up in price – not enough to satisfy everyone, but enough to get the fleet back on the water. With the strike over, we head out of the river, and not knowing any better, we throw out the gear and... take naps. Our first season is all about lessons and opportunities, most of which we survive and learn from...sometimes barely. One early period, Spike, who runs the *Snug Seven* and is in our radio group, is just north of me as we fish near the east rip off Salamatof beach north of the river. It's a slow day, and as usual, I am not paying enough attention to what is going on around me. The tide has just changed and Chris is in the bunk. I've turned the engine off for some peace and quiet, and I'm almost asleep in the skipper's chair when I hear Spike on the radio talking to someone.

"Spike, is that you just north of the *Skookum Too*?"

"Yeah, roger that."

"Getting anything up there?"

"No, but the tide just switched and the rip's starting to work, so maybe something'll show."

"Are you towing?"

"Yeah, just a touch to the west. Looks like Pat is napping. He's gonna be surprised as hell when he wakes up and finds the rip has rolled his net into a ball!"

"Hah. I bet. Well, I may set out above you a ways. Thanks for the comeback. I'm out."

"Roger that. I'm out."

By the time they sign off, I'm on my feet looking out the window at the net, which is starting to look swirled and balled up in spots. Sure enough, just off my starboard side less than a hundred feet, the rip is snaking its way toward me, foam beginning to froth along its path. I can actually *hear* it! It hisses and gives me chills. *Thanks, Spike!* I think as I fire up the engine. I don't know if he knew I was listening or not, but as I tow the net away from the rip, I am grateful for his comment.

One of Chris' gifts is his ability to see humor in almost everything, and we spend a lot of time entertaining each other. We are sitting on deck during a set one calm, slow afternoon eating sandwiches for lunch, when we decide to call home and let Veronica and Gigi know how we're doing. We call the VHF Radio Marine Operator, a land-based telephone service for mariners. For years, the Marine Operator system was the only way commercial fishermen could contact loved ones on land. We'd switch the VHF radio to the nearest operator channel, and contact them to place a call from radio to telephone. The call was always collect, and the person on land had to agree to accept charges. Often times a conversation would already be in progress when you tuned in the radio, and then you'd wait, listening to the conversation until it was finished before calling the operator yourself. As a courtesy to its customers, the operator service would scramble the signal coming from the vessel, replacing it with a busy signal whenever the party on the boat would key the microphone. As we eat and wait for our turn, Chris and I eavesdrop on another call just under way:

ring… ring… ring… click.
"Hello?"
"This is the Nikiski Marine Operator. I have a collect call from the vessel *Northern Star*. Will you accept the charge?"
"Uh, yeah…okay. Sure."
"Go ahead *Northern Star.*"
BEEP – BEEP – BEEP.
"Ohhh, hi, honey… How's fishing?"
BEEP – BEEP – BEEP
"Oh, I, uh, I tried calling earlier because I needed to tell you about the fire."
BEEP – BEEP
"Last night I was cooking dinner, and some oil in the frying pan caught on fire."
BEEP – BEEP – BEEP

70

"Oh, yeah, we're all ok. Dani had to miss her soccer game today, though."

BEEP – BEEP – BEEP

"We're staying at Kenny's, and the soccer field is on the other side of town."

BEEP – BEEP

"Because the house burnt down. I told you that."

… BEEP – BEEP - BEEP – BEEP – BEEP

"I was cooking dinner on the stove, and the oil in the pan flared up and caught the cabinet on fire … and, uh, by the time we realized what was happening, the curtain was in flames, and… and… it all just happened so FAST!"

… … … BEEP – BEEP – BEEP – BEEP

"No. Nothing. We just barely got the dog out."

BEEP – BEEP

"Nooo, I didn't have time. Your guitar was upstairs. Honey, I'm sorry."

BEEP – BEEP - BEEP – BEEP - BEEP – BEEP

"So am I. At least we're all safe. Come home as soon as you can, okay?"

BEEP – BEEP – BEEP – BEEP

"No. The carport fell on the Harley when the house collapsed. The firemen wouldn't let me move it – it was too dangerous – too close to the house."

BEEP – BEEP

"The insurance man said it was totaled."

BEEP – BEEP - BEEP – BEEP - BEEP – BEEP - BEEP – BEEP – BEEP

… BEEP – BEEP

"It wasn't my FAULT! Even the firemen said things like this happen. The kids were fighting, and I just turned away from the stove for a SECOND… Don't yell at me."

… BEEP – BEEP – BEEP

"It's okay. We're all upset." (Takes a breath) "Anyway, we're staying at Kenny's until you can get home and we figure out

what to do. Honey, I'm sorry, but I have to go. I've got to be at the hospital in ten minutes."
BEEP – BEEP
"Oh! Your Dad had a heart attack last night after he heard about the fire. It looks like he'll be okay, but I told the doctor I'd be there to talk to him about what the tests say at five."
BEEP – BEEP – BEEP
"I'll tell you all about it LATER. I'll try to call around eight. I HAVE to go. Bye."
BEEP – BEEP

…click.
"*Northern Star*, will there be anything else?"
BEEP – BEEP
"Thank you, *Northern Star*. Have a good day."

§

Chris and I work well together for the most part, though he chafes sometimes at me taking the role of skipper. He's as big as I am, strong, and willing to do hard work, but he voices frustration with me for wanting to be at the cannery more than he does. His day job is teaching Special Education, like me, but he loves woodworking and carpentry, and just prior to the season we begin fishing together, he finished building his own house off Cannery Road, a mile from where we dock the boat. He loves being at home more than hanging at the cannery, which I love as much as being around boats. I live 15 miles from the cannery, so when I head there I stay as long as possible. If I'm not working on the boat, I'm visiting with new friends or photographing. After a heated discussion, we agree our labor doesn't have to be an equal division of effort or time spent.

The partnership between us is planned to dissolve after the first year. Anyone with a minimum of two year's experience fishing can qualify for a low-interest loan from the state to buy a permit as long as they've been an Alaskan resident for at least five years. Since I have been a resident for four years and Chris only three, we've put the permit in Chris's name with the plan that I will apply for the loan and buy him out after a year of fishing together. By the season's end we've grossed $8,800, less than I made the year before as a deckhand. We definitely need that loan. Chris shops for a boat in the fall and finds an older plywood-hulled vessel he wants. We start negotiating the Gordian knot of our finances – the price of the permit, who paid for what, how much the gear is worth, covering our expenses for this year, who gets what off the *Skookum* – and fail to reach an agreement. The discussion becomes contentious, then outright angry. After weeks of escalation, we finally hire an accountant to sort it all out and come to an agreement on a price. By the time we sign the papers, we aren't speaking, and the friendship never recovers. We've heard similar horror stories about going into business with friends and how things can fall apart. We didn't think that would happen to us. We never consider it again.

Drifting Cook Inlet.

73

Twilight on the Boat

The last of the light
fades from the western sky
until the mountains melt into the dark.
We are rafted to six other fishing boats
adrift on a gentle swell,
stopped on a school of salmon.

The scattered vessels of the fleet
are dark shadows in the distance –
white lights glimmer above them
as they drift south with the ebbing tide.
It's hard to tell where they stop
and the stars begin.

I sit on deck,
lean against the stack,
still warm from the run south
out of the river to beat the tide.
A seat cushion beneath me,
flashlight balanced on my shoulder
reading, trying to wind down
the wire of nerves I always feel
before a big day.

Caught up in the story
I batten out the night noises:
the soft clinking of rigging moving
with the swell; the gurgles,
sloshes of the hulls,
the sigh of the sea so close.

A sound comes behind me – faint at first,
then again, and there, again,
a whoosh of an exhale – a breath –
a gasp for air.

I put the book down and stand,
slow and quiet, to see first one
arcing shape break the surface next to me –
then another: a sliver of light gray
rising from black water.

Belugas! I whisper into the cabin
of my boat and another. Word spreads.
We gather in deep twilight on a dark sea,
stand silent as they rise for air
around us, hunting the salmon
we are stopped upon.

No one speaks.
They are after our fish,
but within that magic,
we don't care.

The night swells
a void above and below,
dark upon dark, each sprinkled
with specks of distant suns –

and a meeting in between,
where we float, and they swim.

Chapter Nine: Take the Wheel

I'm taking a leak off the side of the boat early in the 1981 season as we run south along the east side in a 6-foot sea when the *Skookum* starts turning in circles. *What the hell?* Veronica is pregnant, so she's taken the year off. I've left my deckhand Michael at the helm. His main qualification for fishing with me is that he's one of my best friends. We're both teachers, and he's willing to help me out since I can't find a crew this year. I zip up and turn back toward the cabin to see him standing in the door holding the steering wheel in his hands. "When you asked me to take the wheel," he deadpans, "I don't think this is what you meant." I feel like I'm in a Three Stooges skit.

Our steering controls are locked up. The rudder is stuck hard over. In trying to get the boat back on course, Michael had literally unscrewed the wheel from its post. We put the boat in neutral and re-attach the wheel while we coast to a stop and turn broadside to the waves, but when we try it again, it still doesn't respond. I grab a flashlight and pop the waterproof hatch to the stern compartment – the lazarette – to discover the wooden mounting block holding the hydraulic ram that pushes the rudder when the wheel is turned is shattered. Pieces of it float in the bilge. The ram hangs useless, held only by a bolt attaching it to the rudder. We are done for the day. I climb out as the boat rolls in the trough, trudge into the cabin and call Harold on the VHF. The cannery uses its tenders to assist their fleet if they need help or a tow. The *Beaver* is just heading out of the Kenai River for the opener. I explain the problem and our location. "On my way," he says. "I'll be there in an hour, hour-and-a-half tops. Throw the anchor out if you start drifting too close to shore." Good advice. I hadn't thought of that.

We close the cabin door, shut the engine down and wait, sloshing around under a grey sky and freshening wind. We've been running for an hour-and-a-half with the roar of a Caterpillar diesel filling the cabin. When we shut it off, we immediately notice that our bodies continue to vibrate. Our arms and legs hum internally as if every part of us has been tuned to the pitch of the engine and can't stop. As our ears adjust to the silence, we notice the clatter of dishes in the sink, the roll of buoys on the roof of the cabin, the bilge pump kicking on, the slap of waves smacking the side of the boat. The hull groans as she rolls from side to side. Outside, the wind moans in the rigging. We watch boats throwing bow wakes as they pound into the waves, traveling past us on the way to the fishing grounds. Each one that passes reminds me of the fish we aren't going to catch today. They shrink into the distance, then disappear behind the seas between us and the horizon. It's an ominous, frustrating, lonely feeling. When the fishing begins and reports of catches start coming over the CB, I turn it off but leave the VHF on in case Harold calls.

We've waited almost two hours when I decide to give Harold a call. As I reach for the microphone, I suddenly start sweating profusely and my mouth is full of saliva. Without a word to Michael, I jump off my seat and run out on deck. *I was doing so well*, I say to myself as I empty my stomach over the side. *Sonofabitch!* The feeling after is one of weakness and relief. For a few long, raw moments I feel better. I spit and blow my nose over the side, then head back to the cabin and grab an Oreo to kill the taste. I need to get this radio call out of the way while I can still think straight – before the sickness returns.

"Hey Harold," I rasp into the microphone. "How you doin' up there?" Someone else's voice comes back. "Hi Pat. This is Corey." Corey is Harold's green deckhand, a red-haired kid from Pennsylvania or someplace back east. He's a hard worker with a good attitude, but you get the feeling that he isn't really paying attention most of the time. "Harold's in the bunk. I was just about to call ya. I'm almost even with the east Forelands, right here by the tank farm, and don't see any boats up here at all. Where are ya?"

I take a long breath before answering. Several possible replies fly through my mind before I finally clench my jaw and utter, "Yeah, Corey, we're *south* of the river, down by Humpy Point, not *north* of it. You've been steaming the wrong direction."

Another, longer pause. I can imagine what the kid is thinking. Finally, after a good two minutes of silence, the radio barks, "Yeah Pat, this is Harold. Sorry about that. I thought Corey knew what he was doing. We're headin' the right way now. Probably take us a couple of hours to get there yet." Michael just looks at me as I put on my jacket and head out the door to toss the anchor over. I grab another Oreo as I go. We don't know it yet, but this is one of 1981's good days.

Chapter Ten: Black Monday

The second week of 1981 begins with the forecast for "seas slight to three feet and winds to 15". It's the prediction Veronica and I have been waiting for. Last year she fought seasickness most days on the boat, even after taking Dramamine and other remedies. She's in her first trimester now though, and drugs are not an option, but she still wants to come out with Michael and me for a fish day. "I miss seeing the hits," she explains. "Can we wait for good weather and give it a try?"

When Michael hears that she's joining us, he asks if he can invite his girlfriend Rebecca for the day as well. The four of us head out the river in the first light of morning under gray skies and a stiff breeze. The river mouth isn't bad on an incoming tide, but as we head southwest with the rest of the fleet, the tide changes to push against the freshening wind. The seas grow so rapidly that we're in 5-8 footers before we've gone ten miles. I listen on the radio as Thor and Jim discuss the weather.

"This is getting downright snotty."

"Yeah, there's a pretty good lump in the middle."

"What do you think?"

"I'm going in close to the island. See if I can get in the lee of it and try one at opening."

"Roger. I'm not to the middle rip yet, but it's getting pretty nasty. I'm gonna head east."

"Yeah, ok. I'll let you know. I'm out."

I decide to follow Thor's plan to get in the lee of the island. The only problem is that we have to go through the middle rip to get there, and when it's rough, the middle rip is the worst place to be. The currents and tides stir up steep waves at random, coming from all directions at once. We make way slowly, going more up and down than forward. Michael and Rebecca are braced against each other in the doorway next to Veronica, who sitting at the table, looks distressed and pale.

"Can you slow down for a minute?" she asks. "I have to go outside. I think I'm going to be sick."

"You can't go out on deck in this, Babe," I reply over my shoulder. "Michael. Can you reach the deck bucket? It's under the ladder behind the cabin." Michael scrambles out on all fours, grabs the bucket and crab-walks back in and hands it to Veronica. I hope things calm down soon, for her sake.

They don't. As we run, the waves get steeper and taller until we're riding 20-30 footers cresting and roaring and I realize we're in the middle rip. Occasionally I see the mast of another boat rise above the whitecaps only to drop out of sight again behind the waves. I've never seen water this big or violent, let alone run a boat in it. I'm trying to 'quarter' the huge waves coming at us by going over them at an angle instead of straight on, like Jim taught me. The bow is plowing into the crests, throwing a steady stream of foamy water on the windshield, and the wipers are struggling to keep up. The *Skookum* doesn't have a large or high bow, and it's getting hard to see where the next wave is coming from.

Suddenly we shoot off the top of a 20-footer into the air between it and the next one, and fall to the bottom of the trough before the bow has time to angle downward. Imagine sitting where you are reading this when a giant hand picks up the structure you're in, lifts it twenty feet off the ground and drops it. A frightening BOOM fills the cabin as the *Skookum* shudders with teeth-jarring impact. Books and magazines fly off the dash to the floor. No one makes a move to pick them up. Before I can react, the next wave crashes down upon us and the windows go white. The wipers sweep at solid water as the boat fights her way back to the surface. I can't see where to steer. The windows clear as we launch into the air again. I hear a high-pitched whine as the propeller leaves the water. When the boat slams down, all I can think of is the light oak ribbing the *Skookum* has holding the planks and hull together. *She's not going to take much more of this. She'll break apart.* My fingers are white on the wheel.

80

Mariners have a saying about the water you see in situations like these. *White water is the top of the wave; green water means you're inside the wave; and black water means you're under it.* When the third wave crashes over us, the windows flex inward and go green. The wipers slow against the resistance of all the water. Out of nowhere an inch-wide, two-foot-long piece of brown kelp slaps the windshield in front of me and sticks there until the water slides downward as the boat rises and the wipers sweep it away.

I swallow and look over my shoulder for help, but Michael and Rebecca stare at me eyes wide in terror, faces white. Veronica's face is deep in the deck bucket. Right now, I would LOVE to hand the wheel to someone else. Anyone else. But I realize that as much as I don't want to be, I'm in charge. I'm the only one here that can get us out of this, so I grit my teeth and do the only thing I can think of. I throttle back and turn the wheel to starboard. We slide rather than fall off the back of the next wave. "Fuck this," I say to no one and everyone. "We're getting the fuck outta here."

Easier said than done. The seas are so big I can't risk turning broadside to them. It takes a very long minute, but I finally see a series of smaller waves approaching us. I turn the wheel hard and try to head northeast for the river, but the seas are raging, racing north behind a gale-force wind. The waves are too large to run on that heading. We listen to distress calls on the radio. The entire fleet is running for cover. The 61-foot *Beaver* is rolled on its side as Harold struggles to make it back to the river. "I wasn't sure if she'd come back or keep on rolling," he tells me later. Jim says it's the worst weather he's seen in 25 years. After 45 minutes, I realize we're being pushed too fast to the north to make it across to the river mouth. "I'm going to duck behind the north end of Kalgin Island," I tell the others. "We can wait it out there." I turn the boat northwest.

The waves grow smaller the farther west we go. By the time I make the turn, we all feel a measure of relief except for

81

Veronica, who can't stop throwing up. As soon as we get into the lee of the island, the waves stop. It's a completely different inlet here. We can see setnet shacks sitting serenely below the bluff, smoke rising straight up out of their chimneys. After what we've just been through, the contrast feels surreal. Setnetters dot the beaches around Cook Inlet, fishing nets that are anchored on either end just offshore. They anchor barges carrying fish totes that tenders pull alongside to pick up their fish after each opening. Three other drift boats are tied off to a setnet scow and are planning to stay the night. We radio the setnetter for permission to tie off too. He's been listening to the radio all day so he knows how bad the weather has been. When he hears my wife is pregnant, he asks, "Would she like to get off the boat for a bit?" After throwing up constantly for six hours, Veronica is still queasy, sore and dehydrated. We're both worried about losing the baby. We gratefully accept his offer. Within minutes he pulls alongside in his skiff.

     The setnetter is short, bearded, and talkative. His wife and five kids are Native Alaskans, and don't speak any English. They stare at us as we sit on their bed – the only available seat besides the floor – in his tiny wood stove-heated one-room cabin. The stove is cranking and the cabin feels like a sauna. With the heat, the relief of being safe, and awake since 1:00 am, I rest back on an arm, then my head goes down and I'm gone. Veronica lets me sleep while she and the fisherman chat. Her stomach finally settles down, but she's starving and she's too embarrassed to ask for food. He gets caught up in telling stories and never offers. The scene feels weirder and weirder to her, listening, looking at his family staring at her but not speaking, sweating from the heat, with me snoring on the bed. After three hours, she's had enough and shakes me awake.

     Back on the boat, Michael and Rebecca decide that the day's lesson is how short and fragile this life is. They make love until they hear the returning skiff's outboard. We all wave thanks to the setnetter as he pulls away. We listen to the radio reports still trickling in. Most of the fleet is back in the river, but the fishing day is lost completely – not a fish delivered.

Veronica is ravenous, but her stomach is raw. We sit down to Mac and Cheese, the mildest thing we can find on board to fix for dinner. Once she gets some food in her, she realizes how exhausted she is. Meanwhile, we both comment on how relaxed Michael and Rebecca are. They just look at each other and smile. "We took naps," says Rebecca. Even so, we all sleep soundly through the night.

The next morning the Inlet is beautiful, blue sky, golden sunlight and flat calm as we head home. "Is this the same Inlet?" Michael asks as we shake our heads in disbelief. Veronica and the baby suffer no permanent damage, but it's a long time before she wants to go out with me again, no matter what the forecast. "Winds to 15, seas slight to three" becomes a saying that makes us shudder for years.

Middle Rip, Cook Inlet

It has been cloudy now
a long, long while.
The sea is building.
The unexpected blow
comes from the south,
and is always the worst.

From shore you can't see
the middle rip;
can't tell how bad it is –
waves crashing in all directions at once,
moving mountains of green and gray.

And even if you were there
fighting the wheel to keep her on course,
quartering them up and over, throttle forward and back,
watching more of what's next than what's now,
you couldn't tell whether the changing tide
would lay it down or stir it up more.

I've run away from the middle rip
more than once: turned around, saying,
  This is unfishable!
Gritted my teeth, hung on to the helm
as the boat swung in the trough,
trying to time it so the smallest wave
was the one that hit; watched
out the side window, wishing
we would turn faster – knowing
we couldn't, braced as the wave
slammed the side like a sledgehammer.

I've seen hats, silverware, coffee cups, magazines,
cameras and books slide in synchrony across the galley table,
reach the edge and erupt around the cabin.

I've even set my gear in the middle rip
with a groan as it kicked up –
   Ahh, it'll come down.
I've seen my deckhand crouch
on the back deck, hold on as the boat heeled,
trying to let the net out without a hangup,
with a glance over his shoulder
and a look that asked *Are you insane?*

I have stared dumbly out the cabin door
at towering waves behind him, stern
lifting toward vertical, thinking
   Yes. Yes, I am.

Towing the gear in heavy weather in the middle rip
depends upon your mettle and your nerve;
you know you've got to pick up:
put on oilskins, pull your hat down hard
so it doesn't blow off, button the top button
no matter how tight. The cool press
of rain gear against your neck reminds you
how you wish you didn't have to go out there
into the wind and rollers and make the boat
go stern-first into them.

You open the cabin door. The wind
tries to take your breath, but you suck it back,
clench your jaw, hold the lifeline and dance
across the deck, timing it so the side you're on
lifts away from the water as you move aft.

You pull on gloves as you eye the seas
from the stern of your boat – your boat,
your machine, full of warmth, life
and power to pull in all that net

stretching into the hostile gray glare
until you can't see it any longer –
and your boat can get it all back, and more:
she can deliver you safely home.

And it's you and your boat against all this
space, wind and water. You come alive,
stomp your foot on the treadle – the reel
whines, turns and backs the boat
into the waves. The sea slaps the stern
like an insult, drenching you in ice water.
You duck, come up sputtering, laugh,
whoop, and yell the insult back at the sea!

From shore you can't see
the middle rip;
can't tell how bad it is.

Chapter Eleven: Stick Rips and Luck

After another week of breakdowns and shitty weather, though nothing like what we've started calling Black Monday, Michael and I are waiting in line behind the *Beaver* to deliver, eating dinner. We have 400 fish on board, our highest daily total for the season, but we've paid the price for them: part of our rigging, the forward pole of the starboard stabilizer broke free as we ran home. We almost lost it, but got it on board and lashed it down in a four-foot chop. "Seems like it's always something," I say around a mouthful of fried chicken and rice. Veronica has been making us dinners to heat in the oven during the run home, and by the time we're in the river, they're fully cooked and driving us crazy with the smell.

"I know." Michael looks at his plate. "This is harder than I expected. Every day I feel like I'm going to war."

"I get it," I answer, realizing for the first time how terrifying it must be for him. I feel guilty. He agreed to deckhand for me to help out as a friend. He never had a desire to go fishing, and I know the only reason he's stayed this long is out of a sense of commitment. He doesn't want to let me down by quitting. "It's strange how people love stories about the sea that describe overcoming danger – like the ones Farley Mowat writes – but if they had to live those 'romantic' tales, they'd absolutely hate the reality. They'd never set foot on a boat again."

Michael nods. I can tell my feeble attempt at mariner philosophy doesn't help. After we've delivered and cleaned the boat, he walks up the dock, shoulders slumped, head down. Hating what he's going through – what I'm putting him through – I feel obligated to do something. The next morning, I arrive at the cannery early to ask the Port Engineers for help repairing the stabilizer arm, then head straight to the *Cheechako*.

Dean offers me a cup of 'Cheechako coffee', a unique creation of coffee, Kahlua, brandy, Amaretto and Creme de

Cacao that tastes like heaven and goes down way too easily. After he rescued us last year, we've become good friends. He and his brother Don have fished since their dad brought them up from Seattle to deckhand when they were teenagers. Realizing how little I know, Dean has made me a project. After fishing days, we get together and chat about where I went, what I did, how I did, and how it could have gone better. He teaches me NOT to take naps after I throw out the net, but to watch for hits, tow the net, even cut loose from it and run the boat next to it to chase fish in on a calm day, something I never saw Jim do. We're not in the same radio group, but I have a feeling that might change. Plus, we have similar senses of humor, both like beer and tequila, and we enjoy each other's company immensely.

Dean's deckhand, Danny Miller, has even more fishing experience. Ten years older than we are, he's been crewing for over 15 years. He's a woodworker, knows boat maintenance inside and out, and is soft-spoken and easy going. He's the saltiest-looking guy I have ever seen, with a full mariner's bushy beard, skipper's cap and pipe to complete his look. He's always present when Dean and I drink beer and discuss fishing, and he offers a healthy dose of wisdom and humor about fighting boat problems, rough weather and empty fish holds.

This year Dean has his girlfriend Sarah as a third hand on the boat. She's sweet and a hard worker, but Danny has privately shared with me that, even though he loves fishing with both of them, he sometimes feels like a 'third wheel'. I see that as an opportunity to help everyone.

When Danny leaves the boat for mug-up, I ask Dean, "How would you feel about Danny fishing with me the last few periods of the season? Michael is having a hard time. He feels like he's going into battle every time we go out. I'd like to let him off the hook if I can."

Dean doesn't even think twice. "I'm ok with that if

Danny is. I'll ask him when he comes back."

Michael shows up the next day for a morning of boat maintenance when I tell him the news. "Your season is done." I smack him on the shoulder. "Danny from the *Cheechako* is taking your place." He lifts his head and his face brightens.

"What? You sure?"

"Yep. You're free, man. Get the fuck outta here!" He gives me an exuberant hug. As he rounds the corner past the egg house on his way to the parking lot, I see him skip and hop. I think I hear a "Whoop!" in the distance.

Danny Miller bringing in the net.

By the next period's opening at 6:00 am we are next to the middle rip off the north end of Kalgin Island, but the water is entirely different from Black Monday, sunny with a slight

89

breeze. I feel even worse for Michael. He never had a day like this. We lay the net to the west in a light chop. Most of the other boats are stretched to the south. The tide is ebbing fast. The rip is as wide as a freeway, little wavelets dancing in the sun and a line of foam on its western edge. It's thick with logs, kelp and sticks that the recent big tides have collected off the beaches. Once the gear is in the water, I tow to hold it in the U-shape of a hook facing south to catch northbound fish. It doesn't take long to realize there aren't many hits. We're a little too close to the sticks anyway, so we decide to pick up and move south. Danny takes the boat out of gear and starts picking while I get into my rain gear and boots.

Dressed, I stand on the hatch covers and pull on my gloves. My eyes follow the white corks of the net as they ride up and down the small waves scooting underneath them. The rip is easy to see, clear on our side, muddy on the other, with our buoy bouncing on the whitecaps marking the division. We are way too close. The current is sucking us into the rip faster than I anticipated. I step into the picking well at the back of the boat. Danny stops bringing in the net and ducks under the lines to get on the other side and give me room.

During the past winter I stripped out a couple of shackles of worn, torn-up gear, cutting the knots of twine that hold the net to the lines. I dropped the lines and new web off with a local who had a good reputation for hanging nets. What I didn't realize was that he'd always worked for beach fishermen who never tow their gear. He never hung a net for a drifter. When he saw a weak spot in my corkline, he cut it out and spliced in a new section by laying the two ends beside one another and wrapping them with twine. He covered the butt-splice, as it's called, with black tape to keep it from catching web. What he should have done was square-knot the two pieces together so the line can withstand the stress of a boat pulling it through the water.

In an amazing stroke of bad luck, when Danny stops the reel, the splice has just lifted out of the water at the back of the boat. It hangs just off the stern in the area that receives the most strain from a tow. Neither of us notice it. We aren't looking for a problematic splice. Why would we?

"I'm gonna tow the net away from the rip a little," I say to Danny. He looks out at the buoy.

"How well does the *Skookum* tow?"

"Good enough," I answer, not really knowing and hoping I'm right. I bump the throttle up and put her in gear. When the propeller digs in, the splice parts with a loud *pop!* The webbing shreds like a zipper until the tear reaches the lead line, which parts with another *pop!* The boat surges forward, almost knocking the two of us off our feet.

I stagger to the controls. I throttle back and put the boat in neutral. Danny and I gape as the net folds along the edge of the rip and twists its way into the sticks. "Get to the other end!" Danny shouts as I run forward. I take the three steps into the cabin in one bound, land in the skipper's seat and throw the boat in gear. I shove the throttle to full power and crank the wheel hard over. With a roar and a cloud of black smoke belching out of the stack the *Skookum* leans into the turn. Danny holds on in the stern with a worried look on his face, pike-pole in hand.

By the time we reach the net, the rip has swallowed it all. I maneuver the boat so the stern swings near the buoy, trying to avoid the large logs churning in the waves. Clenching my jaw, I watch Danny through the open cabin door as he leans out and hooks the buoy line with the pole. I put the controls in neutral once again and run to the back deck to help him pull the end of the net on board and tie it off to the reel. The rip hisses and boils, sounding alive and malevolent. Once we have the lines secure, we look up to see our net loaded with sticks, kelp, small branches, large branches, and three thirty-foot logs that are two-to-three feet in diameter – what had once been trees, but are now barkless, limbless waterlogged nightmares, rolling with the current and corkscrewing our net around them.

"Jesus," I say under my breath.

Danny nods his head. "I've seen worse," he says confidently. "We'll get it back." We begin reeling the net on board and picking sticks. It's slow work. The web catches every small branch, every stem, each piece of bark or wad of kelp that it touches. We bend sticks, break sticks, slide sticks through webbing, peel webbing off sticks, and toss sticks onto the hatch covers for the next twenty minutes. We don't throw the sticks over the side for fear they'll be washed back into the net. The pile on the hatch covers gets deep in a hurry. By the time we reassess our predicament we've only brought in 25 feet of web and lines.

Hanging in the gear just off the stern is a large log that resembles a battering ram as it sloshes forward and back. The *Skookum* is stout enough, but her one-inch cedar planks are no match for a waterlogged tree. The leadline is wound around the log in one direction for nearly half its length. Then it joins the corkline and a tangled mass of web, twists around them several times, and continues spiraling in the opposite direction the rest of the length of the log. Getting the net back seems impossible.

"Maybe we should cut it loose," I say dimly.

"Nah, we're ok. I've seen worse than this," Danny repeats, sounding positive. "Let's try stripping the web and at least get the lines back."

We take out our knives and cut away the web, me on the corkline and Danny on the leads. We lean over the back of the boat and pull the lines out of the water as far as we can reach. We lift the lines to try and slide the log out of the hole we've made with no luck. This *is* impossible.

I look at Danny and grit my teeth. This is not the decision I want to make. "We better cut it," I say more firmly this time. "If we leave now, we still have time to get in the river, get more gear and get out here again before the tide goes out."

Danny nods his head again and looks at the mess behind the boat. "Yeah, I suppose we better." He pauses a moment, considering the scene in front of us and shakes his head. "I don't think I *have* seen it any worse than this." At any other time, that would be a good joke.

Without bothering to save the little bit of gear hanging off the stern, I place my knife on the taut lines. Bits of twine on them wave in the breeze. I feel as helpless as they look. I have a sick feeling in my stomach. Not only are we losing most of the day's fishing time, I'm losing $1,500 worth of gear and leaving a mess in the environment. With one slice the knife slides through the lines. The boat bobs free as she sheds the strain of the heavy net.

"I'll call Veronica," I say as I head to the cabin. "I'll see if she can meet us at the dock with more gear." It's hard to keep the discouragement out of my voice. A deckhand never likes to hear his skipper anxious or depressed. Danny's first day with me has turned into a disaster. He's not making any money this way. I wonder if he'll want to stay with me for the rest of the season. Hell, *I* don't even want to stay with me. I beat myself up on the run in, convinced I am a magnet for lousy luck and worse decisions.

Through the VHF Marine operator, I get Veronica on the radio and explain. "Go down to the cannery and get my truck. See if you can get someone to help you move the nets out of my locker to the fuel dock, so we don't have to waste time chasing down the gear. If we can get in and crane it down to the boat fast enough, we might make it out of the river before the tide's too low."

She's obviously worried but holds her questions for later, which I appreciate more than she knows. "I'll call Jon Lillevik," she says. "We'll do what we can."

The river is empty of boats, and I feel conspicuous as we run by the other canneries. We pull up to the fuel dock to find Veronica and Jon waiting for us with three new shackles of gear in bags, one of them already in a sling on the crane. They load them on board in record time. I blow her a kiss, thank them both profusely, and with three new, bagged shackles on deck we race out of the river just in time to beat the ebbing tide.

Half an hour later we are four miles offshore, not another boat in sight. We stop on some streaky water and set the gear out of the bags, stopping to hook the shackles together as we go. We let it soak a few minutes without seeing a hit, then decide to move. Danny picks up the empty net while I call my fishing group on the CB. The strong ebb tide has swept the entire fleet out of sight, almost 15 miles south, barely within radio range. We are the only boat in the upper Inlet that we can see. "*Cheryl Lynne, Skookum Too,*" I call into the mic. "Pick me up, Thor?"

Thor's voice is faint and full of radio static as he answers back. "Yeah, go ahead, Pat."

We exchange information, and to my relief I learn that the fleet isn't catching much down south. Thor says there's nothing down there to run to. He ends the call by encouraging me, saying, "Maybe they'll show up there."

'Yeah, thanks for that," is all I can think to say as I sign off. "I'm out."

Danny finishes picking the set, and we head west to the middle rip again. The sticks, logs and my net have been swept south with the outgoing tide, and the rip is much cleaner and friendlier-looking now. We lay the gear out near it once more.

As we watch the net and drift with the slowing tide, we see an occasional splash on the corkline. Small bunches of fish are hitting. We take a break, have a sandwich and play a half-hearted game of crib, trying to forget the events of the day. Danny encourages me and assures me these things happen. He doesn't seem affected by the loss of a payday, and I'm relieved to know he's still willing to fish with me. An hour-and-a-half later we pull the gear as the day is coming to a close.

§

I once read an essay in *Audubon* magazine about a young man walking in the woods, overwhelmed with a vague and unnamed existential distress. To him, the day was gray. Gray sky, gray trees, gray landscape. Until he sat on a log and a skunk, busy collecting debris for a nest, came near. She was chittering in a way that he interpreted as a kind of singing. At one point the skunk put its paws on the end of the log he was sitting upon, and stared at him for a long moment. Then it went on its way, still chittering, still singing. As it disappeared into the woods, the writer noticed that the day had changed. It wasn't gray at all. The sky was ice-blue, the trees brown and green, the landscape full of muted color. The skunk had snapped him out of his funk and brought him back to the world. The day, in fact, hadn't changed. He had.

§

As Danny and I pick the set, we start to realize there are way more fish in the net than we saw hit. Maybe we didn't want to see how many we were catching because we were so stunned at losing all our gear to start the day. Maybe in my depression and Danny's efforts to cheer me up we didn't pay close enough attention. But as we count them – as bunch after bunch of fish come over the roller and fall into the stern, we slowly realize we've caught way more fish than we expected. To our surprise we end up with almost 700 fish in the net! That's my best set of the entire year, and, we find out later, one of the biggest catches of the day for the fleet! My attitude changes completely, just like that *Audubon* writer. Danny and I high-five each other in the stern and shake our heads. My worst day and my best day of 1981 have been one and the same.

Kenai River entrance buoy with gillnet lines and web.

Chapter Twelve: Metamorphosis

By the end of 1981, we have broken down eight out of the twelve periods we've fished. We've been towed in so often I have my own coffee cup on the *Beaver*. Danny, however, has used his time on board to give me a crash-course in working on the water. The first thing he does is to insist we light the diesel stove to take the chill out of the cabin. "Jim said they weren't safe," I offer as explanation for keeping it off.

"Bullshit," Danny scoffs as he lights the stove with a torn piece of paper towel dropped into the bowl. "I've used these things for years without a problem. And the heat makes all the difference." He's right about that. When we come in out of the rain and wind to a heated cabin, the warmth is a remarkable improvement.

Danny also notices that the hatch cover embedded into the deck in the stern where we pick is notoriously slippery when wet. I've looked everywhere for a decent mat to cover it, with no luck. One particular day, he returns from running errands in my truck and walks down the dock with a rolled-up all-weather mat on his shoulder. "Where'd you find that?" I ask as he unrolls it in the stern. It's the perfect size.

"Safeway," he says.

Confused, I ask, "They sell them at the grocery store?"

"No." He smiles. "I saw it just inside the door. Once I was done shopping, I just went back in, rolled it up like I was taking it for cleaning, and walked out with it. No one said a word." Apparently, my crew's an experienced shoplifter. Who knew? But that mat is perfect, and I keep it for years.

The best piece of good news is that after the season's over Dean invites me to join his radio group. I know most of the guys from cookouts on the beach and boat parties. Dale on the *Seneca* looks like an old hippie with a ZZ-Top beard hanging down his chest and an easy way about him. Wayne on the *Pelican*, in his late 40's, is quiet and reserved, but is quick to offer help and has a deep knowledge of mechanics and engines. Dean and Don's father, Don senior, is the oldest of the group. He is known as "Senior" over the radio. He's a high-school principal in Bellevue, Washington and fishes the *Sumac*. He always fishes with his wife Betty, a primary school teacher. She is a warm-hearted woman who loves her wine and is always up for a visit. She adopts us all and treats the group like an extended family, something I warm to and miss, my own mother dead five years and the rest of my family thousands of miles away. Dean and Don, both of whom I am delighted to call friends, on the *Cheechako* and *Marauder*, feel more like brothers to me. Their cousin Rob, on the *Bluebird* is another likable introvert who Veronica and I both enjoy, but he doesn't fish for Columbia Wards, so we see less of him. He and Wayne and Dale fish downriver for Kenai Packers. Finally, there's Cosmo, our outgoing and funny radio guru, who lives 20 miles south of town near the Kasilof River where he anchors up the *Watersong*.

I am relieved to leave Jim and Thor's group. With over twenty boats it feels too big. Many of the fishermen never share how they're doing, or if they do, they understate what they're catching or report it after the fish have been caught. Others exaggerate their catch numbers to make themselves look better. Rumor has it that some of them go out the day before a period to illegally fish the night before a period. I'm happy to walk away, especially to join people I like and trust, who have a clear policy of communication. Dean sits me down over beers one afternoon before the '92 season gets under way. "After each set, we always get on the radio with our location, length of drift, how many fish, and how many reds. And if you're seeing hits during a set, let the group know right away." We all have scrambled single-sideband radios, so we can talk freely within the group about what we're catching and our location. Cosmo, the group communication maestro, teaches me how to operate it.

Don, Rob and Dean tutor me in boat work, and I soon realize that if I'm going to get better at this, I need to have a boat that's in good shape I can count on. The *Skookum Too* has been owned by the cannery for over a decade, and has suffered for it. The only maintenance she's had has been of necessity – if something broke, it was fixed. Otherwise, she's been left to slowly deteriorate as she ages. Over the next few years, with advice from the Pugh brothers and help from the cannery, I rework as much of her systems as possible. The first job I have on my list is a no-brainer: before the season starts, I have the Beach Gang move the *Skookum* outside the carpenter's shop so Benny and the new shipwright Tim DeLapp can reinforce the ribbing that holds the hull together. Tim 'sister-ribs' everywhere he can get to, putting stout beams next to the weaker ones in the fish hold, engine room and stern. The cabin, bow and area below the back deck where the fuel tanks are can't be accessed. We take what we're given, and hope it's enough. Dean sells me an extra flying bridge he has left over from building the *Cheechako* that somehow matches the exact dimensions of the roof of the *Skookum's* cabin. We bolt it in place, install a steering station, ladder and two awesome swivel bucket seats from the local junkyard up top. I cut a porthole in the roof for a pass-through for the radio microphones, and install deck speakers so I can hear what's said when I'm on the back deck or the bridge. I replace hoses and fan belts, install a new state-of-the-art RACOR fuel filter, replace wiring and fuses with circuit breakers, buy a new reel and drive, buy a small plastic skiff to row to shore at Snug, and hire Tim to build a wooden rack over the reel to hold it. I scrape, sand, and patch holes in the hull and cabin, then paint her sky blue with black trim. I almost change her name to *Silk Purse*, but after all that work, I don't think she's a sow's ear any longer, so I forego the insult.

During fishing closures Dean and I discover that we both love video games. We spend off nights at Sourdough Sal's

Bowling Alley and video arcade, where we pump quarterafter quarter into machines, trying to best each other's score. Veronica struggles with our nightly antics, but Dean often crashes on the couch at the house rather than go back to the boat, and by the time she wakes up in the morning, Dean has coffee going and breakfast on the stove. She knows just how much he's helping us navigate fishing, me on the water and her on land. We build a net rack in the back yard for mending gear, and Dean tutors her until she's an expert at it.

As the boat improves, with Dean's help so do I. The two of us leave the river together most fishing days in 1982, meeting the day before so he can fill me in on what he's heard around the cannery and what he predicts for the coming period. He has years of experience filtering his lens for fish behavior, tides and weather, and I listen intently. On fish days we become a team, and my production skyrockets. I learn where to look for jumpers, when to make a move and when to stay put. I have a better boat that doesn't break down all the time, and I have a good deckhand. Danny Rediske is a former student of mine with several years of fishing under his belt. He's savvy on the water, and earns his keep by working hard, picking fast, and understanding engines way better than I do. When we head out of the river one day early in the season, the high temperature alarm starts blaring a piercing shriek in the cabin. It's the first time I've ever heard it. Danny shouts, "We're overheating! Shut her down!" I do, but the deafening alarm stays on. Danny pulls the fuse on the dash and it goes quiet. We both start tearing up the floorboards to get to the engine compartment. The engine is cooled by a large pump running off a fan belt. The fan belt is fine, but we unscrew the face plate on the pump to discover the rubber impeller is in pieces. I've never encountered this before, so I don't have a spare impeller on board. Danny starts asking me to hand him tools.

"What are you doing?" I ask as he loosens a hose clamp.

"I'm gonna switch the hoses with the wash-down pump so we can cool the engine with that," he replies. "If that's ok." He stops and looks at me.

"Hell yes, if it'll keep us fishing." And it does. He makes the switch in less than ten minutes, and we fish the rest of the day. A year ago, I would have spent the afternoon sipping coffee on the *Beaver*.

By season's end, I have a boat I can believe in, a deckhand I've hired back for the next year, a new best friend, and for the first time, a bank account that's full enough to pay the bills, buy new gear for next year and take us on a vacation. Maybe this fishing business will be okay. Maybe, just maybe I've learned how to catch fish.

Danny Rediske with a King salmon.

Chapter Thirteen: Keeping Track of Dean

Dean Pugh demonstrates how to mend net.

The 1982 season is winding down on a flat calm day with few fish caught by 10:00 am. It's so slow that boats are already starting to head for the river when I get a call from Dean on the sideband. "Yeah, *Skookum Too, Cheechako*. Pick me up there, Pat?" Danny hands me the microphone. We're playing crib and watching the rare splash in our net.

"Yeah, *Cheechako*, go ahead. "

"Where did you get to this morning?"

"Just off the head of the island in the middle. Not much here."

"I'm north of you a bit. Nothing here either. I'm gonna try over west. Too many sticks up here."

"Yeah, Roger that. Let me know if you find anything."

"Will do. Give me your numbers, will ya?" I tell him my lat/long and we sign off. I stare out the door trying to wish a fish or two into the net. When I sit back down, Danny lays down a double-run and we keep playing cards. It's a slow day, all right.

Fifteen minutes later we spot the *Cheechako* running toward us, and I pop out on deck, thinking he's got some fishy information he wants to share with me privately, not over the radio where the rest of the group can hear. Instead, he stops his boat next to the middle of my net. Dean, Danny Miller and Sarah all bolt out on deck where they've stacked a pile of sticks and small logs he's picked out of his gear. As the *Cheechako* bobs next to my net, they heave the sticks overboard – into *my* net! I run into my cabin and yell non-FCC-approved descriptions about what I am going do to him over the radio. I hear him cackling as he finishes, then he idles his boat next to the buoy at the end of my gear. He waves at me right before he empties his 12-gauge shotgun into it. He roars off, laughing through the microphone. I vow revenge – but not over the radio, and after picking small sticks, big sticks, pointy sticks, branches and even a 2x4 with several nails sticking out of it, then hauling in my waterlogged buoy – I focus on tracking him until I get my chance.

By 3:00 pm he's back on the radio telling the group he's heading toward the Kasilof beach south of the river to try and catch a king just outside the set nets. That's a set you have to pay attention to, and I view his distraction as my opportunity. We arrive 20 minutes after he sets out. I notice his boat is on the shore end of his net. We race up to his buoy on the other end, pluck it out of the water, unclip it and put it on board. We wrap the end of his corkline on our stern cleat. I gun the engine,

103

pulling the end of his net back along itself, ruining his pretty little set! "Hahahah! Take that!" I'm puffed-up and proud until I hear his shotgun go off. "Get down!" I yell at Danny. "He's shooting at us!" Danny drops to the deck still holding the end of the corkline with one hand. The other is over his head. I duck behind the flying bridge and keep towing. Another shot goes off. And another. "Jesus!" Danny screams, and I back off the throttle and put her in neutral. I know he's not aiming at us, but I don't want to tempt him. I yell, "Cut it loose, but keep the buoy!" Danny obliges with enthusiasm, and we race away for the safety of the river.

We deliver what few fish we have, saving a couple each to take home. I head to the float, satisfied in our revenge. Danny cleans the hold and is just finishing scrubbing the deck when he notices the *Cheechako* coming up the river toward us. Dean has bragged to me more than once about his extra-powerful wash-down pump with a fire hose nozzle on it for added pressure. It would do a hook-and-ladder truck proud. It easily shoots a jet of water thirty feet. Danny Miller holds it as he stands alongside the *Cheechako's* cabin. The stream of hissing, crackling water twists above the river's surface like a venomous snake. Dean sees us and gooses the throttle, shouting, "Incoming!" We scramble over ourselves to get in the cabin and shut the door, but it's bungeed open and keeps springing back. I scurry back out to release it as the water hits our stern and sprays over the reel. "HAHAHAHAH!" Dean cackles. Spray hits my back as I jump in the cabin and slam the door behind me.

The door shudders with the force of the stream, and water sprays in around the frame. We huddle, helpless in the cabin as Dean slides his boat alongside us. Our side windows jump and flex as Danny points the hose at them. "Not the windows!" Dean yells, not wanting to do any real damage. Danny walks aft to concentrate on the door again.

Out the side window I notice that it's apparently mug-up at the cannery because all the workers are lined up on the dock watching the show. I refuse to lose in front of an audience. I desperately look around for something I can fight back with. I spot the hand-held distress flare stuffed in the egg box on the dash. Sarah looks through the window as I grab it, rip the cap off and go to the door. She yells, "Dean! He's got something!" Dean puts the boat in reverse and starts to back away. Danny keeps the hose trained on the door to keep us from coming out. I watch the stream of water grow weaker, reach its limit then start retreating toward the stern. Before I open the door – let me repeat that – *BEFORE* I open the door, I strike the flare on its starter cap. Orange flame and smoke sputters, then erupts inside the cabin. In my rush, I haven't thought this through particularly well. I push at the door, but the force of all the water hitting it has jammed it shut!

My deckhand shrieks. "JeSUS! OPEN it!"

"It's stuck!" I hit the door with my shoulder, once, twice and it flies open. I bolt out to see Dean standing on the bridge of the *Cheechako* drifting backwards grinning at me. I take two steps, and with the best softball pitch of my life, toss the flare underhanded right at him. "Whoa! HOHOOHOO!!" he screams as a rotating circle of orange flame and smoke arcs its way directly toward his chest. The flare strikes the splashguard at the top of the bridge a foot away from him, hangs there a second then slides down to the bow of the boat where it rolls under the anchor and bursts into flame. Danny runs to the bow as far as the hose will stretch and douses the flare. A huge cloud of orange smoke envelops the *Cheechako* as she drifts downriver and out of sight. A cheer goes up from the cannery workers, and I raise my arms high in victory. Another great day at adult summer camp!

Chapter Fourteen: That Sinking Feeling

The Marauder, Watersong, Skookum Too & Cheechako in Snug Harbor.

1983 begins with one of the most ambitious projects I take on with the *Skookum*. The old fiberglass fuel tank has developed a leak and needs replacing. I contract Lindsey, the cannery welder, to fabricate a new one out of aluminum, and again move the *Skookum* to the carp shop so we can tear out the back deck and replace it again once the new tank is installed. Benny died last spring, so Tim's now the cannery carpenter and he's very good at his job. He also fits in with our group of fishermen, and joins most of our parties. He is as crazy as we are, and we joke around and tell stories while we work. But as cannery carpenter, he's pulled in a hundred other directions doing jobs for the company, other fishermen and the small fleet of tenders Columbia Wards employs. Danny and I spend two weeks of 16-hour days working to disconnect the fuel system, disconnect and unbolt the reel, remove all the hydraulic hoses, prep the hull for the new tank, help with its installation, install new hoses and climb up and down the ladder a hundred times to fetch whatever Tim needs from the shop as he rebuilds the decking. Ten days before fishing starts Danny takes a minute to look around at the gaping hole still in the stern, no tank yet in place, reel on the ground behind the boat, and shakes his head. "Ten days to go? We're never going to make it for the first period."

I've been losing sleep for days worrying about the same thing. It's all I can do to not scream, "Get the fuck back to work then!" But I know better. I take a breath. "We'll see. Just have to keep at it."

The day before the first period Tim finishes bolting down the reel while I hook up the hydraulic hoses. Danny is Crisco-ing the hull. Very few boats are left in the yard, and we're scheduled to be dropped in the water in a few hours. I'm worried about the large gaps in the hull. Since we were working on it for so long, we didn't start watering it down until a few days ago, and we know that's not enough. "When you're done there, be sure to clean any debris out of the bilges," I tell Danny. Pieces of wood, black electrical tape or even screws can jam a bilge pump, and the five we have on board are the last, most important barrier to keep us from sinking during the next few days. We have one in the bow, one in the engine room, one in the fish hold, and two in the lazarette. I'm hoping that's enough.

The boat goes in the water as planned. I send Danny home and spend a few nervous hours at the dock watching for any problems, but the pumps are keeping up with the constant flow of water. I have a restless night, and when I get to the boat early the next morning, I check them all again. Everything seems fine. I spend the day very aware each time a pump kicks on, and more so if it doesn't. We pull some tape out of the engine room pump in mid-afternoon, but we catch the jam before the water's very deep. I'm starting to feel a little more confident after we get to Snug Harbor and raft up with Wayne, Cosmo, Don and Dean for the night. Danny heads to the bunk after dinner, but I drink a couple of beers with the guys and visit.

107

Things feel normal until I step out of Wayne's cabin and see the *Skookum* sitting low in the water. "Fuck!" I yell back at the other guys. "I think we're sinking!" I jump into the cabin and tear up the floorboards. Sure enough, there's a good foot and a half of water under the engine, almost touching the starter motor.

At any other time, I would jump in the water and reach down to unhook the pump from its mount and clear it. But the combination of exhaustion from all the long days and worry, the beer and the stress of fishing today locks me up. Emotionally, I'm on the verge of collapse. If, at that moment someone reached into their pocket and pulled out a $50 bill, I would have gladly sold them the boat and permit.

I can't move. My brain goes numb and I can't think what to do. The other skippers are looking in the cabin, but Rob actually comes in and sees what needs to be done. "Let me," he says as he puts his big hand on my shoulder and steps down into the water. He's wearing boots over his sweat pants, but he doesn't seem to care if he gets wet or not. He reaches under the water and in seconds has the pump in his hand. He looks up. "Turn off the switch." I reach over to the dash and flip the toggle. The red light goes out. He digs at the bottom of the pump and pulls out more black tape, a piece almost six inches long. "Try it now." I flip the switch again and the pump whirs as he holds it. "Ok." I turn it off and he puts the pump back in place. "That oughta do." When I turn the pump on this time, we all hear water shoot from the vent on the outside of the boat. Rob waits long enough to see the water level dropping, then reaches up his hand and I pull him out. "Get some sleep," he says. "You'll feel better in the morning." I feel so relieved I want to cry. Instead, I thank him, but not enough. With this fishing group, never enough.

Chapter Fifteen: Alone on the Fish

It's 4:00 pm on a windy, choppy day. Near the southern end of the fleet, Danny and I have been in the fish all day, picking, laying it back out, picking some more. We find ourselves all alone as we move west of the fleet in a building sea, trying to avoid a large, scattered kelp rip. I am already thinking this will be the last set of the day. Danny is tired after picking over 900 fish, a good day by anyone's standards, and today, better than most. The radio reports are few, and the boats that aren't already heading to the river aren't catching much. I see one, a speck on the horizon north and east of me a couple of miles, but she's the only vessel in sight. We reach water clear of sticks and kelp and set to the west. I see a bunch hit the net in a flurry of foam as we set, but it's quickly lost among all the whitecaps. We lay out the gear while running in the trough, and on the bridge, I'm hanging on to the wheel as the boat rolls left and right underneath me. It's hard enough to keep track of my direction with the compass, let alone look back at the net while setting. Danny has his head down, helping the gear peel off the net in the wind with his hands, keeping a close eye on the blowing web so he can pull the brake on the reel if it hangs up on a cork or a snag. Neither of us can really tell if we're getting any fish or not.

We finally get the net out and head into the cabin. The wind is brisk and cold, with spits of needle-like raindrops mixed in, but the small diesel stove has the cabin warm and dry. Danny asks if I mind if he takes a nap until we pick up. I nod, put my army jacket on over my rain gear, pull on a pair of gloves and a sock cap, and head topside to watch the net. Even after five years of fishing, I still get queasy in the cabin on a rocky day, so I figure I stand a better chance of staying on the grounds and finishing out the period if I'm in fresh air. I go out on deck and put the boat in reverse so I can get some slack in the tow line. I pull it around to the port side and tie it off on the midship cleat

109

so I can tow with our bow into the four-to-five-foot waves, another trick Dean has showed me how to do. I climb the ladder to the bridge and swivel the seat to face the stern, bracing myself with my legs. I hang on to the side of the bridge with one hand and steer the boat with the other. I tow the net, trying to keep the gear from 'flagging out,' or stretching in the direction of the wind and current. The fish run with the waves, and if the net flags, it won't catch much. I watch the gear as it stretches off to the east into a grey, angry white-cap stampede of waves. I can only see the first third of the net clearly. Tiny in the distance, I can barely make out our orange buoy at the end of the net bobbing every now and then. I light up a smoke with a good deal of twisting and turning against the wind to shield the lighter, suck on it and watch. I see splashes halfway down the first shackle. A good-sized bunch there. A few seconds pass. Another, right behind the boat. And another kicking up foam toward the other end of the gear. The bunches light up for just a second, then stop. The fish we're catching can't fight long because of the tension created by the waves and the boat stretching the gear as we tow, so I'm pretty sure I'm *not* seeing at least as many hits as I *am* seeing. This is getting good, and after a particularly large hit, I let out a whoop and scramble back down the ladder to make a fish call.

I key the microphone on the sideband. "Yeah, I'm getting quite a few hits here in the last few minutes, in case anyone is interested." I look out the window at the gear while I'm talking, and a bunch slams into the net about fifty corks out. I love when that happens while I'm on the radio, because then I get to say, "Yeah, there's another good one right now!" Don on the *Marauder* answers, "What are your numbers, Pat?" I tell him my latitude/longitude, and he pauses a second before replying, "Do you see a boat a couple of miles north and east of you? Are you off west by yourself?"

"Yep," I answer. "That's me. Is that you up there?" All Ican see is a gray dot near the horizon in the direction of the river.

"Yeah," he says, "We're clearing out some kelp that hit our gear on the last set. I had to roll it on just to get out of there, and moved west. We're already setting out again. It's 4:30. I don't know if I want to move over now."

"Uh, Don," I say. "This is looking really good here, and they're charging north. Trust me. You want to move over and get in line with me. I'm getting nailed here." I feel a sense of urgency trying to convince him that this is worth the effort. The day is almost over. I know the feeling of being tired and frustrated dealing with sticks or kelp in the gear. But I think, it's rare to be out here all by ourselves on a school of fish. I see another hit, and key the mic again. "Yeah, there's been a couple more since we stopped talking," I say. "And there's another one."

A long pause, and then he comes on. "Ok. We 'll pick up and move over. Let me know if it dies off."

"Will do." I hang up the microphone, grab some cookies and a pop, plug in the external speaker and head back topside. The tow is lifting the lines near the boat out of the water. Fish are hanging in the gear as far back as I can see. We're going to have to pick up soon, or we'll never make it before the end of the period. I look at my watch. It's just before 5:00. We have a little over an hour to go. I watch as Don moves west. I figure I'll wake Danny in five minutes, start picking in ten. Excited, I light another cigarette. The wind whistles around me until I jump down from the bridge and swing into the cabin. "C'mon Danny," I yell. "We've loaded up again! It's time to pick some more fish!" As he sleepily rubs his eyes and pulls on his boots, I call Don and tell him I'm going to start picking.

"How's it goin' up there?" I ask.

"Not bad," he says. "There's definitely some fish here. We've had a couple nice bunches already, and we just got it all out. We'll wait 10-15 more minutes and pick up then."

"Roger that," I'll be on the back deck." Danny and I put on our gloves and rain gear. I take off the tow, put the line back off the stern and let the net flag. Picking while using the net as a sea anchor makes for a more stable deck, and it's impossible to get the fish out of the gear while you're towing. We bungee the door open and hurry to the stern. I estimate we have at least 300 fish in the first shackle thirty minutes later. It's 5:40. We're not going to get it all out of the water by the period's end. If we get caught by Fish and Game with gear out, the entire catch will be confiscated. Though the odds are low of getting caught way out here by ourselves, with all these fish I don't even want to risk it.

"Let's pick as much as we can until 10 til," I say to Danny as we bring on another bunch. "Then we'll roundhaul the rest." He nods and grunts as he bends down to pick a fish. Danny doesn't say much, but he's a hard worker and good fish picker. We both step it up a notch, feeling the urgency. We barely notice the white-crested waves slapping the stern unless one actually sprays us with ice-cold water. The boat is full and heavy, and rolls lazily even in a crazy sea. It makes for an easier working environment, but she's significantly lower in the water. I notice the waves are starting to push the sea into the scuppers, the holes made for water to drain out as we bring the soaked net on board. I have tapered wooden plugs tied to the stern cleats. "Get the hammer," I tell Danny. "Let's put the plugs in." He stops picking and hustles to the cabin. I unlash the scupper on my side of the boat, get down on my knees and lean over the gunwale to guide the plug into place. I reach behind my back and Danny puts the hammer in my hand. A few solid whacks, including one as we roll to the side and submerge the plug, that causes me to splash and soak my own face. Finally, it's secure. We plug the other side, toss the hammer up by the door to the cabin and resume picking. I am wet, cold and tired, but

112

internally I'm celebrating. We are on our best set and day of the season, and no one has come close to reporting this many fish all day. This is the kind of day I dream about each spring. It's 5:55. We pick furiously, swearing when a fish is bagged in the net or is stubborn and won't come out fast. I watch the corks behind the boat as Danny finishes clearing a fish out of the gear, just in time to see another bunch hit!

"We're still getting fish!" I shake my head. "Shit. Why couldn't it be noon right now?"

"Because we'd sink!" Danny smiles. I realize he's right.

"Okay. Let's get outta here. Clear the deck." We pitch all the fish at our feet over the reel into the open fish hold. I press my foot on the treadle that powers the new hydraulic motor and roll the net, fish and all on board. The hydraulic motor is a good one, and even though the fish and gear weigh a ton, we wrap a little over a shackle and some 250 more fish onto the reel. 6:15. We're out of the water. I figure we have close to 2,000 salmon on board.

Without a net to hold her, the *Skookum* drifts sideways in the trough, so I put her in gear, turn her north, put the sea on her stern and climb to the bridge where I clean gurry off my glasses and steer toward Don, who is still picking. Danny starts pulling the net off the reel by hand, picking fish as he goes. Don is just bringing on the buoy as we come alongside, and he's grinning. "That was a great shot to end the day!" He shouts over the wind. "Thanks for that. We must've had 400 on that one!"

"Great! See you in the river!" I yell back. We both duck into our respective cabins and throttle up, heading northeast. I steer and put TV dinners in the oven as Danny clears the fish off the reel and rolls the net back on. The *Marauder* is faster than the *Skookum*, and a better sea boat with more hull above the waterline than we have. He passes us and slowly pulls away as we run home. There are still a few other boats out here, but with the weather turning nasty at the period's end and the bulk of the fleet headed in early, I'm glad Don's with us. The lonely feeling

113

that haunts me periodically over all the years I fish, the one that comes over me when I realize how small a boat I am - a tiny black speck on a great big ocean - feels less strong when I'm running near somebody I know. I never have liked being out here by myself, even with a boatload of fish.

I'm even more grateful for Don's presence when the engine quits about an hour before we reach the river. I'm asleep in the bunk when the drone of the engine goes quiet. "Hey, Pat," Danny calls, but I'm already wide-awake and getting up. It's almost 9:00 pm under gray skies, and the light is dim outside. "What happened?" I ask as I look out the windows. I think Danny shut her down for some reason.

"I don't know," he replies. "Everything was running fine when she just quit." He slides out of the skipper's seat and I climb in. I turn the key. The engine cranks but doesn't start. We click on the cabin lights over the table and the sink. "Let's unbutton her and take a look." I have no idea what I'm looking for, but I'm hoping something will be obvious. While Danny rolls back the carpet and lifts the floorboards in the cabin to allow access to the engine, I call Don. "Hey *Marauder*, *Skookum Too*. I have a problem here, Don."

Steph, Don's girlfriend and deckhand, comes back. "Hang on *Skookum Too*, I'll wake him up."

While we wait, Danny drops into the engine room and starts poking around with a flashlight. "Check the fuel filter and lines," I tell him. "And the solenoid." This engine has a temperamental fuel system anyway, and when the device called the solenoid quits, the entire system becomes paralyzed. It has an indicator switch like a circuit breaker that lets us know when it has tripped, but it looks fine. There are no leaks, no loose wires, nothing that would indicate a problem. I turn the ignition to "On," so the gauges come to life, but I don't turn the engine over, not with Danny so near the fan belts. The needles all snap into place. Water temperature, amperes, everything looks normal.

"*Skookum Too*, what's going on back there?" Don's voice comes over the radio.

"Not sure. She just quit running. We're looking at the engine now. As far as we can tell, everything looks fine, but she won't start."

"I'll come back and give you a tow to the river," he says. "Be there in about ten."

We check battery cables, wires, circuit breakers, in-line fuses to the ignition, fuel lines. Everything checks out. But she won't start. When Don arrives, we rig up a tow line from our bow to his stern, and he stretches the line slowly so it doesn't part. We are under way again, and I sit in the skipper's seat steering so we don't veer off to one side or the other with the swell behind us. The wind has backed off, but the seas are now six-to-eight-foot swells chasing us north. A big one lifts us, and when we ride down its back, the towline dips into it, slicing it like a knife. When the wave catches and lifts the *Marauder*, the line parts with a *thwaannngggg*. Danny and I are on our feet in an instant. I steer the boat with the waves while he goes forward and brings the line back on board. The *Marauder* does the same and swings back around. This time Don ties one of the old tires he uses for boat bumpers between the lines connecting our boats. The tire will hopefully act as a cushion and absorb some of the shock when the line gets pulled suddenly by the wave action. He ties the end to the line on his reel so the tow will be from the center of his stern, allowing him to steer better. Steph eases the boat forward as Don stands on deck directly behind the reel and watches. Satisfied, he walks in the cabin and closes the door. Ten seconds later, the line parts between the tire and my bow, and the tire shoots forward like a loosed arrow. Danny and I both watch in the fading light as it rockets over the reel where Don was just standing, rope trailing behind it like the tail of a kite. It slams into the *Marauder's* cabin door with enough force to bounce back over the reel to the picking deck. "Jesus Christ!"

I shout. If the line splits twenty seconds earlier, Don is dead or knocked overboard.

Steph goes out on deck and pulls in the line hanging behind the *Marauder* again, while Danny does the same on the bow of the *Skookum*. Meanwhile, Don and I discuss what to do on the radio. "The boats are just too heavy in this swell," he says. "I'll try tying alongside." Danny taps on the windshield and points to the bow cleat. As I look, he goes over to it and lifts the back end of it up. The bolts holding it are almost pulled completely through the wooden deck.

The *Marauder* approaches from our starboard side, the direction the swell is coming from. We get lines ready, and Don comes out of the cabin and climbs the ladder to his bridge for better visibility. Steph readies lines on the *Marauder's* deck. The *Skookum* is full in the trough now, rolling sideways up and down the swells. We're in no danger of capsizing, but the motion has the sides of the boat rising and falling several feet with each wave. When the *Marauder* comes alongside, Danny tosses a line onto her stern, then hops over to tie off. Steph, holding a line already tied to the *Marauder's* midship cleat, straddles both the boats and loops the line around our cleat, then back again. Don's boat is fiberglass, the *Skookum* wood. Just as Steph finishes tying the line to the cleat, the *Marauder* is lifted by a swell, and the four-inch-long bolts holding the cleat to the deck of the *Skookum* slide upward through the plank under it like it was butter. Surprised at the force, I look at Steph, one leg on her boat, one leg on ours. I don't even stop to think. I grab her by the front of her jacket, growl, "You're with me!" and pull her on board as the wave rolls under us and boats surge apart. Don guns the engine so we don't crash together on the next swell, and just like that we've switched deckhands.

I make sure Steph is well on board before releasing her. "You okay?" I ask. She nods. We're both shaken by the unexpected display of violence. If she had fallen between the

116

two heavy boats, she'd be crushed or drowned. We watch as Don turns the *Marauder* around to come alongside again, this time to trade people. The boat pulls within a foot of us, and when he guns the engine in reverse, it stops dead. In an instant Steph and Danny switch positions. Don pulls away again, and he and Steph disappear into the cabin. Danny and I do the same. "Well that was fun." I say into the microphone. "What now?" I'm out of ideas and getting low on cleats.

"I don't know," Don says. "We can't tow you, that's obvious. There's nothing left to tow with."

"Let me call Ray," I say. "Maybe he'll have a suggestion." Ray Landry is the cannery superintendent and an ex-engineer. He's seen all sorts of predicaments during his years in the industry, and if anyone can puzzle out what our next move is, it's him. I call him on the VHF and we discuss the possibility of rigging a cradle of rope under the boat and around the cabin to tow with, but that sounds iffy to me. "All the tenders are filled with fish and boats in line to deliver more, Pat." he answers when I ask if one of them could assist. "Besides, I don't know what they can do, anyway. I could send the power skiff out, but we need to wait until the seas calm down." The prospect of trying to set an anchor while loaded, adrift and without power doesn't seem like a good plan at all. It's completely dark now, and the wind and tide are pushing us toward Salamatof beach north of the river mouth, where the shoreline is riddled with rocks. "Let me see if we can figure out what's wrong with the engine one more time, Ray. I'll get back to you."

Don comes on the other radio. "I'll stand by here until you figure out what's going on, Pat." I know that's a sacrifice. It's late, and we're the only ones out here. We're going to be the last boats in the river, and even if we do arrive at a solution, it's going to be hours before we get any sleep. I shake my head at my good fortune to have two brothers like Don and Dean as friends. "Thanks Don. You'll be the first to know if I find anything."

117

I drop into engine room and go back to the beginning. Danny lays on the floor next to me, and together we start inspecting every wire related to the power system carefully. One with white insulation runs from the ignition to the top of the solenoid. "What's that dark line?" Danny asks as I run the flashlight along it. There, about two feet from the solenoid, is a small crack in the insulation. I feel it with my fingers, then bend it. Corroded by who knows how many days of salt water and air getting to it, the wire comes apart in my hands. "Get the strippers!" I exclaim. "And the connectors!" We strip and reconnect the wire and I stand back while Danny turns the key. The engine roars to life. I jump to the radio. "We got it, Don! It was a hairline fracture in the ignition wire! Let's go fuckin' home!"

It's 4:00 am by the time we deliver our fish and head to the dock. I'm high boat for the cannery for the first time ever. As I leave the tender in the dark and motor up to the string of boats tied to the float, I hear a voice shout out, "Goddamn teachers!" It's the guy who believes that teachers aren't as good as "real" fishermen. He's become a friend, but I know his trash talk is tainted with a belief he still thinks is true. I also know he's the kind of guy who watched as we delivered, and knows how we did. Surprised and tired, I laugh a little too loud and reply, "Yeah, and you call yourself a fisherman!" It's a good feeling.

–Interlude –
A Teacher-Fisherman

I never expected to become a teacher. Some people know from the start what they want to do and plan for who they want to become. Not me. I've never been much of a planner. I 'arrived' at teaching in 1973. Fresh out of college, I was hired to teach Special Education at Henry Clay School in inner-city Louisville, Kentucky. My first day was sweltering – Ohio River Valley hot and humid – and I was sweating through my T-shirt as I stapled construction paper to a bulletin board. I was squatted down, finishing, when an epiphany hit me like a school bus: *I'm a TEACHER! Oh my God. How did this happen? How did I get here?* In the context of my life up to that point, the thought held so much power that it knocked me from my feet to my butt.

I sat there and reflected on my own school experiences: the son of an alcoholic mother and a bipolar father (though that term had not yet been coined), I was one of the "problem kids" and had convinced myself I liked it that way. I ran away from home in high school – twice. I smoked, drank, street-raced, skipped classes – anything to defy the rules. The second time I ran away, my senior year, two friends and I broke into the school at night with the intention of getting into the school office, stealing the cash box stored there, and trashing the administration's records. Though our efforts failed due to a well-designed deadbolt, it was more of an act of rebellion than a means to leave town. I hated high school. And five short years later, here I was – a teacher.

I replayed the events of my college life: all I ever wanted to do was write, but I chose English as my major instead of Creative Writing. The first semester of my sophomore year I failed my Spanish requirement. The class started at 7:30 each morning, and I slept in most of the term after late nights studying psychedelics and the tactics of playing RISK. I flunked out that semester. I blamed the failure on my inability to understand how to navigate a foreign language. When I re-enrolled the next fall, I looked for a program that wouldn't require that qualification to graduate. The School of Education offered that as an option, and I enrolled, never thinking about what it meant in terms of a career. Special Education was where jobs were in those days, and when it opened to undergrads to declare as a major my junior year, I signed up. I was assigned as a student-teacher to the school where I was now sitting stunned on the floor. Even mapping out how I arrived here, I was still completely surprised. It felt like I had been acting on stage for years, when suddenly the house lights brightened to show me the role I was playing was now actually my life. I was dumbfounded.

Now what? I felt the existential angst I had carried with me most of my adolescence and into my college years well up inside my chest again. I considered leaving. Just getting up and walking out the door, like I'd done five years ago. Except that decision led to one of the most painful experiences of my life. Running away had hurt everyone in my family. It had hurt me. I realized it was a mistake as soon as I was gone, but I felt helpless to correct it. Leaving wasn't the clean break or fresh start I thought it would be, and I was beyond lucky that my parents found me and allowed me to come home again. I was beyond lucky they forgave me. That experience taught me that walking out now was the wrong answer. I stared at the blank bulletin board and knew I needed to fill it up before I walked away. The only answer that made any sense came when I imagined crossing paths with adolescents who were as desperate now as I was then. I could embrace this opportunity to treat my students with the compassion I longed for during those years. I realized I needed to do that – for them, certainly, but also for me. For the me that was still here inside me, hating school, hating rules, hating authority.

"Be the best damn teacher you can be, then," I said aloud

as I stood and pushed off into my career. "You have to." I made my choice. Now I just had to stick with it.

§

I quickly discovered that I loved the act of teaching. I loved the engagement, the relationships built with young minds, watching them light up when they figured out a piece of the puzzle I was teaching. For me, that was like watching a bunch of fish hit the net. Once I transitioned into teaching the arts – writing, photography and drama – I relished how I could get them to love what I loved: creating. I tried to remain true to the vow I made on the floor of that Louisville classroom in the heat and humidity of the moment. I tried to notice – and help – when my students were struggling in an eddy and not moving upstream. I know I wasn't always effective or successful, but I like to think I was more than I wasn't.

Those moments helped make teaching tolerable when too many poorly thought-out administrative decisions or conflicts with bull-headed colleagues would get in the way of me doing my job. Teaching was the Yin to gillnetting's Yang. Where fishing was organic, always changing and forcing me to be flexible when dealing with weather, tides and fish, the paradigm for teaching was decidedly artificial and contrived, with bells every 55 minutes, policies that came and went every time we got a new principal, headache-inducing 60-cycle-a-second florescent lighting and linoleum over concrete underfoot. The first weeks of teaching overflowed with incessant interruptions and unproductive faculty meetings and were always the roughest waters to navigate. In contrast, one of the things I loved most about fishing was owning my own boat and being the 'skipper' – being my own boss. I loved immersing myself into the natural rhythms of the planet – of knowing the unknowable.

121

Struggling with bureaucracy became a recurrent theme over the thirty-five years I worked in a classroom. It always grated whenever I had to babysit students as they boarded the busses or went crazy at pep rallies. After bad fishing years, I'll admit I felt a relief that I had a steady paycheck waiting for me each fall. But after a good year, I'd go back to school to listen to teachers argue about "tardy" vs "absent", and I'd think seriously about quitting before classes even started.

But then the students would funnel into my classroom. I'd close the door like pulling away from the dock – I was at the wheel again. I'd ask them to think about my class differently. I'd have them stand on tables while I explained how a new perspective could make learning fun and interesting. Again, I'd like to believe it was a successful strategy for the most part. Not always, but certainly more than not. And that's what kept me coming back.

There were important elements of both careers that fit together like the Yin/Yang symbol forms a circle: The seasons for fishing and teaching, for one, are perfectly tuned, at least for salmon. School is out in plenty of time to get the boat ready to fish, and when the fish are gone, there's still time to put the boat away and take a week or two to relax before school started again.

I have boxes of yearbooks, old photos of and by students, and cards and letters from students to remind me that I did indeed have an impact on their lives. These boxes are tangible evidence that I was here – like writing "Kilroy" on the wall. As fishermen, we would scrawl our names and the years we worked on the rafters of the cannery warehouse in chalk – evidence, however impermanent, that we were really there, too.

As a fisherman, it's a source of pride that you are part of the effort to provide a healthy food source for the world. It's a sustainable enterprise if we learn the lessons of how to care for the fish, the waters they swim in, and the land around those waters. As teachers, we feed the lives of our students in ways far beyond the knowledge of the subjects we teach. They swim on, and hopefully the memory of some part of their experience with us remains with them. Eventually, and in more ways than one what we do here ends – and so do we. The world continues to turn in circles within circles. Teaching and fishing for me were two sides of the same coin.

The 1986 Kenai Central High School Yearbook staff photo. I survived.

Chapter Sixteen: Shrimp, Halibut, and Pickle Juice

By 1983 I have been holding two jobs for eight years. Each spring I start on the boat before school is out for the summer, and sometimes I'm still putting it away weeks after I'm back in the classroom, teaching Special Ed. and Photography. The fall transition is always the hardest. Changing my mindset from tides, fish movements and weather to florescent lights, linoleum floors, bells every 55 minutes and faculty meetings is a struggle. I get frustrated to the point of screaming when otherwise intelligent, reasonable people argue for hours over whether the students should be allowed to wear hats. At sea I make my own decisions. On land it's a rare administration I work for at school that I respect or appreciate. In the winter of '83 I tell Veronica that if I'm going to make it to retirement, I need a year off. She's agreeable to the idea, and I apply for and receive a leave of absence, ostensibly to attend graduate school.

I'm dressing in the locker room of the Kenai Rec Center in April after playing racquetball with Jerry Hanson, a teaching buddy and someone whose opinion I respect. We're talking about my plans for the coming year. He asks, "How long have you been in school?"

Not catching his drift, I reply, "Counting Louisville, ten years."

"No," he leans toward me. "All together. Count the years you've *been* in school."

"Ohhhh." I'm starting to catch on. "Um, pretty much every year since I was five. So, 28.

"Exactly. Why would you want to take a year off and *go back to school?*"

That makes me pause. "What would *you* do?"

"I'd travel. Head to Mexico, maybe, where the cost of living is cheap. Go *somewhere*. Do something *else*."

Veronica and I have several long discussions about this during the next few weeks. It's definitely a risk. It's expensive,

124

and I have no guarantee I'll be able to keep the same teaching position when I return. Still, I'd like to try my hand at writing and photography as alternatives to teaching for a living. I can submit stories and photos to magazines through the mail. We can spend a winter in the sun instead of in the long darkness and cold that wears thin on us each winter. The pros of it outweigh the cons, so we change our plans and head south. We buy English/Spanish translation guides to help us with the language, find renters for our house, pack up one-year-old Kessler and fly to Seattle before the snow flies.

We stay with Dean and Don at their home near Green Lake. The two of them have jobs as seafood buyers, and they're gone during the weekdays, but their cousin Rob is in town and he's usually free. He's willing to chauffeur us around and help us buy a used motor home we can afford. The 1966 Chinook we find is funky but in good condition, and just big enough to be comfortable for the three of us. We worry about taking our son to a foreign country, but the more we talk to people who've been to Mexico, the more comfortable we get with the idea. The common phrase we hear is, "Mexicans *love* children."

By December we're camping at Playa Santispac, a beach south of the small Baja town of Mulegé on the Sea of Cortez. For a dollar a day we can park next to a palapa, a shelter made of four poles and a thatched roof. The white sand beach is a mile long with two cantinas serving the dozens of campers and motorhomes parked for the winter or just passing through on their way to Cabo. We're surprised to see that most of the license plates on the vehicles lined up along the beach are from Alaska or British Columbia. We learn the term that describes us all: 'snowbirds' – people who migrate south for the winter.

We're settled in by the Christmas weekend when a fleet of five Mexican shrimp boats appear on the horizon. At the sight of them, everyone on the beach starts running around and yelling. By the time the boats anchor 100 yards offshore, half the beach is headed their way in small skiffs, canoes, kayaks and

125

rubber rafts to buy fresh shrimp, lobster, and to our dismay, even a green sea turtle. The vacationers buy all the product the fishermen have caught in less than an hour. The fishermen take their earnings and disappear for the holiday.

As newcomers we miss out on that first day's bounty. But when the boats return after their next trip, some friends with a small raft buy fresh shrimp for us and another family. I voice my curiosity about their operation. "Wouldn't it be cool to go out with them? I'd love to photograph what they do." A small group of us hatch a plan to ask if some of us can join them for a night's fishing. As another fisherman, I feel a connection tugging at me to go. One of the women in our group speaks Spanish, so the two of us motor out to the boats the next morning to see if we can hitch a ride.

At 10:00 pm that night, five of us are on board as the crews pull anchor. The ships fish all night, using powerful deck lights to attract shrimp as they drag heavy nets through the water. They pull the gear every hour to check the catch. Like fishing everywhere, when the net comes on board, the deck is awash in activity. The fishermen don't wear rain gear, only boots and gloves. They hoist the net with hydraulics and dump the catch on deck. They spend most of the time bent over, sorting shrimp from the flotsam that comes up as bycatch. They push eels, a small octopus, kelp, sticks and jellyfish with brooms and boots through the scuppers and back into the sea. They keep any edible fish to sell, shoveling them into a hold filled with seawater. The work feels familiar, hard and intense until the net is back in the water, when the pace slows and everyone lights a cigarette and bullshits while they clean the deck. I'm photographing the action, but the crew often stops what they're doing to strike poses with each other. The deck lights and fish attract a constant stream of seagulls calling and swooping overhead, trying to find a place to land. I am standing by the rail taking pictures when I hear a whoosh of wings next to me. I pull back from the camera to look a brown pelican in the eye not four

126

feet away. Standing on the railing, he's as tall as I am, and fearless. He tilts his head and snaps his beak at me with a loud *POP*! "No thank you," I say to him and move away. The fisherman watching me raises his eyebrows and nods. "Muy mal," he says with a wry smile. "Their bite is very bad." He waves his deck broom at the pelican and it spreads its wings and floats away.

The fishermen seem happy to have us aboard. My first impression is that their operation is running on a shoestring. The boat is beat-up, paint peeling off the wood and rust streaking the steel. But these guys are genuinely proud of it and are delighted to show it off. When the engineer sees a camera around my neck, he takes me on a tour of the engine room. It's huge with plenty of head room, but stifling hot and smells like diesel. The steps leading to it are slippery with oil. I see hoses and wires laced through the beams held with black tape. Tools line the bulkheads and rags hang on hoses suspended above the generator. It's disorganized to my eye, but to him it's a piece of operational art. He poses erect next to the roaring engine as if he were standing next to a grand prize. I snap the photo with a smile and a nod. I get it.

All night we eat shrimp and visit, the tourists in broken Spanish, the Mexicans in broken English, but we both appreciate how much each other is trying to communicate. Our interpreter helps out when we get stuck, but the crew is friendly and more than willing to visit, even if we don't understand everything. We eat boiled shrimp, fried shrimp, shrimp with garlic and butter, shrimp with lime. We eat so much shrimp we can't eat any more, and they still try to serve us. I bring out some photos I've brought with me of Alaska, and they are amazed at the pictures of snow – *nieve* – and ice – *hielo* – phenomena they've never seen or experienced. At first light we stop fishing and turn for the playa. As we enter the bay, they break out farewell beers and give us each full baggies of shrimp for our families. We offer to pay for the shrimp, but they won't have it. Their generosity is overwhelming, made more so by the evidence that they have so little. We watch the beach swarm with people as the tourists scramble to be the first in line for their catch. We don't feel like tourists anymore. We hug them, shake hands and disembark with waves and shouts of *Gracias!* and *Mucho Gusto!* It's one of the best fishing trips of my life.

Mexican shrimpers in the engine room, 1984.

Kessler turns two on the beach, whacking a piñata with a stick. My first two rolls of mail-in slides never come back, lost in the unreliable international mail. I write in my journal, smoke weed and snorkel daily instead. I find a large conch shell one day, and two of our neighbors show me how to drill it out to make it a horn. For the last month we're there, the three of us

128

start each day by stepping into the water – me at one end of the beach and the two of them spaced out almost evenly along the rest of it – and blowing our conches to greet the sun. The conches produce a deep, resonant sound that echoes across the water… and in my heart. I'm sure we irritate the late-risers, but it's too special a way to begin a day to stop, and no one ever complains.

There's no running water at Santispac. For the four months we're there, we wash Kessler's diapers by hand in a bucket. Disposable diapers are hard to come by, so we use cloth ones. When it's her week to do laundry, Veronica, being the more sensible of the two of us, washes each diaper the same day it's soiled. Being a guy, therefore inherently at a deficit when it comes to domestic choices, I avoid the task for the week while the diapers pile up and ripen in the plastic bucket in the Mexican desert heat. When Veronica tells me we're on the last diaper, I can't avoid it any longer. I pour a generous amount of detergent in a tub, roll a fatty and smoke it all myself before putting rubber gloves on my hands and firing up my Walkman with Sting and the Police. I crank the volume and sing along as I sit, scrubbing cross-legged on the sand in front of the plastic tub and watch the ocean waves, my brain blissfully ignoring what my hands are doing. The best part of washing the diapers out – and let's be honest here, there is nothing even close to a 'best part' – is watching the faces of tourists strolling along the beach as they approach me with curious smiles. When they finally get close enough to see what I'm doing, their smiles change to expressions of horror. I thank the cannabis Gods for good Mexican weed every wash day.

The author, after hand-washing a pail of diapers on the beach, 1984.

By mid-April we have driven 1, 900 miles from the Baja to Seattle on our way home. Don and Rob recruit me to crew on their halibut boat, the 42-foot *Inga E.* We spend the next ten days driving 2,400 more miles to Kenai, and a few weeks later I'm on board, tying lines for a four-day commercial halibut derby. Halibut are flatfish that feed on the bottom of the ocean. The plan is to fish 70 miles off Seward, on the south side of the Kenai Peninsula, where a week earlier Don and Rob tossed out a small string of baited hooks on the way into Resurrection Bay and caught and released several large fish. They mark the spot on the chart. This is where we'll spend the next four days fishing. We have ten miles of tough rope called a groundline on the reel, thousands of hooks, and boxes and boxes of frozen herring that we chop up and use for bait.

Five of us are on board. Randy and I tie hooks onto one end of three-foot long ganyons, which are like leaders made of stout twine. We tie snaps on the other end that we'll attach to the groundline as it pays off the reel when we set. Joe has the least experience and therefore is the 'Master-Baiter', threading thousands of pieces of herring onto the hooks. Rob and Don trade places running the boat, cooking and making sure everything is in good working order on deck. They create a seafood stew called a *Caldo Largo*, or large caldron of potatoes, carrots, celery and an assortment of bycatch we haul in, such as gray cod, ling cod and skate (a small bottom fish similar to a flounder). The pot simmers on the stove for the entire opening, and is added to when it gets low. It's hot, delicious and always ready when we need a hot meal. We leave the harbor late – I am used to this, because Rob and Don are always late for everything – but because we're in a hurry they decide not to top off the fresh water tanks. "We have plenty. We should be fine," they tell us.

The weather is fair for the entire opening. From a reel in the stern, we set twenty 'skates' or sections of groundline 1,800 feet long with 100 hooks per skate. We tie anchors to each end of the groundline that are tethered to buoys with tall radar reflectors so we can find them if the weather turns sour. Each anchor takes 15 minutes to reach the bottom, some 80-100 fathoms (480-600 feet) below the surface. We set out what feels like an infinite number of baited hooks, snapping them onto the groundline every six feet as it spins off the reel. In the wheelhouse, Don decides where to set based on what the bottom looks like on the sonar and writes down the location of each skate. He tells us when to set over the deck speaker. Rob is deck boss and keeps us moving, baiting, tying ganyons, snapping hooks and readying anchors. It's new and confusing work. I feel like a greenhorn again, but we're all boat savvy at least, and learn quickly. We work all day and into the night, taking short breaks for sandwiches and hot burritos. By the time we set the last skate we're working smoothly as a team and though we're all tired from the long repetitive work, we're feeling good about our performance so far.

As soon as all the gear is set, we eat and nap while Don runs the boat back to the first skate so we can pick it as fast as we can, otherwise sand fleas will damage the hooked fish. We're all hopeful as Rob throws the grappling hook over the buoy and pulls the line to it on board. The stories of the big fish they caught here a week ago echo in my head as he threads the line through a power block and starts hauling it off the bottom. But they aren't here. We bring in just a few fish, and they aren't the 100-plus pounders we were expecting. Rob and Don disappear into the wheelhouse to talk strategy while the rest of us clean what we have as we run to the second string. It has more fish, but they are still smaller than any of us expected, averaging less than 50 pounds.

The boat has a cleaning station big enough to hold two fish just forward of the reel. Don teaches Randy, Joe and me how to cut out their gills with a fillet knife, then reach down their mouths and break a membrane deep inside their gullet with our fingertips to grab their testicles and tear them out, or else the fish will spoil. "Wait. What??" Randy says, voicing the thoughts in our heads after Don's explanation. "You're shitting me, right? Rip out their *testicles?!*" Don nods and demonstrates while the three of us shudder and make sick jokes. "Never teach this to my ex-wife," says Joe. But we learn, and try not to think about what we're doing as we work. Once we've cleaned several fish, one of us climbs the ladder into a hold twice as big as a gillnetter's while the other two lower the dressed fish down. The person in the hold lays them on beds of flake ice, shovels ice into their bellies, then covers them completely. We rotate jobs so no one person is doing all the cold work.

The entire process is hard, chilly, smelly, dirty exhausting work. Halibut teeth rake and scratch our fingers and wrists even though we wear tough rubber gloves and neoprene 'wristers' (sleeves) to protect them. Our fingers go numb from punching through hundreds of testicle membranes. Occasionally Don yells "Lunker!" and we all stop what we're doing, grab gaff hooks and congregate at the side of the boat. Looking into the water over the side, a 200-plus pound halibut breaks the surface, and we all plunge gaffs into it and heave it aboard, swearing, sliding on the slippery footing and scrambling out of the way as it falls thrashing over the rail to the deck. "Stay away!" Rob yells at us. "That thing'll break your leg like a matchstick!"

We start catching fish on nearly every hook, and we all know we're making good money. We haul back through the night and the fish pile up until we are knee-deep in dead halibut. Don and Rob stop picking and direct us to drag fish around the cabin to the bow to make room. Our feet ache from standing for hours in rubber boots. Our backs ache from lifting 50-70-pound fish up to the table and down to the hold. Our hands and fingers are cold and cramping. It's chilly on deck but we're all sweating from the effort, and now we're bent over, a halibut in each hand, slipping and falling as we drag them around the wheelhouse. Don comes up behind me as I sit on a pile catching my breath. I look up and shake my head at him. "This is way different than catching salmon!" We both laugh tired laughs. The only thing that keeps us going is the money. The cannery is offering $1.25 a pound for 60-pound fish and larger,
$1.00 a pound for 40-60 pounders, and 90 cents a pound for smaller fish. Even with their smaller size, all these fish mean a shot in the arm financially for everyone. I know this money will help Veronica and I make up for the cash we spent in Mexico. Like everyone else on board, we need it.

We end day two with a nap. Rob and Don wake to the alarm, make coffee and roust the rest of us. They are watching me as I sit on the bunk looking at my hands. My fingers are so swollen I can't feel or bend them. They are so saturated with salt water they're the size of sausages and absolutely white with black lines of dried halibut blood in all the creases. Sitting on the edge of the bunk after trying and failing to pull on my boots, I stare at them with my mouth open, not understanding what's happened. Don and Rob crack up. "Got a problem there?" Don says with a chuckle. He tells me it happens to everyone. The fingers loosen up after I start working again. The nap and some hot breakfast in my belly help too.

The grind continues well into the morning, when Don yells "Lunker! A big one!" We drop what we're doing and watch a giant of a halibut float up like a thick sheet of plywood. It's a monster, weighing 440 pounds, and it's all we can do to hoist it into the boat. The *Inga* has five feet of freeboard, the distance we all have to dead-lift it to get it over the rail and on board. Rob yells "Heave!" and we all lift it a foot. "Heave!" Another foot. By the time it's ready to come over, it's all we can do to hold on. Every muscle in our hands, arms, shoulders and backs is screaming to let go. "One more!" Rob hollers and we all scream as we haul it over the side. Our boots slip with the strain, and as one we all fall back against the bait box, feet against the side of the boat. The giant halibut, already dead, is eight feet long and four feet wide. It lands on top of all five of us, pinning us underneath it. We all look at each other and start to laugh. Don deadpans, "Well, this is how we die. If we're lucky, they'll find us in a week or two, just like this."

"I don't know about you," Randy says, giggling, "but this is as comfortable as I've been all day. If I could just breathe, I'd take a nap."

We all take another break and crash hard in the bunks at the end of the day. No one hears the alarm that was supposed go off after two hours. We're all so tired we sleep six. My fingers are covered in painful scratches. Worried about infection, I rub my hands with Neosporin and put Band-Aids on all the cuts. When I'm done, I have at least one on every finger. Randy awakens with a weird infection in his legs that cause his calves to swell up to the size of his thighs. He can't put any weight on them, so he monitors the radios in the cabin and elevates his feet. Joe pulls a tendon in his forearm from all the repetitive motion of baiting and can barely use it. He spends the rest of the trip trying to shovel ice one-handed. Don, Rob and I hump to retrieve the gear still in the water before the end of the period. We run low on right-handed rubber gloves. All of us are right-handed, and most of those gloves have holes in the fingers from all the rough work. When we run out of cigarettes, morale takes a nose dive. We all smoke, and when we shopped for the trip, we bought an entire grocery cart full of cartons of cigarettes that are now all gone. Don develops a pocket of infection that swells up the back of his left hand. He tries to wash his hands in the sink, but the water spurts and sputters as the tank goes dry. The only thing left to drink on board is pickle juice, but none of us is that desperate. Yet.

We're picking the last skate with Rob running the hydraulic block that pulls the groundline up from the bottom. He leans over to gaff a fish, but just then the halibut kicks and with a splash the hook pops free and sinks into the fleshy meat at the base of Rob's thumb. Everything stops as we head to the galley. We sit at the table, cut the ganyon away and pour Vodka on the wound. Halibut hooks are stainless steel, tough and thick with stout barbs. This isn't going to back out without a significant amount of damage to the flesh and a lot of pain. It's circular in shape, so in order to push it through, we have to cut it first. I pin Rob's arm and wrist to the table while Don slowly saws through the shaft with a hacksaw. Rob grimaces and his face pales, but he doesn't say anything. He swallows a gulp of Jack Daniels before we start, and takes another before we push it through. He's light-headed and weak when we finish bandaging his hand, but he runs the boat while Don and I pick the last string.

Before Rob was hurt, our injuries seemed minor. Even Randy wasn't too concerned about his infection. But Rob's wound sobers us up. If that happens to someone while setting the gear, he's overboard in an instant. He'd drown before we could get the boat turned around. Even carrying a knife taped to your rain gear, which we all do, wouldn't help, and we all know it. I try not to imagine what being dragged through the water by a hook on its way to the bottom of the ocean would feel like. We

135

head to port a few hours early with thirty-thousand pounds of halibut in the hold. Until now we've all been adding up our shares in our heads and counting the money. Not anymore. Now we just want to get home.

On the way in, word comes through the radio – the canneries are plugged and have lowered the price by ten cents a pound for all sizes of fish. To make matters worse we're so thirsty we start drinking the pickle juice and scouring ashtrays and trash cans for cigarette butts long enough to light without setting our beards on fire. For a bunch of guys who just packed a boat full of fish, we're a sorry lot.

Veronica meets us at the dock in Seward. We're not scheduled to deliver until morning, so I call her from the grounds. She drives my truck over, and we rent a hotel room for the night. I shower, we push the two double beds together and I fall into her arms as if it's the last wonderful thing I'll ever do.

We wake up when the sun spills around the curtains, have breakfast at a local restaurant and head to the boat. Once we pull the *Inga E* to the dock and open the hold, there's more bad news. Our average poundage is less than we thought – 30 pounds for dressed fish. Then we find out the worst news of all: the access panel sealing the hydraulic lines running through the fish hold has come off, allowing the hoses that heat up when the hydraulics are used to burn enough of the load that the cannery will only buy our fish as 'seconds', dropping the price even lower, to 66 cents a pound. The little remaining air goes out of all of us. This puts Rob and Don in the red, with a boat payment, food expenses, fuel, insurance, crew shares, and a mountain of work behind us adding up to not enough money to break even. We all go numb. To say we're devastated is an understatement, and there's not a thing we can do about it.

Don is sitting at the galley table with a blank stare when I walk in after hosing down and scrubbing the deck. I ask him if it's okay for me to head home with Veronica. "Yeah," he says. "Doesn't make any sense for you to ride around to Kenai with

136

us." We shake hands and he helps me load three small fish into my truck as a bonus to my $400 share. I put them under a tarp in the back of the pickup. Veronica drives us the three hours home while I sleep. I dream of stuffing myself with shrimp, drinking beer and laughing with a bunch of fishermen from Mexico.

Pat with a halibut on the Inga E in the Gulf of Alaska, 1984.

Chapter Seventeen: Whirlpool

The 1984 salmon season is forecasted to be slow, and it lives up to the prediction. Veronica has decided to fish with me for the season, and though she is willing and excited, she fights seasickness every day we're on the water, and tries every remedy possible, including a prescription for a behind-the-ear patch that looks like a circular Band-Aid, with the drug Scopolamine embedded in it. It holds off the nausea, but makes her constantly thirsty, dizzy and tired. Rather than quit mid-season, she toughs it out in hopes she'll get used to the water.

We are running north along the eastern edge of the south Kalgin bar in a flat calm sea when we see what appears to be a small whirlpool in the water ahead of us. Even though the tide is running out hard, Cook Inlet is not known for any phenomena like a whirlpool, so this gets us a little spooked, and we approach it cautiously. It's maybe six feet across, and spinning in the center of it is a small buoy and a piece of twisted line. I move the boat alongside, and Veronica picks up the line with the boathook. We try to pull it out of the water enough to lash it to the line on our reel and use the hydraulics to lift it on board, but it won't move at all. I have to keep adjusting the boat by bumping the throttle into gear when the tide starts pulling us off it, and the whole operation becomes an ordeal. Plus, the eeriness of a whirlpool where there shouldn't be one has me a little weirded out, so we give it up and head north again. We never do find out what that was all about, and none of the fishermen I ask about it have ever seen a whirlpool in the Inlet.

The Scopolamine doesn't solve Veronica's seasickness problem, though it does help mine. She spends several periods picking fish, stopping to throw up over the side, then turns back to picking again. She feels terrible, and I feel terrible for her. When we hire Craig Phillips to help out for a day, she sees how much more she could be doing if she weren't so sick, and decides not to deckhand for me from then on. It's a painful decision for both of us. We entered into this business with the idea that we'd fish together, and raise a family of fishermen, like some of our friends are doing. Now she's stuck on land while I have all the fun. She dives into providing "Land Support" by mending gear, shopping and prepping meals for the boat, chasing down parts we need from town and helping with the boat work and clean-up. To ease the disappointment of not fishing, she comes out on the calm days, and often meets me at the dock after a period. And of course she joins us for mug-up whenever she can.

The extra added benefit of Veronica staying home is for child care. We think we have a good nanny when we start the summer, but Kessler is two-and-a-half, and is just starting to talk. When we come home after a fishing period early in the season, he uses a racial slur in conversation that shocks and outrages us both. We realize that it could only have originated with the nanny. We fire her and scramble for child care for the next few weeks until Craig jumps on board for the remainder of the season and she can stay home. In all, Veronica's role change becomes the right decision.

Chapter Eighteen: Changes

Dean decides to sell out after the 1984 season. He's been considering it for a while, but when his winter job situation changes and he becomes a full-time fish buyer, he figures he needs to make that move. Of course, he's right, but it still stings. Michael Burgener, my friend and deckhand from 1981, moved away a year earlier, and I missed him desperately. This feels like a pile-on, though I know they both have their reasons.

Dean and I talk frequently on the phone in the fall and winter, mostly about the logistics of selling the boat and permit. I find him a buyer: George Clouston, a shop teacher at the high school where I work. But late in the spring of 1985 I make the mistake of heading to the cannery before anyone has arrived from down south. I find a ladder leaning on someone else's boat in the yard and drag it through the crusty snow to the *Skookum*. When I unlock the cabin door and step down into the musty air, I recite my end-of-winter mantra, "Hello boat!" The stove stack rattles in the chilly wind like an answer, and I suddenly feel sorry for myself. My best summer friend and mentor is gone. I wonder if I'll be even half the fisherman without him.

Over the years, I've gotten the impression that for a lot of skippers and deckhands, fishing is simple. They get up from their beds and go to work at the cannery or on the fishing grounds like they would if they were headed to any job. For me, that's never been the case. I have a healthy respect for the water, but deep down I think the feeling is closer to fear.

When we build a new house less than a mile from the cannery with a view of the Inlet, I spend dozens of nights staring at the ceiling, listening to the wind blow as a front or storm moves up the Inlet. I can hear the engines of boats as they leave the river in the early morning, and the more their drone fluctuates, the more I know they're plowing into big waves. It isn't fear of dying that grips me. It's the apprehension that I'm in for an uncomfortable day fighting seasickness and the elements, when it's already a challenge for me just to find the fish. Dean's presence and help has masked that for me. With him coaching me, I didn't feel so alone out there. Without him, I'm back to square one. I'm able to share my fears with Veronica, and she's often awake beside me listening to the weather spatter on the bedroom windows. "You know, you don't have to go," she whispers as she snuggles me. "It's ok."

But as Thor says when we talk on the dock while a storm lashes the Inlet on a fish day, "You have to poke your nose out to see what it's like." Over time, I come to agree. The worst weather is often between my ears.

Don Pugh on the Inga E, 1984.

Don shows up a month later, in mid-June, and we immediately pick up where we left off. We're at the bar one night shooting pool when someone asks where Dean is. We tell him, and he looks at me and says, "Lost your running mate, eh?"

141

It's meant as a joke, but it still smarts. I look at Don, put an arm around him as he goes all sheepish and shoot back, 'Yeah, but I've got a replacement!"

He looks at the floor. "I was afraid of this."

I hug him tighter. "You're it, baby. We're best buds now!" The other fisherman laughs at us. Neither of them realizes how much I mean what I say.

Chapter Nineteen: Blue Water Melancholy

Like a lot of fishermen, I save my permit cards issued by the state before each season. It's the end of September when I add one more to the stack I keep on a shelf above my desk with a sigh. I know this feeling. Everyone's gone home or back to their non-fishing lives, including me. As rough as this business can be, I long for it during the winter like an addict. "I'm going down to the boat for an hour or so," I tell Veronica as I put on my jacket. "I'll pick up the groceries on the way back." Kessler's down for a nap. She knows how I feel this time of year and hugs me as I leave.

It's cold, yet I drive to the cannery on this gray day as if it's the middle of the run. The fish are long since up the river, spawned out and dead, their carcasses providing nutrients to the lakes and rivers of their birth. I am filled with emptiness, and I wonder if I can regain some of what I feel I've lost by going where I think I belong. The asphalt road past the new subdivision is deserted, puddles in the shade on the pavement rimmed by early winter's ice. For a moment I glance into the woods I'm driving past and look for a moose. The birch and aspen, their autumn glory fading on the ground around them, stand silent and bare. Most moose are still up in the hills escaping the fall hunt. Too late for fish, too early for moose. Briefly I wonder where the Kenai Flats caribou herd goes in the winter, but the road distracts me as it turns to gravel. I take a right to the cannery and stop at the entrance to unhook the unlocked padlock hanging off the steel gate blocking the gravel drive. The padlock is always left looking like it's locked, but it never is.

I open the gate and ease through. I stop the truck in the dust, get out, push the gate shut again and drive down the hill to the boat yard. I slow down as I pass the winter watchman's house, but his truck is gone. He's probably in town. I have the entire place to myself. *Perfect. If I'm going to come down here*

143

and make myself feel like shit, then at least I'll be alone so I can do a good job of it.

I turn the truck left and creep down the line of boats on either side of the pothole-ridden lane. The truck bounces and lurches when all I want is a smooth, contemplative ride. Instead, I'm treated to a jarring journey between puddles and continuous holes in the gravel. I'm forced to pay attention to where I'm going, not reminisce over where I've been. I twist the wheel trying to find an easier path and finally come to grips with the fact that there won't be one. I pull off to the side and kill the engine. Leaving the keys in the ignition, I grab my gloves and get out.

I take a deep breath, hoping for a scent of the sea. The air is fresh, blown in from across the flats, but there's no salt smell today. A flicker of disappointment travels through me. I'd been hoping to use that scent to reconnect to the water. Instead, I stand firmly on land; all too much on land. *Shit.* It's not even October yet. *It's going to be a long winter.* I listen to the gravel crunch under my feet. I'm heading toward the river. At least it will still be there – steady and flowing, like this blood pulsing in me, like this feeling.

I reach the wooden boardwalk, and it feels odd. My winter boots are foreign here. Better to walk here in a Romeo – a deck slipper – or even tennis shoes. A sensation that should be received by my feet can't get through stiff Vibram soles. Again, something I want to feel is stopped short. *What the fuck?* I start to notice a pattern. I'm forcing it. I'm looking too hard for something that's not about this place, but about a time. At least that's what I begin to realize, even if the thought isn't completely formed yet.

By the time I come back to myself, I have walked all the way to the edge of the dock. My boots have taken me off the wooden boardwalk onto the concrete pier until I'm at the railing. I have been looking at the river, but haven't really *seen* it, muddy and swollen with the autumn rains. This is not the river

144

of summer, blue of sun or steel-gray of summer storm. No, it's brown and full of the debris it's sweeping off its banks, out of reach all year until now. Soon freeze-up will insist even this stop, but today the river flexes its muscle and surges by like liquid wind, smooth, sweeping, powerful. This is not the river salmon dream of returning to when they are far out at sea, not the river of jumping fish and lazy, drifting boats. This is not the river that laps at the hull or floats implacable gulls by on the incoming tide. This is a river of strength and change, surging and carving a new year out of old banks. I'm helpless to do anything but watch. Summer's river and I have had conversations about life, death, replenishment, the future. There is no talking to this river. It has neither the time nor the patience to suffer such discussion. It is a river on a mission.

I watch as if I were seeing this for the first time. I realize that's exactly what I'm doing. My thoughts of melancholy are swept away like flotsam in the roiling current, and I become spellbound, having found a different road, a different cannery, different air, a different landscape, a different life here, right now, in front of me. It truly isn't about last summer. It isn't about the past at all. It's about me paying attention to the now I need to see. Fishing happens in different ways during different seasons. I came here fishing for confirmation of a shallow, blue-water melancholy. Instead, I've caught murkier, deeper waters. I watch the river for a long time before leaving.

Chapter Twenty: Fishing Naked

I'm at the Vagabond, a small Alaskan pub near the cannery housed in a log-and-plywood cabin a block from my house with a single pool table, four sit-down tables and a dozen barstools. It's between fishing periods at the start of the 1985 season, and the place is full. Fishermen, cannery workers and tender skippers and crew sit or mill about, sharing stories, booze, beer and cigarettes. The only woman in the place is the owner behind the bar, keeping us all on a short leash.

The small barroom is loud. Cheers go up over the pool table whenever someone makes a good shot. Everyone is talking over the guy next to him. I'm at the bar, listening to the friend of a friend pontificate about his fishing technique. This is one of a half-dozen places fishermen frequent when letting off steam, and when the liquor and camaraderie begin to loosen otherwise tight lips, tidbits of valuable information drop to the floor like nuggets. "Last period, one of the guys in our group was off the head of the island at closure," says a flannel-clad deckhand from under his mullet. "He saw jumpers – three and four in the air the whole time – in that little rip that forms up there on the flood." He nods as he takes a gulp of Budweiser from his glass, eyeballing his audience. "We're headin' there next opener. I shit you not." We all nod back and log that into the database inside our skulls. In two or three days those fish'll be long gone. But it's good information we can check out on a slow day.

Someone mentions the weather forecast. "Supposed to be hot as fuck next week. That'll drive the fish down. Maybe even keep 'em from heading to the beach." Salmon like a certain temperature of water, so there could be some merit to that.

"I hate picking on a hot day," I shrug. "I sweat like a motherfucker in rain gear."

Mullet man chimes in. "I seen my skipper pick in hip boots. He says it's way better. Cooler. You don't gotta wear bibs." The bib-overall style of rain gear we wear is made of neoprene and doesn't breathe at all. On a hot day, it's like working inside your own personal sauna.

"I have hip boots," I say. "Might give that a try." I raise my glass toward him in thanks. Like most bar advice, his idea is worth exactly what I pay for it.

The forecast for the 1985 salmon season is depressing. Sockeye salmon return to the rivers four years after they hatch. The 1981 escapement up the Kenai was poor, so the prediction for this year is for a low return, and the locals know it. As a result, three weeks before the season's scheduled to begin I'm still without a crew to help me with boat work, and I'm starting to get concerned. I've promised Veronica I won't go fishing alone. Though a lot of fishermen do, we've talked it out and agree that it's too dangerous to take the risk. Still, I should have a deckhand by now.

A few days later, I'm under the boat changing zincs when this short, skinny kid I've never seen before stops by for a chat. "How's it going?" he asks in a soft-spoken voice.

Annoyed by the interruption and anticipating what he wants, I barely look up. "Not bad. How you doin'?"

Encouraged, he bounces on the balls of his feet "Good! This place is amazing! I'm Joel. My girlfriend and I just got here from California. She's working for the cannery on the slime line," he smiles behind a full beard. "I'm looking for work as a deckhand."

I perk up. "Got any experience?"

He shakes his head. "No, but I learn fast."

"Most guys want crew that know how to pick fish and tie lines. Ever been on a boat?"

"No, but like I said…"

I turn back to the zinc. "You'll have better luck getting the cannery to hire you," I dismiss him, conveniently forgetting my own attempts at getting hired in Haines a decade ago. "I could use a deckhand, but I don't want to train somebody."

147

His face falls, but not into defeat. Jaw set, he looks determined. "I don't want to work for the cannery. I want to work on the water." He pauses, then starts to walk on. "Thanks anyway."

"Good luck." As he leaves, I think about how I could use someone, even a greenhorn, to help with the fish hold full of boat work I have to do in the next three weeks. I remember I currently have no prospects. "If you don't find anything, check back in a couple of days," I call after him.

That evening I exhaust my last remote possibility of finding a crew. No one, it seems, wants to fish for 10% of a small catch and a low price. When Joel comes back around, I offer him an hourly job helping me get the boat ready to fish, with the promise that if he works out, I might hire him for the season.

During the next few weeks, I give him jobs I don't want to do, like sanding mildew growing underneath the varnish on the mahogany ceiling of the cabin, chasing down spare fan belts, oil and other supplies all over the cannery, getting gear from my locker in the warehouse. The cannery frowns on him sleeping with his girlfriend in the henhouse, the bunkhouse for women, so I agree to let him stay on board while he's working for me. We visit as we haul the electronics, tools and sleeping bags from my pickup to the boat. I learn he's a graduate student studying Literature at UC-Irvine. He's definitely book intelligent, but doesn't have much to offer in the way of boat sense. What he lacks in salt, though, he makes up for in hard work. He never complains, does most jobs faster than I anticipate, and goes beyond the assigned work, organizing junk drawers, putting away tools and cleaning in his time off. Plus, though he lacks the aggressive attitude and stout build most skippers like to see in a deckhand, he's a nice guy. All things considered, I decide to hire him as crew for the season.

A week before the first period, Veronica and I take Joel and his girlfriend out for ice cream and break the news that he's got the job. They are both ecstatic. We shake hands on how long I expect him to stay (until the season is over and the boat's put away), his pay (10% of the gross), and how it will go. My mantra for hiring crew is, "I can't promise you anything as far as wages. That all depends on how many fish we catch. I do promise that we'll stay safe, have fun, and catch fish – in that order." It's a line I use throughout my career, and I mean it. I'm not, nor do I want to be a 'screamer' on land or at sea, yelling at my deckhands when they aren't fast enough or make a mistake. I want my crew and I to be a team, doing our best, enjoying each other's company and catching as many fish as we can. I won't risk our lives for a bigger payday. Joel is glad to hear that, and we enter the summer full of optimism.

The season starts slow, which is fine by me. The fewer fish there are to catch early on, the more time I have to teach Joel how to pick. By the time he's showing promise, ADF&G, worried about the poor return up the Kenai, decides to limit the area we can fish. They draw a line east-to-west across the Inlet south of the river, from Humpy Point (Cape Kasilof) to the northernmost tip of Kalgin island. We are restricted to fishing south of that line. That way the salmon north of it can make it into the river to spawn while the fleet's harvest will provide data to Fish and Game about how many sockeye are left in the lower Inlet.

On the first fishing day after my bar conversation with mullet-man, the weather is clear and warm. The tide is flooding, and we hear of a few fish being caught close to the line. We set out a few miles south of it and drift north, not seeing many hits. When we get a mile from the line, I put Joel in the stern. "You pick up the gear," I tell him. "If there's more in the net than we've seen, I'll jump in and help." Sure enough, the first shackle has a lot more salmon than we expect – all down low in the web. "I'll be damned. They've been hitting deep all along," I say. Joel looks at me over his shoulder. "I'll get my gear on. Be there in a

149

Joel Reed on the stern of the Skookum Too, 1985.

sec." As I duck into the cabin, I think, *Time for those hip boots.*
I'm actually proud I remembered they were on board.

We pick almost 300 fish out of that set. Wearing nothing
but the ridiculous, stupid and ineffective hip boots, I get
absolutely soaked with seawater, blood, gurry, slime and scales.
The boots keep my legs dry, but the rest of me is a disgusting
mess. As soon as the last of the net is on board, I tell Joel, "I'm
going to run south for 45 minutes or so, change clothes and do
this drift again."

He's pitching fish into the hold. "I'll clear the deck, then I'm going to lie down and take a nap in the sun while we run, if that's ok."

"Sounds good," I say, already peeling off my soaked shirt and hanging it to dry on the cabin door, which is bungeed open. I step down into the cabin and grab my day bag from under the bunk. I peel off my clothes as I throttle up the boat and turn her south. At the same time, I pluck the microphone for our group radio from its perch and report my set's location and catch. It's the biggest report of the day for our group, and I feel proud, especially when Rob asks me to repeat my location. If good fishermen like him are interested in my information, I must be doing something right.

I steer us south, weaving between boats and nets. I'm down to nothing but my socks when Wayne comes on the radio and gives his own fish report. "I'm right by Pat." he says. "Gonna run south and throw it out again." I look out the door while he's talking. His boat, the *Pelican*, is just off my starboard stern, maybe a quarter-mile away. *Ohhhh,* I think. *Perfect.* I grab the mic. "Hey Wayne. Can you see me?"

"Yeah, I see you, Pat."

"Got your binoculars handy?"

"Right here. What's up?"

"Train them on my back deck. I wanna show you something."

"Ohh-kay?"

I pick a course that is clear of boats and nets as far as I can see, center the wheel on that heading, then dash out on deck to moon Wayne. I mean, why not? I'm already 'dressed' for it. But I only have a short time to do this, as the spin of the propeller will swing the *Skookum* off-course in less than a minute. As soon as I'm on deck, I realize there's a problem. Joel is in the way, spread-eagled face up on the hatch covers, sound asleep. He doesn't move as I step out of the cabin and look for a place to stand while I aim my ass at Wayne. I quickly determine that the safest place to pull off this maneuver is pretty much right over Joel's head… right over Joel's face. But, hey, he's asleep, right? Knowing Wayne is likely looking through his glasses at me right now and there's no time to waste, I assume the stance with a chuckle of self-satisfaction and begin 'waving'.

The guys in my fishing group are my type of people: quick-witted and irreverent. Practical jokes, trash-talking and jibes are frequent when we get together. Once they hear my deckhand for the season is a greenhorn, a college student AND a Literature major, they decide he is an easy target. Mostly they treat him well, but when they get him alone, they plant seeds of paranoia about how "Skippers can change at sea. Oh, he might be a stand-up guy on land, but some guys – not saying Pat is like this at all – SOME guys go nuts out there, alone with their crew on a boat, miles from anywhere, making their deckhands do all sorts of things, treating them like shit. And watch out for 'boat initiations.' You never know what someone might pull." Joel never mentions this to me, but when the boat begins to swing while I am semaphoring my message to Wayne causing my shadow to cross over his face and his eyes open, I'm sure every seed they planted bore immediate fruit.

I'm still bent over when I notice a blur of movement behind me. In an impressive flurry of speed and agility Joel has scrambled to his feet and made a run for the cabin. Certain his skipper has gone rogue, he thinks better of being trapped inside with no way out, and instead detours almost overboard, turning to gape at me from the other side of the cabin door, eyes wide, white-knuckled fingers curled around the edge of the door, toes barely on the boat.

I figure he needs an explanation, but I'm oblivious to what he must have seen when his eyes opened from his nap. I offer up my best rationale and point to the *Pelican*. "Wayne's right over there!" What I fail to remember is that Joel and I have

152

known each other a little less than a month, and we've been fishing together for less than two weeks. He has no idea who Wayne is. I can almost see smoke curling from his ears as he stares at me in fear.

By now the boat is well off-course and accelerating into a sweeping turn. I have to get in the cabin fast. I make a dash for the door, running directly toward Joel and scaring him with the quickness of my move. He jumps backward, hands still holding the door, body almost going horizontal over the water. I watch him land back on board as I rush down the steps and grab the wheel, getting us on course again. I look back to see him, still frozen in place peeking at me from behind the door to see what his psycho-skipper might do next. Suddenly it hits me what his reality has been since he was so rudely awakened from his nap, and what he must be thinking. I turn forward again, wave my arms in the air and shout, "NUDE FISHING!!"

Chapter Twenty-One: Karluk Reef

Remarkably, Joel returns next year. I explain that I really wasn't 'initiating' him into the fishery, and he finally sees the humor in what happened that day. By the end of his first season, he is an accomplished crew, and I am glad to have him on board. We're running with the stabilizers out in a choppy sea back to the river one evening after a slow day. We're a few miles from the mouth, but the wind has me off-course, pushing the boat too close to the setnets, so I turn to the west, not realizing I am heading right over the sandy low-tide shallows called Karluk reef. As we run, I notice the boat seeming to strain to make headway, and then pull to one side or the other. At the same time, I start hearing an unusual sound, a *whannng,* almost like a washtub bass, but deeper.

Stabilizers are metal or wooden poles on either side of a boat with a heavy metal 'fish' lowered into the water at the end of the poles. The fish we use are designed like a simplistic airplane to provide resistance against the roll of the boat and create a smoother ride in a rough sea. See the Glossary at the end of the book for a photo.

As I look around trying to figure out where the strange noise is coming from, I see one of the fish fly out of the water, race forward, almost even with the bow of the boat, and land again with a splash. I glance at the depth finder. We're only in 10 feet of water! It's almost low tide, and we're right on top of Karluk Reef! The bottom is shallower than our scope for the line coming off the stabilizer arm, and the fish are digging into the sand like anchors until the forward motion of the boat pulls them free. Once released, they leap forward with a *thwannnng,* and launch out of the water. I immediately stop to haul in the stabilizers and stow the fish. I'm embarrassed to make such a rookie mistake. Until now, I've never given Karluk Reef a thought. No more.

Chapter Twenty-Two: The Good, Bad and Almost Ugly

Don calls me in the spring of 1987 and asks me to fly to Seattle and help him drive his truck up to Kenai before the season starts. In early June, we find ourselves listening to U2's *The Joshua Tree* and bouncing through British Columbia on the Cassiar Highway. I catch the flu just as we depart, and though we have an uneventful trip – which is rare for us – I hack and sneeze the entire way. By the time we get to Tok Junction, we're almost broke, so we decide to share a room at the local dive of a hotel. They only have one room left. For ten bucks each we get two twin beds on either side of a night stand covered in cigarette burns, a single bare light bulb hanging from the ceiling, a sink that's disconnected, and a shower down the hall that only has cold water. The room is warm and dry but when we sit on the beds the mattresses are so soft and the springs so shot we almost touch the floor. We're grateful to be warm and dry, and fall asleep laughing at ourselves. "Fishing is so profitable!" Don chuckles. "Everyone should do this!"

We start the season in late June, and before we know it an oil tanker gets in trouble in our back yard. Waiting to deliver a load to the refinery at the north end of our fishing district, the *Glacier Bay* anchors in an area south of the river to wait on the incoming tide. When it swings on its anchor as the tide changes, it smacks an uncharted rock and leaks a million gallons of North Slope crude oil into the water. The state scrambles to set up a 'zero-tolerance' fishing policy to keep us away from the oil, forcing the fleet south into a corridor along the east side of the Inlet with threats of confiscation of all fish and gear that gets contaminated. The run starts strong and keeps building, and the impact of the oil ends up being minor for most fishermen. The price for sockeye is high, opening at $1.10 a pound. Our price is often determined by what Bristol Bay's run is like. They start fishing two weeks before we do, and if their run is strong and floods the market with salmon, our price goes down. But this year, their run fizzles, and our price soars. We sell most of the season's catch at a buck-forty, and Don and I joke that after the season we should go back to Tok Junction and pay for that room with a single fish each. In an amazing turn of events, each fish coming over the stern is the equivalent of a ten-dollar bill. Only a few guys catch oil in their gear, and for their trouble the oil company buys them new nets and pays for the lost fish. Except for the oil, hell, even with it, it's a fisherman's dream season.

I've hired Tim, the cannery carpenter, away from the company to be my deckhand, but we struggle to define his role when we're in port. Ray, the superintendent of the cannery doesn't help as he keeps asking Tim to do carpentry jobs when I'm not around. I expect Tim to be working on the boat, but I often show up to find him gone, our projects incomplete or not even started. He feels obligated to the company, and we have a few frustrated arguments about that, but when we're at sea we work well together. More than anything we're friends. Despite our differences, he's a good hand, we laugh a lot, and he's damn good luck. Day after day we leave the river and catch way more fish than we expect. We don't know it yet, but we are fishing what will be the largest return of red salmon on record for Cook Inlet.

I'm in the stern on a calm day under blue skies. We're fishing 2 ½ miles offshore inside a 3-mile corridor along the east side of the Inlet. The boat is drifting south on an ebb tide in the late afternoon. I am warm in the sun and making money. I have found the fish today, picking more salmon than I ever imagined catching here. We've been given several extra days of fishing time because of the strong run. Fish bound for the Kenai River run up the east side, but never in this close, usually staying five or more miles off shore. During the past few days, they have charged toward the beach and into the corridor where we've been fishing, plugging our nets day after day. Everyone is delighted except for the processors who have been caught off-guard and are desperately trying to keep all the fish from overwhelming their facilities. They are hiring extra help, pushing their cannery workers for 20-hour shifts, even flying ice-filled totes full of unprocessed fish to plants in Bristol Bay to ease the load.

The fleet has been at it for four straight days. Typically, corridor fishing produces a hundred fish a day. Most guys come out for the flood tide and only fish until slack water six hours later. We often use the time allotted in the corridor to catch up on naps or choose not go out at all, instead mending gear, doing boat work, or tending to other non-fishing related business. But this is not a typical year. The fleet average is 1,100 fish *inside the corridor* on the first day, and from then on no one stays at the dock. After four days straight, most crews are exhausted. We are no exception. I'm running on fumes and Tim is sick. He's been so woozy on the back deck that I send him to the bunk as we run south for the day. I'd like to get below Humpy Point for the opener, so Tim can get a few hours rest before we set out.

I'm wiped, and the drone of the engine has me zoned out and running on automatic, watching the occasional boat go by me, and adjusting my course to avoid the setnet buoys off the point, when I see what appears to be a swamped gillnetter ahead and a little east of me. The silhouette is bow down, stern and reel in the air. I steer toward her for a better look before calling anyone. From a mile off, I can't see anyone on deck. I switch the VHF to channel 16 and turn the volume up in case they got off a mayday, but there's no chatter as I get closer. Then it hits me: it's not a boat at all, but the northernmost of a series of rocks that appear at low tide called "The Sisters". I'm running right for them. I immediately slow the boat and turn back to the west. I've heard stories of guys running aground after thinking they were recuing a boat in distress. I'm glad I'm not one of them. I'm wide awake as I steer away.

I wake Tim to help with the opening set, and send him back to the bunk as soon the gear is in the water. There are enough fish that I wake him to help pick throughout most of the

157

day, and he doesn't look any better. By the time we're on the last set of the day, I'm determined to pick it myself and let him rest until we deliver. The tide is running out hard, and with my slow boat, even if I leave the grounds an hour early, I'll be one of the last boats in. I already have 800 fish on board, which will slow me down even more. As if that's not enough reason to get to picking, I know the tide is beginning to take us away from shore as I get close to the bottom of the corridor. The current down here is influenced by the land mass of Anchor Point, the cape that pushes westward into the Inlet. Soon I'll be riding it over the three-mile line. I'm picking alone, so I start earlier than I normally would. I've seen maybe ten hits on this set in the past hour, singles or small bunches. I expect maybe a hundred fish at best. When I begin rolling the net in, I'm shocked to see fish heads lifting out of the water in a solid, silver rope. By the time I have the first shackle of gear on board, I've counted 300 fish, and there's two more shackles to go.

Worried that I might be getting close to the line, I run into the cabin to check the radar. I'm still a quarter-mile inside, and as I make my way back to the stern, I watch boats a half-mile outside of me drifting south, not picking up yet. *I can get this in without having to wake Tim up*, I think as I take one more glance around. A small tender is chugging its way north a mile south of me on a heading that will take him just outside my net, but there's no reason to be concerned. On a day like this with barely a ripple on the water, tenders will often anchor up in a convenient spot and take fish from boats that want to deliver and spend the night out here. The word has come over the radio that we are fishing again tomorrow, so I imagine our tenders are nearby as well. We're low on fuel, so we have to go back to the river anyway. Tenders carry fuel, but aren't allowed to dispense it when they have fish on board.

I bend my head to pick a wad of fish that comes over the roller and when I look up again, the tender is closer. It looks like it's heading right for the end of my net. I decide to give him a little room, lock the reel and put the boat in gear, towing to the east. The net straightens out behind the boat but is so loaded that I don't want to tow too hard and wash fish out of the gear. Besides, the skipper on the tender, I can see now that it's the *Beagle*, a 50-footer owned by Kenai Packers, should be able to maneuver around my net with ease. I stop towing and start thinking about picking, but the tender, bow wake foaming, isn't slowing down, and he's heading right at my net! I consider towing again, but quickly realize that there is no way I'm going to be able to get out of his way. I can't comprehend what he's thinking. At the last second, I see someone run out of the cabin of the *Beagle* and look over the bow at my net. I scream at him, "HEY! What are you DOING?!? What the FUCK are you DOING?!?!" Then I see it: an anchor line coming off the front of his boat! He isn't running at all. The tide is ebbing so fast that it's throwing a wake on his bow – creating the illusion that he's motoring ahead when in fact I'm the one moving. As the net nears his bow, I pull my knife out in case I have to cut it loose. I yell again, louder. I say the same thing, but this time I mean *What the fuck are you doing anchoring INSIDE the corridor?!* For a surreal moment, I watch other boats outside of us drift serenely by as our net gently hits his anchor line, then folds around it. We begin to swing to the south like we're on a pendulum. The net between us is well over 100 feet in length, but it still takes me a few seconds of holding my breath to realize we aren't going to slam against his steel hull with our wood boat. As we swing close, I am struck by how solid and tall the *Beagle* is compared to my low, 32-foot wood boat. A few feet different and we'd be splintered and sinking, with Tim still in the bunk. The *Beagle's* skipper comes out on deck and looks over the rail at me as I stand in the stern, my jaw open. I look up at him and raise my hands, palms up. "Now what?!" I yell. He doesn't answer. Instead, he looks at his crewman, who is gaping at us from the bow. "Get the boathook," the skipper growls at him. "Lift it up and cut it."

159

I look around to see Tim come stumbling sleepily out of the cabin. "What's going on?" he asks. His eyes widen as he comprehends our predicament. "Get your rain gear on," I reply. "I'm going to need you back here."

The boat lurches as the deckhand cuts the gear and we spring free. I step on the treadle and the reel responds, pulling the net and fish on board as we drift away. The hydraulic motor in the engine room whines with the strain of wrapping the gear and fish onto the reel. Lines and fish slap the deck again and again as they whip around. Tim jumps into the stern with me and shakes his head. "I can put my rain gear on later. I go to sleep for a couple of hours, and this is what you get us into?"

"Just take over here," I reply, motioning to the treadle. I'm still trying to sort out what this implies for the rest of the day and tomorrow. It's clear we aren't getting any sleep tonight. "As soon as it's all on board, we need to chase down the rest of the net," I say, and look past the stern of the *Beagle* to see my buoy and a half-shackle of gear drifting south with the tide. "There." I point. "Keep an eye on it." He takes my place in the stern and I take off my jacket and bibs and climb the ladder to the bridge. Tim finishes reeling and we race to catch the rest of our net, picking it up from the buoy end and splicing it to the cut end on the reel. The reel is full of fish and web, so we pull the last of it by hand, dumping fish, lines and web in a tangled mess in the stern.

Once we finish, I call Louie Gebenini on the VHF. He's the skipper of the *Chisik Island*, one of our tenders. I ask if he's taking fish on the grounds tonight. He gives us his location with an affirmative. He's anchored already, 45 minutes away. Tim puts on his rain gear and picks the fish off the reel as we run heavily to the *Chisik*. If we can deliver our load and run in, we should be able to fuel up and switch nets in time to catch the tide and get back out here for the opener tomorrow. We'll be the last boat in the river, but that might be a good thing. If everyone else is done for the night, we won't have to wait in line for the fuel dock. As a former cannery carpenter, Tim should be able to commandeer a forklift or a Cushman golf cart that the Port Engineers use to run around the cannery to haul the nets to the boat. It's a plan.

We arrive at the *Chisik* before Tim is done clearing the reel, but a couple of other boats are already unloading. I throw a couple of burritos in the oven after we tie off and help Tim finish. We have over 1,600 fish for the day, but we've also caught a serious liability that could cost us fish tomorrow. I explain to Tim how everything developed as we bag the nets. I get angry all over again. I can't BELIEVE a tender skipper would be so stupid as to anchor inside the corridor, and then STAY there as the fleet drifted down on him! By contrast, Louie is anchored at least five miles off shore. I vow to have a talk with the skipper of the *Beagle* – and his boss – after the fishing slows down.

We spend the next few hours waiting, eating dinner and delivering our fish. The *Chisik* lowers a brailer into the hold and we take turns pitching them by hand. It's back-breaking work, tossing 1,600 seven-pound salmon by hand into a brailer in a chilly and cramped fish hold. My back is screaming as I get the fish ticket from Louie and step into the *Skookum's* cabin. The sun is low in the sky when we cast off. We are still 30 miles from the river, and though the tide has turned and will help us home, it'll be ebbing by the time we get there. The tides are especially strong this week – Louie told us he clocked the one this afternoon at seven knots, which explains the bow wake on the *Beagle* that fooled me into thinking it was under way. Neither Tim nor I recall seeing an anchor light or any other indication from her that she was a stationary object.

Tim is feeling better after his extended nap and a meal, but I am absolutely wiped from all the adrenaline of almost colliding at sea. If our boat had slammed against the side of that tender, I am certain it would have been with enough force to break us apart. In that tide, even with boats all around us we

161

wouldn't have had a chance. I thank the fish gods as I replay the day's events over again in my mind while changing into sweats. Tim turns up the stereo for the ride home. The bunk is like a giant cradle as the boat knifes through a smooth sea. Bob Marley sings over the roar of the engine. I am asleep in seconds.

By the time we get to the river, it's 1:00 am. Tim wakes me as we near the cannery. The water is black and there's a chill in the air, but the lights from tenders, loading docks and boardwalks reveal the ongoing frenzied activity. I was expecting things to have slowed down, but it's obvious that I've gotten that wrong. The lines to deliver are still eight or nine boats long on each side at the tenders, and at least that many waiting for the dock. The fuel dock has two rows of boats three deep tied to it, with four others floating in the river waiting their turn. We aren't the only ones going without sleep tonight.

I decide the best approach is to get in line at the fuel dock, since the boats delivering will be headed there once they finish, and the line won't shorten until morning. We idle in the river for 20 minutes against the current to protect our spot in line until the boats at the fuel dock untie and leave. We tie off to Thor on the *Cheryl Lynne,* the outermost boat in the front row. I ask him if that's ok, since the customary etiquette on a normal day at the fuel dock is just two boats. He doesn't mind. He's sent his crew to town for groceries and that should take a while anyway.

When the cannery bulldozed the 'ways' years ago, they bought a Travel Lift, a huge machine designed to lift boats out of the water with straps and carry them around the yard. Operated by the Beach Gang, it's driven above the river on two concrete piers. The *Skookum Too* and *Cheryl Lynne's* bows are obstructing the launch area for the lift, which has a boat in the sling while a few of the beach gang are under it in a skiff cutting web out of its wheel. Thor and I chat as we wait for the boat inside him to finish fueling. I tell him the events of the day and find out how the rest of the fleet did. Turns out we had a better-than-average catch, but it feels far from it with the loss of our gear. A shackle costs over $500 each, and we've lost two of them today, one that was cut in two, and another that was worn already, but was severely beaten up by wrapping it on the reel while it was full of fish.

Fatigued even after my nap on the run in, I sit on the hatch covers and watch mindlessly as Thor begins fueling. I'm a little apprehensive about how long this is going to take. Tim has disappeared – he has gone to my locker in the warehouse to grab two new shackles and take them to the delivery dock upriver. There we can use a crane to load them onto the boat and take the old ones off. We'll have to get the old gear off the dock so it's not in the way of the forklifts racing around the cannery moving fish to and from processing. By the time we're done with all that, we'll still have at least a two-hour run to the grounds. We'll be lucky make it in time for the opening set, which is often the best of the day. Every minute that goes by with no Tim in sight raises my blood pressure and stress level.

Fueling the boats takes time. The pump is slow, and most boats carry 300-500 gallons of diesel or gas. Thor finishes filling his starboard side and is beginning to fuel his port tank when a large silhouetted figure appears at the top of the fuel dock. "*Skookum Too!*" it bellows. I look up. It's Emery, the beach boss, a burly man with a bad attitude and the authority to manage the boats and fishermen while they are at the cannery. Rumor has it that Emery was hard-drinking and rough in his younger days. He's let the drinking go, but he still comes across as gruff and impatient, especially with anyone who doesn't know what they're doing. I steer clear of him for most of my ten years fishing, but have to intervene when he hassles Joel the year before Tim becomes my crew. That doesn't go smoothly and we carry some residual tension because of it.

"*Skookum Too!*" louder still. "We're launching a boat in ten minutes! As soon as the *Cheryl Lynne* is done fueling, get out of the way!"

Even during the best of circumstances, I bristle at being ordered around. I'm quicker to anger after a particularly bad day with little sleep, exhausted and already anxious about the immediate future. Several boats hang in the river now, waiting for my spot at the fuel dock, willing to cut in line if it looks like I'm leaving. When Emery shouts at me in front of the other fishermen, my response is visceral. "I'm not done fueling!" I yell back a little too loudly. "I'll move when I'm finished!"

Emery's barrel-chested silhouette puffs up on the fuel dock. "You haven't even started!" he hurls back at me. "We're launching a boat here! Get the FUCK outta the way… NOW!"

With Thor and the crews of the boats around us all watching and listening, I pretty much come unglued. "Fuck OFF, Emery! I've been here for over an hour, and I'm NOT giving up my spot! I'll move as soon as I'm done!"

Emery stiffens and stares. As soon as the words leave my lips, I regret them. "Nice move, Pat," Thor mumbles as he sits on the gunwale holding the fuel hose. He glances up with a smirk. Emery turns on a heel and moves abruptly away. I feel weak.

"I didn't handle that well, did I?" I ask as the reality of confronting my mortality lands on me. Visions of flying off the dock into the river at Emery's hands flash through my mind. Visions of Emery's *hands* are even worse– his meaty fist hammering my jaw is a far more likely scenario.

Thor shakes his head. "Not particularly." He gives me the fuel hose and screws his filler cap back on. "I'd just get fueled up and outta here as soon as I can if I were you." He disappears across the boats and up the ladder.

I fuel the boat in the silence and dark of my own mind, hoping I won't have to see Emery again until next season, if ever. No one else speaks to me as I sit in the shadows of the pilings. The tide is going out fast, and I feel like it's carrying me with it. I keep looking for Tim to show, but he's probably waiting for me at the upper dock. Half an hour later, tanks full, I look around for him one last time then cut loose and move the boat out into the river. Thor and the other boat follow suit, and we all go our separate ways. Thor turns downriver and joins the growing procession of boats headed back to the grounds. I idle toward the upper dock and look for Tim on the boardwalk. *Where the hell is he?* I put the boat in neutral and rig a spring line to tie off to a piling, then maneuver against the dock and tie up.

After adding a bow and stern line, I climb the ladder that goes up the pilings to the dock above. At low tide, it's a twenty-foot climb in the dark on a steel ladder with round rungs coated in fish slime. It's not something I enjoy doing, especially in my current state of exhaustion, but I need to find Tim and get these nets switched out, so up I go. As I near the top rung the dock comes into view. Tim is nowhere to be seen, but two guys are talking to each other in the light of the sorting table some twenty feet away. I don't recognize the taller of the two, but the other one is…sweet Jesus… *of course…* Emery.

For a long moment I consider going back down the ladder to hide on the boat until Tim shows up. I *really* don't want to end up on my face, one more dead fish laying in the slime on the dock, but this confrontation is inevitable. At the least it'll be an appropriate ending to the story I'll tell about this day. I have to do this and hope for the best. I swallow and walk over. Emery looks up me, and once he realizes who I am, his smiling face turns dark. I stick my hand out. "Emery, I'm sorry. I've had an incredibly shitty day – we wrapped a tender anchored on the grounds today – and well, I just snapped when you told me I had to move. Sorry."

My hand hangs in the space between us as Emery stares at me, not smiling. *Here it comes,* I think. *This is gonna hurt.* He turns to his friend and breaks into a wide smile. "You know what this guy said to me tonight?" he turns to me, reaching out and shaking my hand. "He told me to fuck off! In front of everybody at the fuel dock!" His friend looks at me, then says,

165

"He's not very bright, is he?" They both laugh and Emery pulls me in and slaps me on the shoulder. "It's alright. These things happen. I know. Trust me, I know." I shake my head and laugh too, but for a different reason.

Emery and I will have a good relationship until he retires in 10 years. At this moment though, my legs go weak with relief. I tell him about our day and ask if he's seen Tim. "Right over there!" He points over my shoulder as Tim comes around the warehouse on a converted Cushman golf cart with two nets in the back. He jumps out of the cart, unaware of any of the events of the past two hours. "Couldn't find the keys to your locker," he explains. "Had to take your truck up to your house to get the spare."

I shake Emery's hand again while Tim looks on with a curious expression. Emery walks away with his friend, and we get to work swapping out nets. I look up from the crane controls to see a boat slide downriver in the early light of dawn, heading out. In a few minutes we'll be right behind him.

§

Running home from the grounds ten days later with another load of reds, Tim steers while I sit at the table and inspect the season's fish tickets I've shoved in the back of the log book. I suddenly realize we have already more than doubled my best year, and there's more fishing yet to come. I count them again in disbelief. I show the results to Tim. We celebrate by mooning the first boat that passes us: *The Mayflower*. My friends and neighbors Rich and Marcia King fish her. I don't see Marcia as she snaps a photo of us waving our butts at her with our pants around our ankles, boat running itself, low in the water as we steam home. I keep that photo above my desk for years afterward.

166

Skookum Moon, with Tim DeLapp, 1987. Photo by Marcia King.

No Place to Hide
~ For Frank Mullen

I've been selling to cash buyers for the last two weeks,
Frank says, standing in the cabin of my boat.
We are close to the beach in the mouth of the river,
barely floating in seven feet of water.
Slack tide. A shackle of his gear hangs limp in the water
off my bow, waiting. His deckhand stands in his skiff
tied alongside.

We've been fishing now, what, 12 straight days?
I nod and we both take sips of beer. It's another sunny day.
For the first time in weeks fishing is slow.
Each day, by the time I deliver and clean up,
it's too late to take the cash to the bank.
He sighs and looks out the door at his crew.
They both look as ragged as I feel.
Why don't you just have Janis take it?
He turns back, raises bushy eyebrows
under his blood-stained white halibut hat.
She's in Ireland for the month.
I can't leave it in the house.
What if someone breaks in?
And I can't keep it on the boat.
It's driving me crazy.
He takes another swig and looks out the door again.
his deckhand looks up, shakes his head.

What are you doing, then?
He barks a short laugh and leans in.
I'm putting the cash in plastic bags
inside empty coffee cans.
I bury them at night in the garden.

He lowers his voice to a whisper.
I've got 60 grand in the ground.
I keep a map in my wallet.

168

He shrugs. *I don't know what else to do.*
It's my turn to laugh. *You're shitting me.*
He holds up an open palm like you'd swear an oath.

This is the smartest man I know when it comes to money.
In ten years I'll hire him to be our financial advisor.
He shrugs again. *Janis'll be home next week.*
Who's gonna look in my garden, anyway?

Frank Mullen and Andy Mack,1987.

We shake our heads, chuckle some more, tell
a few more stories. We're crumpling the cans
when the group radio crackles: *Fish and Game*
just announced an opening tomorrow, boys.
Better fuel up and get your groceries.

Frank unties the skiff and starts the outboard.
He waves as they pull away. *Thanks for the beer.*
See you out here tomorrow!
I can't resist.

I don't think so, I respond.
I'll be in your garden with a backhoe!

169

Chapter Twenty-Three: Graveyard of Dreams

It's the middle of the fishing season. I have boat work to do and errands to run. My first task of the day brings me to an isolated part of the cannery, where the old, decaying fishing boats are stored, sitting on 55-gallon drums. I walk by wooden hulls covered with peeling paint and rust streaks. Warped plywood cabins look down at me with cracked and broken windows. My boots are wet with morning dew as I pick my way around the flotsam: rusted exhaust stacks and rotting lumber lay next to overturned fish totes and forgotten storage boxes. The boats add litter of their own: caulking hangs between the planks of the hulls, corroded antenna mounts cling to the side of the cabins, a tattered rag of a windsock sways in the morning breeze.

I come looking for a brass, two-inch fuel filler cap that can replace the one my deckhand knocked into the river last night. I look for a ladder to use to climb aboard the boats, but they are scarce here. This is the boneyard: a graveyard of dreams. Not unlike a ghost town, these old boats have been replaced, retired and forgotten. Soon they'll be bulldozed and burnt. A few may suffer a final indignity and be cut apart and converted into a hot tub or a child's playhouse before they too end up in the fire pit.

I find a beater of a ladder and tug it out of the weeds that are covering it. I set it upright against a rotting hull and test it. Seems solid enough. I climb up to the deck and almost tiptoe to the stern. This feels like a violation. I know these boats have been scavenged, but it feels wrong somehow to take something without permission, even though there's no one to ask any more.

I notice a faint glint in the sun. There they are: two corroded brass filler caps just the right size, sealing rotten fuel lines that lead to empty tanks. The key I brought with me even fits the holes in the cap I decide to take. I turn it, and after a moment's resistance the cap gives way and comes loose in my hand. I drop it in my pocket and look at the gaping hole I'm leaving behind – the wound I've created. I feel a twinge. Some part of me wants to cover it somehow – to stop the bleeding of the past dripping into the future. My hesitation melts as I realize I have a lot to do this morning. I climb down the ladder and head back to the boat work that will fill this day. Each step carries me further into that future, each a step closer to the season that will leave me up on barrels of my own.

K-6 in the boneyard, CWF, 1985.

Farewell

~ for the Skookum Too

She was my first boat,
a Gerry-rigged derelict
with a sketchy past.
Perfect for a guy like me,

Never built to fish—
she was a wooden plug
used to make a form
for 32-foot fiberglass hulls.

But somewhere along the line
the company got greedy
and decided to sell her too.
Maybe that's where she got her name.

By the time I bought her from
the cannery, she'd been around
the yard more than a few years,
and looked it.

I got a deal, I thought.
Her engine was pulled for a rebuild,
and the cannery guaranteed it to be
working before the season started.

But after dozens of years as a leased boat
with no preventative maintenance, and decades
of fixes addressing symptoms, not causes
of bigger issues, I was in for a bouncy ride.

Electric, hydraulic, fuel, steering – every wire,
hose, a few planks in the hull, and damn near
every bolt would need to be upgraded
or replaced over the next eight years.

I was aboard when they installed her engine.
I was aboard as engineers hooked up her systems.

I added a flying bridge,
sister-ribbed the fish hold,
installed a new reel drive,
hydraulic motor and hoses,

new steering ram and controls,
new fuel tanks, filters and hoses,
a new stove, new batteries, electronics,
wiring, water tank… and hoses.

What I didn't know
(which was pretty much everything),
I learned – not from YouTube or Google,
but from old-timers, experienced skippers and crew,

and fishermen friends who as a joke
locked me in the lazarette,
yet taught me how to tighten
the packing on a stuffing box.

By the time I sold her
to raise cash for a new boat,
she'd caught me tons of fish.
Ours had become a love/hate affair.

We knew each other's strengths
and failings. She brought me through
storms I didn't think she'd weather.
We'd seen each other at our worst

and at peaks of fishing proficiency
I never thought I'd attain.
The guy who bought her
fished for a different cannery.

Walking the dock in Ninilchik
a couple of years later,
I recognized her from a distance
like an old lover.

But when I got close, I saw
her paint was chipped and peeling.
Her sides were coated with rust.
I rested my hand on her gunwale

and apologized.

I never saw her again.
He ran her on the rocks
near the Barren Islands on a halibut trip
and left her there.

None of us
gets to choose
how it ends,
only how it goes.

Chapter Twenty-Four: The Old and the New

As soon as the 1987 season ends, Veronica and I start looking for a boat builder. As much as I have come to appreciate the *Skookum's* ability to catch fish, her speed is becoming a liability. New boats are arriving each year with engines and designs that allow them to run faster and haul more fish. The fastest boats on Cook Inlet are traditionally bow-pickers, vessels with their reel forward instead of aft, propelled by high-performance twin outboards in the stern. They are twice as fast as most of the fleet, but the high-performance outboards are constantly in need of service. They also use gas and are more likely to catch fire and explode. They are definitely less popular than the heavier, slower and safer diesels.

In the mid-eighties all that changes. The Bellingham, Washington-based shipbuilding manufacturer Uniflite begins powering its vessels with a new generation of lighter, higher horsepower turbocharged diesels made by Caterpillar and Cummins. Uniflite's hulls are 'planing' designs, made to lift themselves to the surface of the water when running at cruise. The reduction of drag when they get up 'on step' drastically increases their speed. Compared to the average 10-knot boat in Cook Inlet, these boats are twice as fast. That means the Inlet is half its size to a fisherman in a hurry.

I make fun of the first Uniflite I see. It doesn't look nautical at all. It resembles a box on the water, with sharp, square lines and a stubby little bow. Instead of the smooth, sweeping lines normally associated with a sea-going vessel, it looks decidedly awkward and out of place. But when I watch one roar past me like I'm standing still while the *Skookum* is running at seven knots, my attitude changes. When two of them dock at our cannery in '87, I talk to their skippers, get a tour, and become serious about making a change. The price is lower than I expected too, enticing me even more.

I discover that the plant had a fire in 1980 that destroyed most of the molds, but the 32-foot version survived. During the winter, they sell the mold to an independent boatbuilder named Rodney in Beaverton, Oregon, a suburb of Portland. Rodney worked for the company, and he bought the mold with the dream of becoming his own contractor.

We have a dream too. Over the past few years Veronica and I put most of the money we make into a 'Capital Construction' tax shelter for small business owners to use for major projects. After a few phone conversations with Rodney, we order a new boat to be delivered in time for the 1988 season. He's already got two other orders from friends of mine who fish for our cannery, so we're third in line.

In March of '88 Rodney gives me a call. "Hull's all laid up and prepped. We're ready for the engine," he says enthusiastically. "Where do I pick it up?"

"Engine? I thought *you* had engines."

"Nope. You have to buy it first. Then they deliver it. I been waitin'."

"Ok. Who do I call?"

He gives me a number. "That's the Caterpillar outlet in Seattle. You're lookin' for a 3208 Turbo."

"Roger that."

When I call Caterpillar, I discover the cost of the engine is $25,000. Most of the money in the bank is already committed to building the rest of the boat and outfitting her. I hadn't realized the engine wasn't part of that expense. "I'm going to have to talk to Ray," I tell Veronica, "and see if we can borrow the money from the cannery." Canneries have a long history of financing their fishermen in exchange for loyalty. "If I'm going to ask him to loan us this much, I think I'll do better in person." We decide I'll fly down to Seattle over Spring Break.

The headquarters of Columbia Wards/Wards Cove Packing Company is on the east shore of Lake Union in downtown Seattle. It's a huge old building, part warehouse, part offices, part dock on the lake. I stay with Don while I'm in town. He drops me off for my appointment with Ray, then heads out to run errands. The worn wooden stairs of the office make me feel like I'm walking into a mausoleum. How many fishermen have climbed these stairs before me, looking for help with their finances?

"$25,000?" Ray asks. "That's a lot of engine." He shifts in his chair. I get the feeling neither of us are comfortable doing this.

"I know, but it's the one they recommend. With these engines, the boat'll do twenty knots."

His face lights up. "That would get you on the fish in a hurry."

"I nod. "That's the idea." We both chuckle. The ice has broken.

"So," he rubs his hands together. "What do you have for collateral?"

"Uh, collateral?"

"We need something for you to put up against the loan. Do you have an engine number?"

"Ummm, no. We haven't bought it yet. That's what this loan is for."

Ray sits back in his chair. He's been a cannery superintendent for years, worked for the company as an engineer for many more, flies his own airplane up to Alaska every year. He's seen and done things I can only imagine. Now he has to deal with my naïve approach to all things fishing. He sighs and leans forward, opening the leather ledger-style checkbook on the desk in front of him. Looking down at it, he shakes his head as he picks up his pen. "Our accountants aren't going to be very happy about this, Pat." He writes a check payable to me for $25,000.00, carefully tears it free and hands it to me. "Just call me with the engine number as soon as you know what it is, ok?"

"Absolutely Ray. Thank you so much!" I am overwhelmed, and even though I've never liked Wards Cove lowballing us on price every season, I vow to sell my fish to him without complaint for the rest of my career.

Ray Landry, Superintendent of CWF, in his office, 1994.

When Don picks me up, I show him the check. "You know," he says, "we could turn that into 75 grand if we use it for cocaine!" We have a good laugh, but I wonder if he's completely joking. Hell, I wonder if *I* am.

The rest of the spring is spent playing phone tag with the builder. He paints a rosy picture about how the project is coming along. I head to Beaverton at the end of May with Tom Burck, a colleague and ex-Navy friend who teaches shop at my school. He's coming along to help finish her off and run her north, but we discover Rodney hasn't worked on the boat at all since dropping the engine into her. He's weeks away from beingdone, and we barely have a month until fishing starts nearly 3,000 miles away.

We dive into work that should have been done by Rodney. We labor for several 18-hour days hooking up wiring, fuel lines, gauges, a head. The list seems to grow rather than shrink. Tom welds a mast together out of aluminum, and we bolt it to the deck behind the cabin. Rodney installs the fuel tanks and builds and fiberglasses the decks. He's also trying to finish the other two boats, one of which is almost complete, the other, not so much. I begin to wonder if we're going to make it at all. When John Noble, one of the other skippers, calls me to ask how it's going, I tell him I'm concerned Rodney isn't going to make it. We're all planning on making the run up to Alaska together, so all the boats have to be done on time. "I think he's bit off more than he can chew. It's gonna be tight," I say into the phone.

The next morning Tom and I show up at 7:30 am ready to go, but find the door to the shop is padlocked. Rodney comes around the corner and announces we can't enter.

"What? Why?" I ask.

"Because you told John I wasn't doing a good job." His voice is aggressive and belligerent. "You said you didn't think I was going to get the boats done on time, and now he's threatening me with a lawsuit! So, you can't come in here until we're done."

I'm stunned. Tom looks ready to punch Rodney, and the only horse he has in this race is that he wants to go home soon. It's been too long already. If Rodney won't let us work, then neither John's boat or ours will be done on time. "Ok, then," I reply, my voice rising. "Give me my money back and I'll leave.

Otherwise, let us get the fuck in there and get to work."

Rodney blinks. "I'll let you in if you promise no more phone calls to John."

"Sure," I lie. "Whatever. I just want to get this boat finished."

"Me too," Rodney says, and unlocks the padlock. Things are tense the rest of the day, but we inch our way closer to being out of there. Tom welds the mast together and mounts it on deck, installs most of the wiring, hooks up the fuel systems, and works his ass off for three weeks, when all he signed on for was to help me bring the boat north. I'm incredibly lucky to have such a good friend with me.

After two weeks of insane work, we sea trial our brand-new, navy blue Uniflite on the Columbia River with a Marine Surveyor on board. The boat starts right up on the first try, purrs at idle, roars at cruise and outright screams at top speed. She clocks 21 knots on the river. The surveyor asks me, "What's her name?" For a short-lived moment I consider naming her the *Aunt Judy* after my sister. But knowing better, I reply, the *Veronika K*, with a K, not a C," which is how Veronica's name is spelled on her birth certificate. I sign the papers and we make arrangements to trailer her to Seattle. Tom and I ride in the cab of the semi all the way to Lake Union in Seattle. We're on our way.

The next week, Tom stays on the boat while Don drives me around Seattle to buy tie-up lines, buoys, life rings, spare fan belts, flashlights, flares, survival suits, cleats and bilge pumps and all the other supplies and food we'll need for the run up. After three hours in Doc Freeman's Marine Supply, I spend over $3,000.00 worth of boat gear. I walk to Don's truck with a knot in my stomach. I have never owed so much money. How will I ever pay it all back? I have a hard time catching a breath. Not counting the 25 grand for the engine, the boat and my loan total $84,000 before I even get her to Cook Inlet. I climb in the truck and slump over. I'm spending money I don't have. I can't imagine what Veronica is going to say. The most debt I've had to this point is our house, and it was way less than this. I can't live with my family on a 32-foot boat! What am I...suddenly Don punches me hard in the arm with a meaty Norwegian fist. It hurts and snaps me out of my funk. "Jesus!" I snap at him. "What was that for?"

"Quit worrying. It's only money."

"Thanks, asshole," I reply, rubbing my arm. "That helps a lot."

"No, really," he says, dropping the shit-eating grin. "When I bought the *Marauder*, after the first season I didn't have enough money for a plane ticket home. I was sittin' on the steps outside the cannery office with my head in my hands when Joe Fribrock, the superintendent back then, saw me and sat down. 'Tough year?' he asked. I nodded. 'That happens, you know. Don't worry. There's always next year. You'll be ok.'

"I said, 'Joe, I don't even have enough money to fly home.'

"'Ohh,' he looked at me. 'That *is* a tough season.' He stood up. 'Stay here,' he said, and disappeared into the office. A minute later he came back out and told me I had a plane ticket waiting for me at the airport.

"And you know what?" Don says to me as I rub my shoulder. "He was right. It'll be ok. You'll see."

The pep talk helps. At least I can feel my chest loosen and the knot in my stomach ease. When I call Veronica, she's sympathetic and understanding. "You have to have that stuff for the boat, right?"

"Yeah."

"You'd have to buy it sooner or later anyway, and it's cheaper in Seattle. You're exhausted. Get some rest. We'll get through this. Just come home safe." I'm weak with relief. Talk about lucky.

Chapter Twenty-Five: Running North

Tom and I work on the boat in Seattle while we wait for Rodney to finish John's *Susan Marie*. By the time he shows up a week later, we're prepped and ready to go. Tommy Hansen has his boat, the *Denali,* outfitted as well. None of us have made the trip from Seattle to Kenai before, through the Inside Passage and across the Gulf of Alaska. Don volunteers to join us since he's made the trip several times with his Dad, and on the *Inga E* with his cousin Rob. We're all grateful for an experienced guide, and head out of Seattle through the Ballard Locks into the waters of Puget Sound on a beautiful sunny day in early June. We're all curious about how seaworthy our new boats are, and the run to Friday Harbor in the San Juan Islands is the first leg of the trip on open water.

The Uniflites all have short bows, so when we encounter a chop, the boats throw spray on the windshield. What we don't realize until we get to Friday Harbor is that Rodney has forgotten to seal the decking to the hull after screwing it in place, and all three boats leak water profusely into the fo'cs'le. The bunks, sleeping bags, pillows, cushions and clothes lying there are all soaked. We drag everything out into the late afternoon sun to dry, cursing fucking Rodney as we work. We share and use multiple tubes of 3M 5200 marine silicone to try and seal the gaps between the decks and hulls under the rubber rub-rail that cover where they meet. It's slow, imperfect work, and when we stop each day for fuel or for the night, it's a ritual for the crew of each boat to come out of the cabin with more silicone to apply. 'Fucking Rodney' gets blamed for everything that goes wrong during the trip up, whether it's his fault or not.

One morning after a stay at an abandoned cannery on Vancouver Island, Tommy and John are leading our little procession of boats out the channel into Johnstone Strait when we hear a loud *CLUNK* from the stern and I suddenly can't steer. I put the boat in neutral as Don and Tom run out the door.

182

I call Tommy and John on the radio. "Uh, guys? I have a problem here. Lost my steering." I see them both slow down and start to turn back.

Don yells from the stern, "Try bumping it in reverse!" I do. Another clunk. "Forward!" I push it into gear again.

I hear Tom say, "There! Look!"

"Try the steering now!" Don yells. "You kicked out a 2x4!"

I do, and the steering works again. "It must've been wedged next to the rudder," Tom speculates. "It was only a couple of feet long. Good thing it wasn't bigger." We leave the piece of wood floating in our wake.

We push hard for several long days in a row, counting down to the first period of the season and hoping we can make it in time to try our luck with these new speedboats. Overall, we are pleased with their performance. They fly over the surface of the calm water we encounter, and we make good progress, stopping nightly at out-of-the-way docks and abandoned canneries on the way. One particular night we feel our way into a small bay after dark in a pounding rain. The *Veronika K* is the only one of the boats in our little group that has a spotlight, so we lead the way. The chart shows several small rocks that are a danger at low tide, and though it isn't fully out yet, the tide is ebbing, so the taller of those rocks could be hazardous to us. Tom puts on rain gear and goes up on the bridge, sweeping the powerful spotlight 20 feet in front of the boat as he looks though the downpour for any rocks nears the surface. I wonder how he can see anything at all. In the cabin, Don checks the chart frequently while I idle ahead with the window cracked so I can hear Tom if he yells. We are headed for a small public dock, and though we can barely make out a light on shore, we don't know if that's the dock or someone's cabin. Suddenly Tom's boots are pounding on the roof. "ROCK! Rock to port!" I put the boat in neutral and steer to starboard. Don stares toward shore, jaw jutted out in concentration.

"There!" he says, pointing. "That's it. Turn to starboard."
I can't see a thing. If he's wrong, we could hit a rock or run
aground. But it's Don, and when it comes to being on the water,
I trust his judgment. I turn the wheel.

As we swing, Tom starts slamming his boots on the roof
again, causing us both to jump. "ROCK DEAD AHEAD!"

"Jesus!" I say, putting the boat in neutral again. "How
close?" I yell out the window.

"Thirty feet! Keep turning and you'll miss it!"

Don and I give each other a look, hearts pounding.
"Almost there," he assures me as the dock comes into view.
After we're tied up, there's none of the usual visiting. Exhausted
and relieved, we hit the bunks early and drift off to the white
noise of rain on the roof.

The Denali and Susan Marie running north in SE Alaska, 1988.

The next day breaks sunny and calm, and we cruise north
on a calm Chatham Strait. The land is remote, with few villages,
houses or signs of civilization at all. As we near Icy Strait and

the jumping-off point to crossing the Gulf of Alaska, we come upon three humpback whales swimming in our direction. The biggest of them turns our way and places himself between us and what appears to be a mother and calf while they swim on. We all cut our engines and take photos of the big guy until he determines we're no longer a threat and swims off to join the others. We're all smiling at the encounter. There's a chill in the breeze, but we're glad to be surrounded by mountains above a blue sea in a wild land.

The day we pull into Elfin Cove to reports of a gale raging on the Gulf, an 80-foot tug-and-barge that left the day before it turns around because the seas are too rough. The forecast is poor for the next few days, so we hit the local rec center for basketball and showers. The village is tiny, built on a rocky shore with boardwalks and trails instead of roads. The people are friendly and welcoming, and one of the guys on the basketball court strikes up a conversation with Don about the NBA finals game coming up. "I manage a bunch of condos tourists rent during the summer," he says. "I still have a few that are empty. If you guys promise to leave it as clean as you find it, I can open it up so you can watch the game." We jump at the chance, and the next day finds most of us rooting for the Lakers over the Pistons while we munch chips and drink beer on the floor of the condo.

Another day goes by. We're all going stir-crazy, but the gale has yet to blow itself out. It's June 22, and Don decides he has to get to Kenai to get his boat ready. I still want a third hand on board for the Gulf crossing, so when Don sets up his flight to Seward, I have Tim fly out and take his place. We all see Don off with handshakes and waves, and the following day we head out into the remnants of the storm, bound for Yakutat. Large swells race under us from our stern, but they are wide rather than steep, and negotiating them is actually easy. Each boat has a 55-gallon barrel of diesel fuel lashed in the stern to supplement the 300 gallons in its tanks. We only bring one hand pump to transfer the fuel from the barrels to the tanks, thinking we can pass it back and forth. When we get low on fuel, we all slow down wait while one of us uses the pump. Then we place the pump in a plastic bag, tie a small buoy to it, and hand it back and forth with a dip net. If the pump gets dropped, someone is getting towed to Yakutat. Fortunately, we're careful enough to do it right.

We stop in Seward for fuel. We say goodbye and I offer a huge thank you to Tom when his wife Liz drives over to take him home. The whole ordeal has been hard on them, and I'm glad we're still friends at the end of it. Tim and I head out of Resurrection Bay, make the turn around the southern tip of the Kenai Peninsula and head into Cook Inlet. It's the first fishing day of the season, and the Inlet has prepared a fitting welcome for us by gifting us the worst weather of the entire trip. The waves attack us on the stern. Uniflites have square sterns that take weather poorly unless loaded. We have no fish on board and little fuel, so we're ultra-light, and we get pushed, turned and rolled constantly. At one point I get so frustrated fighting the wheel that I make the mistake of thinking this new fast boat can outrun the steep 10-footers pummeling us and push the throttle higher. The next wave grabs us in its teeth and rolls us so hard to port the I come completely out of the skipper's chair. I stand on the SIDE of the cabinet next to me, trying to turn the wheel back to starboard and reach the throttle to back off our speed at the same time. Tim, his eyes wide, is sitting at the galley table with his back against the port side, feet stretched out on the seat. When I glance at him, I see green water race past the window behind his head. "Jesus!" I yell, just as we stop broaching and roll back.

"Nice ride," Tim deadpans. "Do that again!"

"Fucking Inlet," is my response. "Welcome home!"

Chapter Twenty-Six: Truce

1988 is another perfect season, mixed differently. We don't have as many fish as '87, but the price is better. Cash buyers, competitors of the canneries who anchor in the river and offer ten cents more a pound, are a presence in the Inlet. The cannery price for reds opens at $1.40 a pound. The amount climbs all summer, and by season's end we're pushing $3.00. The boat average for the season is well over $100,000. The corridor once again produces large catches of fish, and fishermen and cannery workers alike are exhausted but happy. Even with all the work, there's still time for the occasional shenanigans.

I love trash-talking with Don about almost anything. From fishing prowess to who is better looking, we're constantly trading barbs. In the same vein, we start threatening each other with comments about who is better at pranking. Dean and Don have a long history of going after each other. Dean once dumped a bucket of flake ice through the access hatch on the bow of the *Marauder* while Don and his girlfriend were recreating in the bunk. Don retaliated by fiberglassing Dean's boots to a piece of plywood the night before a fishing period. Now that Dean's gone, Don and I become each other's targets.

One night before fishing, Danny Miller, now Don's deckhand, warns me to be sure and check my net carefully as we make the morning set. "He's up to something, but I can't tell you exactly what. Just check it – go slow when you make the first set."

Don lives on his boat at the dock, but I spend my nights at home in my bed like most local fishermen. After I leave, Don and Danny peel my net off the reel until they get to the end of the first shackle where it's clipped to the second with stout stainless clips at the leadline and corkline. Don unclips both sets, then rolls the shackle back in place. He leaves the river early the next morning, before I get down to the boat. He tells Danny that he wishes he could see the look on my face when I set my gear and my first shackle falls into the Inlet without warning. He listens to the radio intently after the opening begins, waiting for me to come on and yell at him, but I have other plans.

When we discover what he's done, I know exactly what he's expecting. I tell Tim that we're not getting on the radio for the next four hours at least, even if someone in our group calls us. We fish all morning, and together we concoct a story. It's after noon when Don comes on the radio. "Anybody heard from Pat today? He's been awfully quiet all morning."

"Now that you mention it," Wayne answers, "I haven't heard a word. You on here, Pat?"

I desperately want to reply, but I decide it'll be more effective to wait. Plus, I know my silence will drive Don crazy. It's 2:00 pm by the time I pick up the microphone. We've picked the set we've been on, and I wait until I have the sound of the boat running in the background to make the call more effective. To make the story even better, I know everyone out here is having another good day. "Yeah, *Marauder*, *Veronika K.* You pick me up, Don?"

"There you are! Where did you get to, Pat?"

"Oh, Jesus Christ, we've had a morning from Hell. I was in a crowd of boats setting on a bunch of jumpers at opening when my net came apart somehow, and everyone was packed so tight around me that when I tried getting it back on board, I got web in the wheel. I tried kicking it out, but it was wound so tight that it tweaked the cutlass bearing on the shaft. We were vibrating like crazy when we put the boat in gear. We were lucky to be just outside the river, so we got a tow back to the cannery. They hauled us out right away, and I grabbed a new shackle while Tim and Bill Wegner fixed the bearing. We're just getting back out here. What's going on? Any fish anywhere?"

The radio stays silent for a looooong time. "Holy shit, Pat. That's terrible. There were fish earlier, but it's slowed down. I'm sorry that happened to you."

188

In my best magnanimous voice, I reply, "That's okay. It wasn't your fault. I'm just glad it wasn't worse. If they had to pull the shaft we'd still be at the cannery."

Again, a long pause. When he comes on this time, the tone of his voice is subdued. "Yeah, Roger that. Maybe some fish'll show on the flood."

"I hope so. Looks like we missed a pretty good day," I reply, filling my voice with perky optimism. "Ok, we're gonna try one up here. I'll let you know. I'm out."

By the time the period ends and Don gets back to the dock, I've already delivered and cleaned up. I act like I'm just about to leave when Don pulls in and motions me to join him in his cabin. He grabs a couple of beers and hands me one. I've never seen him look so downtrodden. He's had a full six hours to beat himself up over this, and he looks like he's done a spectacularly good job at it. "Pat, I have to tell you something," he says, looking at the floor. "Last night I unclipped your first shackle and rolled it back on the reel as a joke." His head drops as he looks at the floor. "It was meant to be a joke. I'm so sorry you went through all that."

"What? YOU unclipped it?" I laugh. "Bullshit." I want him to say it again, and he does.

"No bullshit. We did it after you left last night. Really. I'm sorry. "He reaches into his shirt pocket and hands me his pink receipt from delivering his fish. "Here's my fish ticket. You missed a really good day. I'll go up tomorrow and tell Ray to put half those fish in your account."

I open the ticket and stare at it, trying hard not to laugh. "You fucker," I say as I look up. "You *fucker*."

"I know, I'm sorry," he says again.

I fold the ticket and slide it back across the table to him, then smile. "Gotcha!"

He looks bewildered, which Don does well. "We didn't break down. We didn't lose the shackle or any of it." I tell him what really happened, and that we had a good day too.

189

"You asshole," he says finally. "I felt TERRIBLE all day! Shit!"

"Good! You deserved it. Truce?"

"Truce."

Pat and Tim DeLapp, 1987.

A week later, at the end of a good day on a glassy Inlet, we are sitting on a set along the middle rip, catching the occasional single. I'm on the bridge in the sun, fish hold mostly full, enjoying the last few moments of the day, when a 'Russian' boat zooms up, drops his buoy ten feet from the other end of my net, and makes a set to the west of me. I immediately become irritated. The Russians, most of them from a community of "Old Believers" of the Russian Orthodox church, live at the head of Kachemak Bay east of Homer. They have huge fiberglass boats, and often fish with their families aboard as crew. They have a reputation as aggressive, sometimes ruthless fishermen, but are well respected as being very good at what they do. I am irritated at this particular guy because he's spoiled my bliss. Now I have to pay attention. As I watch, he finishes setting, then he buoys off the end of his net, and returns to the end close to my net. *This is so totally unnecessary,* I think. I decide to go give him a piece of my mind.

I put a buoy on the end of my net and motor over to him. He's sitting on his seat on the flying bridge, watching his crew work on deck as I put the boat in neutral. "A little close, don't you think?" I yell as I point to the small gap between his bow and my net. He swivels his chair forward to look, the swivels back to me. "Not so bad," he answers in a thick accent.

I am trying to think of what else to say when I notice what his family is doing: he's caught so many fish that his fish hold is full and he's deck-loaded. They are all grabbing fish and walking them forward to balance the load. I realize that with a boat as large as his, he's probably got 4,000 or more salmon on board. I've been having one of my best days, and just cracked 1,800.

I gesture at all the fish on deck. "Nice day!" I say. He swivels again to face his back deck, then swivels back. With absolutely no change in inflection, he yells, "Not so bad!" I shake my head, wave and go back to my net.

191

Chapter Twenty-Seven: Pompadour

The advantage of a fast boat changes my fishing style. On full Inlet openings, I hire an extra, experienced hand on board so I can spend more time listening to the radio and zeroing in on where the fish are while the crew picks. The boat helps me get on the fish before the fleet arrives and catches or scatters them, and having two good fish pickers to clear the gear in a hurry makes us quick to move when we need to. It's an efficient combination.

We fish 21 days straight, sometimes just Tim and me in the corridor, sometimes the full Inlet with the extra crew. To keep up (we tell ourselves) Tim and I do cocaine. Lots of cocaine. We laugh about it, saying it's a great fishing tool, but in reality, it gets in the way of the rest of my life, particularly on shore with Veronica. I'm testy and irritable with her and the kids when I'm home, and I'm of little help around the house. When she mentions it, I get defensive and the discussion quickly devolves into a fight, but part of me knows she's right when she says I have a problem. I just won't admit it because I want to do more cocaine.

I'm fortunate that the source for buying it dries up at the end of the summer. I realize later I was heading down a dark road, and had the drug been readily available to me all year long, I would have been hard-pressed to stop. During several fishing periods, Tim and I start each set with a line, do lines running out the river, more during the day, and even more running home. The drug certainly has us in its grips, and the summer flies up our noses along with a couple of thousand dollars.

Sometimes guys can make too much money. Fishermen aren't immune, and I certainly wasn't. Halfway through the season I'm driving to the supermarket for groceries when I see a life-long dream of mine with a For Sale sign parked across the street from the bank. I call the number…

192

Pompadour

Name the year that is especially good:
high price and fish fill the gear wherever
we set the net. We watch the bank account
grow ten grand a day. 1100 sockeye one opening,
1600 the next. The cocaine dealers make as much
as well-paid crew; park trailers in the yard
next to empty campers owned by fishermen too busy
to sleep. We're glad they do. Makes our dropping
a couple hundred a week into their pockets easier.
They even take trips with their best customers–
faux-deckhanding on fish days and providing free product.

Everyone knows. No one cares. Toot becomes a tool
for exhausted crews and cannery workers
spending 22-hour days on the slime line.
After a shift one night, Peggy naps in a pickup bed,
one leg hanging off the tailgate when a car backs into her.
She doesn't do coke.
Some of us think she should have.
At least she'd have been awake.

I run into town for supplies a few days later,
and collide with a lifelong dream:
chromed-out Honda 750 *Shadow*,
parked in the grade-school lot across from the grocery.
She has the saddle-seat lines of a vintage Harley,
a pompadour of a sign pinned to her handlebars–
FOR SALE: $3,000 or Best Offer. Leave message.
I use the pay phone outside the store.
We agree to meet when things slow down.
Planned in a cocaine haze, I don't mention it at home.

We use toot like rain gear.
Put a line on the table every time we pull on a jacket.
Suck lines into our noses
as we work rubber gloves onto our wrists.
Do a line running out the river,
before the first set,
before the first pick,
running on a fish call,
talking on the radio,
with coffee.

Stop for a bite almost never,
talk fast all day about anything,
about sex, about more cocaine.
When we crash, the lights don't just go out,
they blow. Alarms blare,
we get up, do it again.

Absent at home,
all we're about
is heading to the boat
to catch more fish
and do more coke.

We sell to a cash buyer after one trip–
I jam crisp hundreds into a plastic grocery bag,
stuff it under the seat of my blue Ford pickup
parked in the cannery yard, then go out fishing
'til the end of the week. Once the reds run out,
I meet the bike's owner in town.

My ass in that saddle feels like a hand in a glove;
I hear the engine purr, go for a wind-in-my-hair ride–
never think once about how good my choices are.

I hand him the cash and drive home.
I already own the leather–
a black helmet with a skull,
my ensemble's complete.

Cocaine logic is the perfect solution
for the building seas of marital disaster:
30 one-hundred-dollar bills in an envelope,
her name on it. *Spend it any way you want, sweetie.*
You might anticipate how that worked out.
I don't.

She puts the money in the bank.

Name the year that was especially bad:
this is the low water story of that summer.
I bump bottom with that bike, as off-course
as Joe Hazelwood skippering the *Exxon Valdez*.
It takes me years to realize how lucky I am to miss the reef.

Chapter Twenty-Eight: Rain Dream

It's fall, so it's easy to find myself in a coffee shop writing about rain. Coffee seems to go best with rain. I wrap my fingers around the cup, more to connect with what a rainy day feels like than for warmth. I watch the downpour dance on the sidewalk and street outside the window. The glass streaks with rivulets of water running to the ground, and the scene before me dissolves into streaks of a chilly Alaskan rain running down the dusty windshield of a dry-docked boat in the spring. The sound of the drops is drowned out by the *thumpa-thumpa-thumpa* of the rotating diesel stovepipe cap and the low moan of the wind in the rigging.

§

A gust throws spatters on the window and I'm standing in my oilskins on the flying bridge looking down over the bow. Raindrops sting my face as the boat slices through the waves. The rhythmic diesel roars in my ears, and I notice soundless circles dancing on the side of a glassy swell: expanding then disappearing into ripples of newer drops. Light upon dark upon light, it's a silent ballet in a world filled with more urgent noises.

The swell rolls away, and I awaken on another morning to a muted patter on the roof of the boat. Barely audible, the rain utters a gentle whisper that I just might understand, if only I listen hard enough. I walk outside into a soft downpour that speaks in voices I have never before encountered. In the predawn light I watch the water dance in tiny liquid explosions of gravity on a gray mirror of ocean. The boats of the fleet, dull and oblivious, sway heavily on their anchors in the near distance, dark gray forms against lighter grays of water and cloud, all connected, shrouded, washed in rain.

The sound of hissing is faint. At first I don't hear it under the thrumming of drops on the deck, pinging on the metal mast, plopping off the rigging, off the gunwales into the sea. All that is more conscious, more evident. Underneath it all is a hiss: a lighter, softer white noise. It is as if the sea and the sky are conversing in an altogether foreign language. A language so primal as to be all but inaudible to my modern ear filled as it is with noises and sounds I not only help create, but inspire.

Buddha speaks of the seeking of silence – an inner peace that is heart and soul of existence. For a few moments, standing on deck, for a few heartbeats on a silent boat floating on a quiet sea, I eavesdrop upon another dimension. I sway heavily on an anchor of my own, hooked deep, listening to forces surrounding me like an ocean.

§

The rain eases and the clouds lift. As the sky brightens, I slowly become aware of rain-soaked socks chilling my feet. I blink away my reverie to notice fat drops of water dripping from the brim of my hat. A shiver raises the hair on the back of my neck, and with it I turn and open the cabin door. It's time to brew the morning's warm coffee with water that's fallen from the sky. I listen to the waning drops patter upon the roof as they mingle with the sound of coffee dripping into my cup.

Chapter Twenty-Nine: Group Dynamics, Part 1

When Dean sells out in 1985, his deckhand, Danny Miller, starts working for Don. Danny is the ultimate crew. He is mechanical, handy with wood and fiberglass, can pick fish fast, and knows what to look out for in terms of other boats, fish, and hazards like sticks or kelp. He can cook, and he always makes a point to clean the boats he works on exceptionally well. He is also a good friend to both of the brothers and me. One of his best talents is listening.

As the 1988 season develops, Don is slipping more and more into a funk about the changing fishery. Gone are the days of dock life, where the majority of the out-of-town fishermen lived on their boats and socialized between fish days. The cannery has put in housing for fishermen, so most out-of-town skippers don't live on their boats anymore. The fishery is transforming into a money-making enterprise instead of a lifestyle, and nowhere is the change more evident than on the *Marauder*. When he built it, he chose it for its seaworthiness and ability to pack fish, not for speed. But the speedboats starting to populate the fleet are racing to fish the *Marauder* either can't get to because it takes too long, or she arrives too late, after the fish have already been caught by faster boats.

Done delivering, I tie alongside the *Marauder* at the dock after one particularly frustrating day for Don, and instead of he and Danny coming out of the cabin to help us tie off, I see them sitting at the table deep in conversation. When Danny comes over after a half an hour, his face is grim. "He's seriously thinking about selling out."

"Let me talk to him," I say, hoping this isn't real. Don and I have become best friends, and I really don't want him to leave the fishery. I grab a couple of beers and head to the *Marauder* as Tim and Danny sit down on the *Veronika K.* "Danny says you're thinking of pulling the plug," I hand Don a beer. "What's going on?"

198

"Everything," he starts, and it all pours out. His frustration with the fishery, the loss of boat life, and the temptation of the current high price for permits after two incredible seasons. "I just think it's time." He puts the boat away a week later, taping a 'Boat and Permit for Sale' sign to the bow before heading to the airport. By the end of September, he has a buyer, and I am sick over his departure.

Our fishing group has slowly disintegrated. Senior and Betty sold out the year before. Dale disappeared without a trace during the offseason a few years ago. Wayne died of a heart attack during the winter of '87. After Don leaves, Rob, Cosmo and I are the only ones left. We invite a few guys from our cannery to join us: John Efta, a former student and his dad Leonard, have lost their group too. I don't know what kind of fishermen they are, but I've known them for years, and they're good people. Along with a couple of other boats, we put together a ramshackle group that lasts two years. One, if you don't count 1989. In March of that year the Exxon Valdez fetches up hard aground on Bligh Reef in Prince William Sound and costs us the entire season.

Chapter Thirty: Exxon: The Lost Season

On Good Friday, 1989 the *Exxon Valdez* runs aground on Bligh Reef in Prince William Sound. Mike, my deckhand, is in his last year of high school when asks me in April if I think the spill will impact us, asking, "Do you think we'll fish this year?" I've already made up my mind. "I can't see how," I answer. It's a prediction I hope I'm wrong about, but it comes true. Cook Inlet is hundreds of miles away by water from the Sound, but by July so much oil is in it that not only can't we fish, we are so far away from the spill's 'ground zero' that the oil company doesn't even attempt a clean-up. The state reinstates its policy of zero tolerance from a few years ago, and each day before a scheduled fishing period, it sends test boats out to the areas in the Inlet where the fleet would normally fish. If the boats catch any oil, the period is cancelled. Over a million gallons of crude oil in the form of tar balls drift into Cook Inlet. By the time they arrive, they have 'neutral buoyancy', meaning they don't float on the surface, but hang about six feet deep unless they encounter kelp or sticks. Or nets.

The drift fleet sits at the dock, boats ready to go, hoping we can finally get to fishing. Each night before a scheduled fishing day, we buy groceries and make sure we're ready to go the next morning. But all we get to harvest is anger and frustration as test after test finds oil. Exxon sets up a claim office in downtown Kenai, but there isn't a fisherman who doesn't feel like he's in the welfare line looking for a handout as he waits in line for a check that is too small handed to him by a claim officer who makes him feel like he's a freeloader. We walk out the door with jaws clenched and the old adage running through our minds: "Oil and water don't mix."

On July 19th ADF&G tells the drift fleet they aren't going to have a season this year, and close the Inlet down. Meanwhile, the setnetters who fish along the eastern shore are

having a record year. They are harvesting the fish they'd
normally get as well as all the fish the drift fleet would catch.
We haven't had one storm all summer, so the oil remains in the
center of the Inlet, leaving the beaches, where the setnetters fish,
clean. Fish and Game, trying to avoid a huge over-escapement
into the river, lets them fish every day for weeks. I talk to a
friend at the store who is crewing for a setnet site along
Salamatof beach north of the river. He tells me they have
already put up over 700,000 pounds by July 21st, with at least
another week of fishing yet to go. The price is holding steady at
a dollar and a quarter. The setnetters are literally becoming
millionaires, and we haven't caught a single fish.

The F/V Denali next to an oil tanker in Cook Inlet.

I have an old tar ball of Valdez oil I dip-netted out of the
Inlet later that summer when we took the boat down to Homer to
get away and at least enjoy being on the water in Kachemak
Bay. It's ugly, but it reminds me of what happened that year,
and for years represented the hope I held that Exxon would
eventually get spanked by the justice system for its policies and
incredibly irresponsible actions that led to the disaster in the
Sound. When the Supreme Court struck down that hope in
November of 2008 and handed back Exxon four-and-a-half of

its five-billion-dollar original trial judgement, the last of that hope slipped out of the bottle. Nothing to do about it now except write. Like a lot of guys, I'm used to clenching my jaw.

The Blockade

Once the season is cancelled, something many fishermen anticipated, the rush is on to put the boat away and fly home. A small group of locals, however, feel that a response is needed to force Exxon to clean up Cook Inlet. I help organize a meeting where we hatch a plan to publicize our predicament in order to stimulate some action, and we agree to contact as many skippers as we can to blockade the oil terminal dock 20 miles north of the Kenai River in Nikiski, where the next tanker is scheduled to pick up bunker oil soon.

By July 21, with short notice, we've only recruited 15 boats willing to participate, and we leave the river at noon with the intention of meeting the tanker and creating a scene that we can film and photograph for the news services. My old deckhand Michael Burgener's brother Mark is a good friend and a videographer, and he agrees to come along and tape the event from the *Veronika K.* Another fisherman, Rich King, is with a film crew from the Governor's office in a helicopter overhead, and other news crews have been offered spots on other boats. I also have Frank Mullen, who was instrumental in organizing the protest, on board.

Before we leave, we draw up and disseminate a list of "concerns" to be carried by all boats participating in the blockade. It says:

> The oil companies have lied to us in three ways:
> - They told us they wouldn't spill oil, and that was a lie.
> - They told us they'd clean any spill, and that was a lie.
> - They told us they'd compensate those damaged by the spill fairly, and that is proving to be a lie as well.

202

The decision to blockade the Nikiski dock is based on the desire to:

- create pressure upon oil companies to implement a serious oil clean-up effort on Cook Inlet;
- encourage Exxon to deal equitably and fairly with the settlement of claims resulting from the Exxon Valdez oil spill and its effects on the Inlet's fishery;
- remind the public that British Petroleum and Tesoro and others have yet to negotiate any settlement to fishermen as a result of the 1987 Glacier Bay spill on the Inlet and that spill's impact upon our fishery;
- and to point out that there is still no real capability to clean up a new oil spill [in Cook Inlet].

As the tanker nears, the boats begin to move in close to the docks. As we do so, we notice four men on the dock, one in a Coast Guard uniform., writing down boat numbers and names. Soon after that, the Coast Guard announces its presence on the VHF, and says we are in restricted waters. They order us to clear the area. Our small group of boats is quiet over the radio in response. Frank and I feel that someone needs to find out what can be the consequence of our actions, so I pick up my microphone and ask the person making the announcement to identify himself. He refuses.

Then I ask him why he would not identify himself, and he replies that it was due to security considerations. I ask him what laws we would be in violation of, should we refuse to move, and what the penalties for those violations are. Again, he refuses to answer over the radio and remarks that he will tell me in person if I motor over to the dock. After a brief discussion with Frank, I decide to find out what our group is risking.

We pull the boat close to the dock and learn that upon refusing a direct order from the Coast Guard, we are subject to up to five years in jail and a $50,000 fine for obstructing a navigable waterway – a federal misdemeanor. At that time, we assume that our boat is the only one that has received a direct order, and we tell the Coast Guard officer that we'll stand off, but we can't speak for the rest of the boats. The Coastie, a Lt. Wilson, is apparently there for the routine inspection of the tanker. He voices his sympathies for our concerns, and requests to come aboard. Frank whispers that he can take command of our vessel if he is allowed on board. Lt. Wilson smiles and nods in a not unfriendly way when I deny him permission.

We idle away from the dock, switch to the VHF channel our group is on and inform them of what's been said. I tell them we are staying out of the way of the tanker as it approaches the dock, and advise them to use their own best judgment. After a long pause, an unidentified voice says, "I dunno. I think I might be having a fan belt problem soon."

The tanker is now close in on the fleet, and the show begins in earnest. The tanker skipper, on his first run to Cook Inlet, is advised from shore to "Keep her coming –Dead Slow. They've been warned away. They're just playing chicken with you." The fishing boats crowd around the tanker; one even bumps her. I remark to Frank that the entire scene feels symbolic of the roots of this struggle: the giant is, in reality, unaffected by the small craft buzzing it. The 800-foot tanker just keeps on coming, implacable, unstoppable, just like the oil spill itself, just like the industry. What chance do we really have?

The futility of what we've done follows us all the way back to the dock. We're tying up when a stranger asks if we were one of the boats involved in the blockade. We answer yes, but we're not sure what good it's done. He says he's an Exxon stockholder from New York City, and he thanks us, saying, "It got people's attention." We thank him for saying so, and feel a little better for our efforts.

The next evening, we get 10 seconds of national news coverage on NBC Nightly News, and 30 seconds on our local ABC channel. Nothing else changes. No serious cleanup is ever ordered for Cook Inlet, and no charges are filed against the fishermen after the blockade.

Fallout

Innocence in your eyes,
you ask,
   Daddy, we will be safe from the oil?
I swallow hard.
How can I say to you,
   No! One day it or something like it
         something we have created
         something I have given my blessing to
         (if only by my silence)
         will kill us all.
instead I lie,
   Yes, punkin. We'll be safe.

Chapter Thirty-One: Radio Fish

After the Exxon spill, our fishing group breaks apart again. The radio communication is so bad during the 1990 season that Rob and Cos decide to fish by themselves. I want to be part of a bigger group. For most of the next winter I try to navigate my way to more than a 'group' of guys who fish together. I know what I want. It's what I had – a community. I want to fish with people who are also friends, who socialize, laugh, have fun as well as fish together. I ache for the summers I spent with those two idiot brothers. I have one friend I can ask, Rich King: a neighbor who fishes for my cannery with group of guys I know and like. I ask him, but they're not looking. "We'd love to have you, Pat," Rich tells me, "but we pretty much have the right number of boats already." *Shit.*

Tommy on the *Denali* hears that I'm looking. He's joined Jim and Thor's old group and invites me in for a second go. I'm leery, because the communication in that group has been an issue, but I decide to give it a try.

In the spring, I hire Craig Phillips as my crew. I know Craig from the theatrical performances we've both been involved in during the winters in Kenai, plus I taught with his dad. He's young, energetic and easy-going. He works hard for me, and we have great conversations about acting and art. He introduces me to new music as we run to and from the grounds or while we work on the boat. Through him, I learn about DePeche Mode, The Indigo Girls and other groups that become instant favorites. I listen to music constantly. When I'm working, driving, relaxing at home or even teaching, I've always got something playing on the radio, boombox or stereo. It's a good thing Veronica likes music as much as I do. It's a constant in our lives.

Craig and I head out one period in mid-July to a foggy morning. Fog is rare in Cook Inlet in the summer, and the few times I fish in it, I find it's easy to get disoriented. The radar on the *Skookum Too* was impossible to use in fog. I had to stick my face into a rubber eyepiece because the screen was so faint. The sweep of the arm was slow, so it took forever to see what was in front of you or which direction you were headed. The new Furuno radar I install on the *Veronika K* is worlds better – bright and fast. But I quickly learn that it is more about me getting disoriented than the equipment's fault. Fog just makes everything more difficult, and I never learn how to fish efficiently in it. When we make the first set in the middle of the Inlet alongwhat I think is the middle rip, I am less than confident I'm in theright spot. Tommy is on fish, and has put out a call. The Loran strength is iffy, so I'm not sure if his numbers match mine, but Iknow I should be close. I just can't tell for sure because the fog is so thick I can't even see half my net once it's out.

Fifteen minutes go by, and we see maybe two hits, and aren't even sure about that. I listen to Tommy talk on the radio about the fish he's catching, and convince myself that we're in the wrong spot. We pick the gear and have over 50 fish. Craig thinks it's pretty good for a short set, and suggests we lay it back out, but I'm so anxious I don't listen, and we head farther south, where I think Tommy is. It becomes obvious before too long that I've made a mistake. The fog is too thick to go exploring, and I've lost track of the rip. I almost run over a couple of nets that appear out of the gray mist in front of us, and in frustration put the boat in neutral and check the radar for boats around us. I think I can see a clear spot just to the east, so I head to it and out of frustration throw the net out again and wait for the fog to lift and listen to the radio. Another mistake.

The more I listen, the more I become convinced that we're not in the right spot again. The fog does start to brighten a bit, and I see scattered boats in every direction. Tommy's caught 350 on his first set, the best set of our group, but another report comes in five miles north, so we pick up and head for it. By the time we get there, it's died off, so we run farther north and set off the rip to nothing. Nada. No fish. We wait twenty minutes while I rack my brain wondering what the best move is. Craig keeps to himself as his skipper dives deeper and deeper into his neurosis. "Let's try the east rip," I say finally. "Might as well go exploring."

Over the next nine hours we listen to the radio for any scrap of information. As soon as someone says anything even remotely like they're catching a fish, I pick up and head that way. We run east, back west, south, and north again. We set out for ten minutes here, set for five minutes there, for a half-an-hour when we see a hit. Each time we pull up and run again. We set all the gear out most of the time, half of it sometimes, only a shackle if I'm desperate and just checking a fishy-looking streak.

Toward the end of the day, we find ourselves lined up along the middle rip below Kalgin Island with 50 or more boats stretching north and south as far as we can see, each vessel just far enough from the next one to not be corking them off. I get antsy again, so we pick up and head north. Before I do, I check the Loran for my location, and write it down for the log I keep. I run for ten minutes at the helm in the cabin, then run up to the flying bridge for a better view. From there I realize that the entire fleet – or most of it – is lined up along both sides of this rip. I don't see any spots available to the north at all, but there's one opening a mile to the south of me. We turn around and run to it. After we set out, I go to the cabin and check the Loran. The numbers look familiar. I check my notes, and sure enough, I'm back where I started.

That's it. I'm done. All my running has cost us a shit-ton of fuel, and we have fewer than 90 fish in the hold. I estimate the fleet average to be over 500. I give up, sit in the skipper's seat and shake my head. I feel awful. Not for me. For me I feel foolish. But for Craig, who has worked his ass off all day for a percentage of my self-induced insanity, I feel, I *know* I've let him down. No skipper wants to disappoint his crew with a bad performance. Breakdowns and bad weather are one thing. Being lousy at catching fish is something else entirely. I feel…guilty. It's a lesson I should already know. The adage sticks with me this time: 'You can't catch fish if your net's not wet'.

We return to the cannery and I give Craig all the fish he can carry for the freezer at home by way of an apology for my poor performance. "Nothing to apologize for," he says graciously. "We all have bad days. We'll get 'em next period." I vow to do just that.

Running on a fish call, with Mt. ReDoubt volcano to the west.

Chapter Thirty-Two: Group Dynamics, Part 2

By the end of the summer, I'm ready to move on from Thor's group for a second time. One of the group's more abrasive members accosts me over the radio for sharing information with another fisherman from outside the group. The information I shared was that I wasn't catching anything, and that, coupled with the fact that I hate anyone telling me what I can or can't do pisses me off. When that same guy catches 900 fish on a slow day a week later and tells the group about it after it's over, I am so furious I announce to Tommy and Thor on the dock the next day that I'm leaving. I'll fish alone before I fish with that guy again. I start looking once more.

The best part of the next year, 1991, is that I've hired Don to be my crew. After a few years away, he misses fishing, and the fact that we can fish together is an extra enticement. It's a tough season with few fish, but I get through it mainly because he's there. With the fishing closed most days, we drink whiskey at the Vagabond and listen to stories told to us by one of our favorite cannery old-timers, Louis Clark. We play pool and shoot potato guns at beer cans on a fence in the back of the Albatross bar. We visit Good Time Charlie's strip bar more than once.

When we do get to fish, it's often a decent shot on the morning set, then slow fishing all day. Anticipating having Don aboard, I have stowed Halloween masks under the bunk, and when a buddy of ours, Jeff Snyder, swings by while he's looking for fish, Don and I put them on. When we come out on deck, Jeff roars with laughter and yells, "Get the camera!" to his deckhand.

An early Halloween: Pat and Don on the Veronika K, 1991.
Photo by Jeff Snyder

He snaps a photo of us, then he and I switch boats while he and Don pick my gear and I take pics and drink one of his beers. Somehow, Don and I scratch out enough fish to make the summer feel almost normal. Then the worst happens.

Chapter Thirty-Three: Jeff

Jeff Snyder shooting tequila out of a squirt gun, Cook Inlet, 1991.

Don lives on the boat for the season, inspiring many impromptu parties, several of which I miss because I'm living in town, which irritates me… but not seriously. It's disconcerting to come down to my boat to find it trashed, beer bottles everywhere and my deckhand hung over in the bunk. But it's Don, and within a few minutes he's telling me what happened and we're laughing at the stories. I get my revenge one night when we're hosting a dozen fishermen and women on board and I yell, "Everyone throw something at Don!" and with enthusiasm they all oblige. It's one of the few highlights of the summer. There certainly aren't many on the grounds.

Stuck in the corridor fishing one period in July, we aren't catching anything, so we say "Fuck this", pull the gear and run out to the middle on a gray, drizzly day over water like glass. The sea has a slight swell to it, and the rain pops small circles on the waves. We're both on the bridge, standing in our rain gear, checking to see if any fish are jumping out here, but we really aren't looking. We're both seeing a different world, one where we can always stand on a boat slicing through a calm sea, salt air in our nostrils. It feels to me like we're seeing ourselves through the lens of the changing present, looking back at the past. I think to myself that I could do this the rest of my life. I say as much to him, and he nods imperceptibly, his jaw working as he stares out at the low clouds and empty water. A few long seconds later he goes into the cabin. We never do see any jumpers.

Our fishing group and a few good friends all get together for a bash toward the end of the season at Cosmo's house in Coho, twenty miles south of Kenai. Cos has a fish tote full of heated water for a hot tub, with a bilge pump for a Jacuzzi, a barbecue full of fish and coolers full of beer. We splash around, drink and laugh into the wee hours. Jeff is not one of our fishing group, but he's a close friend to many of us and he's having a good time. I have a new medium-format camera, and I snap several portraits of him messing around with my sons. He's younger than we are by a few years, has a quick, wide smile. Tonight, he gets pretty hammered, becoming loud and out of control. He's in training to become a firefighter, so he's in good physical shape, and though we try to stop him he doesn't listen and trashes Cos's place until it gets to be too much, so several of us usher him away and convince him it's time to leave before he does any real harm. We drive him home and put him to bed in his trailer at the cannery.

He comes down to the boat the next day, hung over, wearing sunglasses and groaning. We all inform him of his out-of-line behavior, and he's definitely embarrassed. "Do I need to go apologize to Cosmo?" he asks us, sheepishly. We can tell he

214

wants us to say no, but the answer comes back a unanimous yes. He leaves immediately. I notice his sunglasses on my boat later that afternoon.

If he is anything, Jeff is genuine and kind. He adds a richness to the flavor of cannery life, and has a lightness about him that everyone feels. He's everybody's little brother. He lives in Anchorage with his wife Jo, who is pregnant with their first child. He's finishing his fireman training, flying back and forth between Kenai and the city as often as he can, living in a trailer at the back of the cannery between periods when he's here. Everyone has a Jeff story. They're all funny. One summer he invites us all to the Nightwatch, the nicest bar-restaurant in the area for a Saturday night party. He's the self-appointed 'Event Planner and Drink Coordinator,' so he goes to the bar early, orders 18 Howitzers – a drink he invented, consisting of Kahlua, Baileys, Grand Marnier, and Drambuie topped with Bacardi 151 rum all layered in a shot glass – one for each of us, ready when we arrive for dinner at 7:00 pm. He pushes tables together and even puts name cards on the places where he wants us to sit. He puts the drinks on our plates at 6:45 and waits. Only no one shows. An unexpected fishing opening announced by Fish & Game has us all scrambling to fuel up, buy groceries and leave the river before the tide is too low. His deckhand finally realizes where he is and calls the bar to tell him what's going on. Since he's already paid for the drinks, he decides they shouldn't go to waste, so he sits at each place-setting, has an imagi-conversation with each of us about the fact that we're not there, and tosses back our Howitzer. "I did it for you guys," he says later. He cabs it back to the cannery, stumbles drunkenly onto his boat, tells his deckhand, "Take 'er out! Yer'r the shkipper today!" and face-plants in the bunk. His deckhand fishes the entire period with Jeff passed out.

He heads to Cosmo's, we find out later, and makes amends, staying and helping clean the mess he created and more. The next day he runs his rusty, smoking truck out north to

215

pick up a spare propeller he's had reworked. The truck tends to stall, so he often doesn't come to complete stops at the stop signs. On the way back he coasts through a sign and onto the highway in front of a Volvo cresting the hill. The Volvo doesn't even have time to hit the brakes. It T-bones the truck on the driver's door, killing Jeff instantly.

I swear I see him the next morning standing in his overalls with his back to me as I ride my bike past the machine shop. I think how I'll come back and harass him after I check on the boat. But Don and a couple of other fishermen are slumped in the cabin, and when they tell me the news, I can't believe it. *I just saw him.* I think they're bullshitting me, but no one is smiling. *I just saw him!* I stare at the sunglasses he left on the dash. *He was just here.*

It's the end of the season for us. I don't have the heart for it anymore. Don waits until after the funeral to fly home to Seattle. I put the boat away slowly, by myself, and spend long hours thinking about selling out and walking away from this godforsaken business forever. Depressed and lonely, I wander up the trail from the boatyard to see if Danny's still around. I don't look at Jeff's trailer when the path goes by it. Danny fishes for Tommy now, and we don't see each other as often as we used to. Still, we're good friends. He knows me as well as anyone, sometimes better than I know myself. We play cribbage in his trailer and smoke a bowl from his corncob pipe. I tell him how I'm feeling. I'm not looking forward to any more seasons like this, and can't see my way to making it fun again. School is starting in a couple of weeks, and I'm looking forward to that even less. Danny lights his tobacco pipe and looks at me from under bushy eyebrows. "Which would you rather do?" he asks. "Quit after a losing season, or keep fishing and hang it up after a good year? Which taste do you want in your mouth when you walk away? How do you want to remember fishing?" It's a question I take with me into the winter, and after printing photos

216

in the darkroom of Jeff for Jo and all his friends, the answer has me back again the next spring.

Not that the winter is easy. Over the years I develop a Thursday night routine when I'm teaching. I spend the evening in town, grading prints and working on my own photography in the school's darkroom until 10:00 pm or so, when I give Thor a call. Most of the time he's available and we meet at one of the bars in town. Thor favors the 'triangle' of Larry's Club, The Rig and the Rainbow bar, with an occasional stop at Kenai Joe's. We meet at his apartment or at one of the bars where I nurse a beer while he sips on a rum and Coke and waxes poetic about his favorite topics of art, basketball and fishing. During the long, dark months when the boats are up on barrels and covered with snow, it's my only connection to fishing, and in 1991 I'm in need of it more than ever. Some nights, though, Thor doesn't answer when I call. In hopes of finding him, I spend hours driving around Kenai in the dark, looking for his car in parking lots. Those nights are hollow, lonely evenings. I don't want to drink by myself – drinking isn't the reason I'm out here – and I don't have anyone else to call. By midnight I'm home, more depressed than ever.

Overboard

It was a cannery truck, we said afterward.
Unreliable. It would stall when he slowed down.
He probably coasted through the stop sign.

Bone cancer doesn't relent, the doctors told her.
Go. Live. Enjoy the time you have left.
For five years she did exactly that:
dove the Great Barrier Reef,
went to China.
Fished the lake behind her cabin with her niece.
When she was done, she slipped away overnight.

It doesn't take much –
a gentle roll of the boat as the wake
passes; the brush of an elbow,
and the power drill, set too close to the edge,
tips and tumbles overboard.
You see it roll: watch without
moving, frozen in a dream.
It doesn't even complete a full circle
before it hits the water – that flashlight –
or 10-inch crescent wrench, or your cell phone
slipping out of your pocket as you bend down –
in the air before you know it.

It lands on the water's surface
like you land on the bed after a long day,
blankets fluffing, rising as they are displaced,
absorbing the impact and falling back again;
only the water receives and moves aside, and your knife,

the one you spent all those seasons sharpening,
the one you got in France years ago, on vacation –
a gift from the vendor who loved that you were
a commercial fisherman and insisted you take it –
is suddenly out-of-reach, beneath the surface, fading,
getting smaller and dimmer as it recedes from you
and all your memories of it, out of your grasp
forever in an instant,

like your friend who tipped over the edge after the struggle
to hang on to the rail while the disease rolled under her,
or the buddy who was brushed away in the morning light
when a car crested the hill and elbowed him into the air
before he knew it – a short fall into deep water.

Pat Dixon and Thor Evenson, 1990.   *Photo by Veronica Kessler*

Chapter Thirty-Four: A Better Taste

After the '91 season, I hunt for a different group to join. I call Rich again, and this time his response is more welcoming. "We lost one of our guys this year. There's a good chance you could replace him." They talk it over and welcome me in. Rich is joined by his close friends, most of whom I know already. Chris Kempf on the *Excalibur*, Lee Todd fishing the *Snug Fifteen,* and Gary Seims on the *Kazor* all have reputations as good fishermen. I learn that Chris's uncle is Gene Kempf, who helpedJim and me on the big day fourteen years ago. Fishing can be a small world.

1988 is the parent year for 1992, and the '88 run and escapement were big, so Fish and Game is predicting a banner season. Most of the global fish pack is depleted, so the price is good too, opening at $1.25 per pound for reds. Deckhands are easy to find, and I hire two guys I know and like for the big days, Rob Ernst and Craig Phillips. Rob is a former student with several years of experience on boats. He's the full-time crew. Craig fished with me in 1990, and only wants to work the big days as a second hand.

I pick up a third crew member when our niece Sharon Roufa, fresh out of college back east, calls looking for a summer adventure. She starts the season living with us and working on the boat. We're excited to get to know her. As a greenhorn, she has a lot to learn, but as a graduate from an Ivy League college, she is reluctant to admit it. She's young, smart and attractive, though she doesn't know her way around boats. Rob is one of the smartest people I know, and graduated from Amhurst. The two of them hit it off instantly, but the dynamics change from a focus on fishing to intellectual discussions. One period I come out of the cabin to find that instead of watching the net for hits, they are engaged in a philosophical discussion about life, and can't tell me if we're getting any fish or not. She also struggles with gender issues of being the only woman on the boat. We butt heads about her duties while fishing when she gets offended that she has to prepare lunch while Rob and I pick fish. I explain that she's less experienced, and speed is necessary when picking, but the exchange frustrates us both. When the run fails to materialize as expected and Fish and Game shuts us down, Veronica offers her a job at the music and book store she manages. Sharon jumps at the chance. Years later she apologizes profusely and we laugh about that summer. But for now, all of us are relieved.

Hiring both Rob and Craig is one of the best decisions I make in my entire career. The two of them are fish-picking machines, and I trust them on deck completely. I pay more attention than ever to the chatter on the radios and watching other boats as they head off on fish calls. This arrangement puts us on more fish than I've ever caught before. I am high boat at the cannery three different periods. After four periods of great opening sets and full fish holds, I miss the fish completely at the beginning of the next period. Craig and Rob give each other a concerned look when I say, "Nothing here. Pick it up. We're gonna move southwest a bit." There's a call on the radio that sounds as promising as anything I've heard, and it's just ten minutes from us. When we make the next set, the gear lights up with hits.

"NOW we're talkin'!" I yell at the guys from the bridge. Bunches are hitting all up and down the net. "That's more like it!" Rob and Craig smile at each other in the stern and nod, then run at me, climbing the ladder to the bridge. "What the fuck are you doing?" I yell. They laugh and open the cooler where they've put a six-pack of Michelob for the occasion.

"We knew you could do it! Five periods in a row!" They open the beers and raise them at me. "Here's to our skipper!"

I laugh and reach in the cooler to join them in celebration. It's 7:30 am, but the beer, like the fishing, tastes clear and bright.

Danny was right.

Rob Ernst and Craig Phillips on the Veronika K, 1992.

Waiting to Deliver

On the good day
when boats return home
low in the water, holds full,
nets wrapped around salmon
rolled on the reel,

after picking half the net,
and laying it back out
while the fish keep hitting,
then running to the other end
and doing it again, all day long–

no time for breaks, a sandwich
or even water, your face, beard
and glasses streaked black by gurry,
dotted white with scales, back
aching, fingers and wrists sore,

you find energy reserves –
threads of adrenaline buried deep
sustain you 'til you've made the run home
and toss a line to the boat you tie behind,
the last of a dozen hanging off the port stern,

fifteen feet from a matching group
tied to the starboard side of the tender
taking fish anchored in the middle
of the river. This day of donkeywork,
this day of absolution isn't over,

won't be for hours. At the back
of the queue, you know you'll be here
past dinner, past dark, maybe past dawn.
You'll eat a baked potato and a red salmon
garnished with lemon, onion and butter

less than two hours from the time
you plucked it alive from the sea.
You'll wash it down with a cold beer
from the cooler, watch the sunset
and think how this is the best,

most complete life you can imagine.
Salt air cools as shadows lengthen
and the water changes from blue to black.
You trade bunk time with your deckhand
and fall asleep before your head

hits the pillow. The smack of a boathook
on the bow wakes you both as the next
boat in line cuts you all loose to go deliver
and those of you still tethered together
like a serpent in the glare of arc lights

work to move up– fighting the current,
pulled and yanked off-course by boats
fore and aft, bumping throttles forward,
neutral, reverse, trying not to ram the one
ahead of you, hoping the one behind you

does the same. Your deckhand fends off
as you swing too close to the vessels sleeping
to starboard, until the lead boat tosses
a line around the tender's cleat again
and you all slide back in the current like a sigh.

Engine after engine goes silent, lines creak
around the cleats as they stretch taut.
Your crew slips into the bunk while you
settle back in the skipper's chair,
light a smoke and sip a cold cup of coffee.

You're still waiting. Waiting to deliver.

Waiting in line to deliver fish to the tender, Kenai River, 1982.

Chapter Thirty-Five: The Connection
~ for Kessler

The season is winding up, and as my deckhand, I look to you for help.

"Tomorrow's the first big day," I remark as we head out to the net rack. "We've gotta get this gear on and go for groceries. I want to leave the river tonight."

Your face falls, but I haven't noticed.

"I'm not feeling so good," you answer, and I see your scowl. I'm in my skipper mentality, what your mother calls my 'jerk mode', so I'm quick to assume the worst: I think you just don't want to work. After all, you're 13 and though you like making money, you'd rather play video games than help out. It's just my first wrong assumption of the day.

By the time I chew on that for a while, I'm angry at you. We work the gear in silence. I stew over what to do. I need the help, but I don't need the distraction of an attitude. You committed to working for me for the season, and I want to teach you to live up to your commitments. Isn't that what being a dad is all about?

I'm even more upset, and we haven't spoken a word. You go through the motions, but the tension between us is thick. We'll argue this out later, after the nets are on the boat. We drive to the cannery in a thick cloud of dust and silence.

Home, hours later, after dinner, I'm starting to pack up. "Got your gear together?" I ask, knowing you haven't.

"I don't feel good," you answer from your bed. "My stomach hurts and I've got a headache."

"Look," I say, walking into your room, "I need your help tomorrow. I'm sorry you feel bad, but you promised me you'd come, and we need to get going. We have to get out of the river before the tide's too low. You can sleep on the boat."

"I don't think I can do it, Dad!" Your voice rises as you start getting upset. "Can't you just go without me?"

"No," I answer, my voice getting louder, too. "I need you tomorrow. I'm counting on you." I walk out of your room and down the hall toward mine. "It's gonna be a big day, and we really need a third hand to pitch the fish, and that's you. Come on. We don't have time to argue!"

"No, Dad!" you yell back at me, coming out into the hall. "I can't go! I don't <u>feel</u> good!" You run back into your room and slam the door.

"What the hell? I mutter under my breath. "I don't have time for this." Your Mom, hearing the loud voices, comes down the stairs. "What is wrong with him?" I start with her, "Is he...?"

"Hold on a minute," she says in a soft voice. "He knows how big a day it is tomorrow. Something else is going on." She heads toward your room.

"Wait," I say. "Let me." I walk into your room and see your body under the covers, facing the wall, lights off, shades drawn. "Hey," I say, trying to sound calm. "What's really going on? Why don't you want to go?"

"I TOLD YOU! I DON'T <u>FEEL</u> GOOD!" You pull the covers tighter. "LEAVE ME ALONE!"

Angry all over again, I yell back, proving I can yell louder, "HEY! Just get dressed and let's go! Stop this ACT! Get out of bed NOW! Come ON!"

I raise my arms in exasperation as I march out of your room and down the hall again. Veronica just stares at me as I stomp by. She disappears into your room.

I'm angry, embarrassed, confused. I throw my clothes into my day bag like they were trash. I can't BELIEVE this. Not now, not TODAY. I shake my head. Tomorrow is forecasted to be big, and could make the difference in how we do for the season. It's too late to get anyone else, and I need the help! Why are you doing this?

I hear voices coming out into the hall. I step into the doorway to see you, tears running down your cheeks standing in front of your mother. She puts a hand on your shoulder, "Go on. Tell him. It's ok."

"Dad," you say, with a look that goes right to my core, "I don't want to go. I don't want to do it." You stop for a breath and look down. "I just can't stand all the killing."

...and I am no longer in the hallway with you. I am on the back deck of the first boat I fished on, the North Sea. Fishing my first season as a crew, no longer a 48-year-old skipper with two children, but 27 and as green as can be, I am watching hundreds of salmon come over the stern, and I am stunned at all the death. Some of the fish come aboard already dead; most of them will die soon; some struggle, some accept it, some are puzzled. Some actually look like they know what's happening and are resigned to their fate. If fish are like people, I think, then it's in this: they die in as many ways as we. But the part that's hardest to accept is that I am partly responsible for their deaths. Confronted with this terrible sense of guilt and shame, I come closer to quitting fishing forever on this day than on any other for the next twenty years.

My anger and frustration melt like spring ice. "I understand." I say softly, because suddenly I do. "I understand completely." We hug and talk. I tell you of that day, how I had a hard time with the killing too. I explain the nature of it, how I came to understand I was harvesting a source of healthy food just as the fish were at the end of their lives anyway. You listen. We arrive at a compromise.

"So you'll help with boat work when we get back to the dock?"

You nod and look very serious. "Yes. That'd be way better."

"It's a deal. See you tomorrow."

I lean over and give you a hug goodnight. Standing at the

foot of your bed, arms folded, your mother smiles.

Kessler steering the Veronika K, 1993.   Photo by Veronica Kessler.

Chapter Thirty-Six: 911 or Greenpeace?

Tired of fishing and needing a break for a summer, in 1993 I strike a deal with Danny Miller. He agrees to fish the *Veronika K* while I take a summer off. It's been a rough year at school, and the forecast is for a slow year fish-wise. Even so, Danny has been a deckhand far longer than I've been a fisherman, and I am comfortable and confident that he'll do well. We agree to pay expenses first, including crew share for his son Dusty, then split the profits down the middle. I help with the prep work on the boat, but don't need to show them both the ropes. Danny has been fishing with Tommy on the *Denali*, a sister ship to mine, so he knows how the boat behaves. We install the electronics together, and as they load the gear, I begin to feel like a fifth wheel, so I roam the cannery with my camera, taking portraits of fishermen and cannery workers. I'm in heaven. No pressure, and someone to do the work while I get to photograph the people and scenes I have always wanted to shoot, but never could while I was getting the boat ready. Before long I have guys like Emery and Ray posing for me. The permit card arrives in the mail a day before Danny and Dusty have the boat ready to go into the water.

I snap a shot of father and son standing proudly in front of the boat as it sits in the sling of the Travelift right before we launch, and we all climb aboard. Little Mike fires up the diesel on the Travelift, and puts it in gear. As we creep out above the river, we scramble to be sure everything is ready. I put my camera on the table in the cabin, far from the edge so it's safe if we bounce at all. We loop lines through the stern and bow cleats to tie to the dock. We tie off buoys but keep them on board so they don't interfere with the launch. We pull the floorboards in the cabin that cover the engine so we can check it once it's started. We double-check the seacock valve to be sure it's open so we'll have cold seawater pumped into the heat exchanger that cools the engine. We open the lazarette hatch in the stern and place a flashlight nearby so we can check the compartment for leaks around the rudder shaft. I yell at Mike over the engine noise, "When we hit the water, hold us in the sling until we check her and start her up!" He nods. It's a drill he knows well, having launched hundreds of boats. The boat sways forward and aft as we stop at the end of the launch. Mike pulls a lever and the Travelift belches black smoke. The boat begins to lower and lurches to starboard. I look up at Mike and spread my arms, right one lower than the left. Mike sees the signal and adjusts the controls to even us out. The Travelift's hydraulic motor whines higher and we descend faster.

Dusty and Danny Miller in front of the Veronika K, 1993.

232

The tide is running out, and once we touch the water the current grabs us. Danny and Dusty fend us off as we push against the pilings of the fuel dock. I slip into the cabin and turn the key. The engine roars to life. I grab another flashlight, drop onto a piece of plywood we have in the engine room bilge to stand upon, and start checking the engine for leaks around the fittings and hoses. Danny and Dusty are doing the same in the stern. "Good back here!" Danny calls. Everything looks good around the engine, so I climb out and go on deck. Mike is watching our dance intently. I climb the ladder to the bridge. Closer to him now, I give him a thumbs-up and yell, "Looks good!" He smiles and tips his hat.

"Good sailing!" A push of another lever, and the straps lower more, releasing us. I feel the boat float free of its cradle, and I bump the engine into reverse. Danny and Dusty fend us off as we slide backwards into the river. We swing around the last piling as the current grabs us, and I put her into reverse and back into the river. Once clear of the pilings, I shift to forward and idle into the current. Danny comes up to the bridge with me, and I suggest he take her to the dock. He's got over twenty years on the inlet, and knows boats better than most skippers. He takes over and I help Dusty tie off.

Once we're secure, the three of us stand in the stern and discuss the workings of the reel. Dusty has never been on a gillnetter before, so Danny and I start by explaining boat safety to him. "Never hurry to the point of recklessness," I say. "You can hurry if a situation requires it, but the faster you go, the more you can get into trouble. Take the time to check things out before you leap." Danny agrees, and we begin our explanation of the hydraulic reel and treadle controls. Danny is bent over showing Dusty a fitting he'll need to grease, when the bow of the *Pintail*, a company tender that Don and Tim have bought and now run, slides into view from around the dock as they motor upriver. Don is at the wheel, and I immediately see the light is perfect for a portrait of him, golden on his face. *If I can get my camera in time*, I think, *this'll be a great shot!* Forgetting everything I just told Dusty, I leap onto the hatch covers and bolt into the cabin as fast as I can. Danny and Dusty look up at me, wondering what just happened. I race down the steps into the cabin and before I can stop myself, realize I've made a horrible mistake: the floorboards are off, exposing the still-running engine! With nowhere to go, I try not to step on the engine, and instead launch into and across the open space I was standing in just minutes ago. My left shin slams against the 3/4-inch plywood edge of the floor on the other side, and I scrape it to the bone as I fall into the compartment. I land on both feet on the plywood at the bottom, inches away from four fan belts running at 600 RPM's. My leg feels like it's on fire, and I can't put weight on it at all. "Jesus!" I yell. "Danny!" I try to hoist myself out of the compartment, but the pain is too great. Danny pokes his head into the cabin.

"What are you doing?" he asks, smiling.

"I fell in here - slammed into that edge!" I yell. "I think I broke my leg! Turn off the engine!" Danny hurries to the dash and turns off the key. I am feeling weak with pain. "Fuck, man," I say, "Just as we were talking to Dusty about safety! Case in point. Don't race around."

Danny shakes his head. "What were you doing, anyway?"

I look up and see the Pintail go past our window. "Trying to get my camera so I could take Don's picture." I feel like an idiot. "I need to get out of here."

"Wait a second," Danny says, and puts two floorboards back in place so I have somewhere to pull myself. I lift myself out and slide back on them while Danny sends Dusty for help. My leg screams as I lift it out of the engine compartment. Danny puts the last floorboard in place. I lay back and rest the bad leg on the good one as he gets blankets and pillows to stabilize it and make me comfortable. By the time help starts to arrive,

Danny has cut away my bloody jeans and taken off my boot.
All I can think of while I wait is the throbbing. Ray, the
cannery superintendent, comes in and shakes his head at me.

"What did you do, Pat?" I flush with embarrassment. Ray is
like an uncle.

"Something pretty stupid, Ray. And I didn't even get the
photo."

He nods in his usual, calm way. "Don't worry, Jeannie is
calling Veronica, and we have an ambulance on its way..." he
turns to Danny "...though I don't relish the idea of getting him up
that ladder."

Danny looks out the door with a grim expression. The
ladder/gangplank to the dock is aluminum, with wheels on the
bottom so it can travel along the float as the tide rises and falls.
It's low tide, and the ladder, all 30 feet of it, is nearly straight
up. We hear a siren in the distance, getting closer.

I am a big man, 6-foot-4, and weigh in at 235 pounds.
Carrying me off a boat and across a dock when everything is
level would be bad enough. Once the paramedics get me
strapped to a backboard, they have to lift me and pass me out of
the cabin door just to get me outside, no easy task. By now there
are easily a dozen people – fishermen, crew, paramedics and
cannery personnel all lending a hand however they can. My leg
is immobilized in an air cast, and I am strapped snugly,
including my arms, to the board in three places. I feel helpless in
a very surreal way as I am passed off the boat down to the float.
I watch the men lifting me look at the gangplank (a ramp with
handrails and wheels at the bottom so it can raise and lower as
the tide lifts the float) with concern. A fall from up there could
severely injure if not kill the victim, and the gangplank is too
narrow for anyone to be on it next to me. The people carrying
me, at least six of them, will have to go up on the outside of the
rail. With another person at my head and one at my feet,
hopefully we all can make it without mishap.

"We'll have to have someone up top to pass him to," says Ray. "We can't climb over the safety rail at the top while holding him." A few of the men go up top. "Ok," says one of the paramedics, "Everyone ready? Let's go!"

I am jostled and pulled, accompanied by the grunts and sounds of straining men as we head up the ladder. The ladder bounces and sways under the strain, and the men I can see are holding onto the backboard's handles with one hand while hanging on for dear life to the aluminum pipe handrail with the other. It is slow going. About two-thirds of the way up, almost 20 feet above the water, the backboard lets out a sickening loud *crack!* Everyone freezes. For a moment we all look at each other, then someone starts to laugh. Instantly everyone is tryingto stifle a laugh while hanging on. A vision of falling, face-first,strapped to a backboard, into the Kenai River flashes through my mind. "If you fuckers drop me," I say to snickers all around,"I will come back from the dead and haunt you all."

"Let's get it together, people," says the lead paramedic with a smile. "We *all* want to live through this." They sober up and hoist me the rest of the way up. I get handed to the men waiting on the dock, and they hoist me, backboard and all, onto a gurney waiting at the back of the ambulance. As the paramedics unstrap and slide the board out from under me, I thank everyone for the help and ask Danny to take care of my camera. Ray comes over and shakes my hand. "You know Pat," he says with a grin, then looks around to be sure everyone's listening, "When I heard it was you who was hurt, for a second I wasn't sure who to call: 911 or Greenpeace!" I wait for the laughter to die down before I reply, "Fuck you very much, Ray." I smile all the way to the hospital.

The leg isn't broken, but the wound has taken all the skin off my shin so the bone is indeed exposed. I spend most of the summer nursing it and hobbling around the cannery with my cameras. It isn't the relaxing year I expected, but I still get a lot of photography in and spend time with Veronica and the boys.

Dusty and Danny have a decent season and take great care of the boat. At the end of the summer, I'm feeling well enough to ask Don and Tim if they can take me to Snug Harbor on their west side run picking up fish from the setnet sites, then come get me on the next run four days later. I spend the last fishing period of the season over there, staying in the cannery bunkhouse and visiting with the watchman, his wife and their setnet crew between photographing every inch of the place. One of their crew is Linnea Kistler, a former student of mine and the grand-daughter of Joe Fribrock, who started and built the Snug Harbor cannery. Rich and Rob Levenhagen have both told me stories of encountering Joe's ghost there, so when I'm in the fisherman's bunkhouse photographing the hallway and the door I've opened for light swings closed, I don't even raise up from the viewfinder. "Hi Joe," I say to the empty hall as chills caress my back and arms. "I know your grand-daughter, Linnea. I'm just here taking a few pictures. I'll be gone in a few minutes." I wait. Nothing happens, but the chills subside. I look up and tiptoe down the hall and open the door again. Outside it's bright and sunny, and flat calm. Not. A. Breeze. When Don and Tim come get me a few days later, I tell them the story. They just nod. "I've heard about Joe's ghost," Don says.

Chapter Thirty-Seven: Fire on the Boat

Brannon Ames and Dylan on the Veronika K, 1995.

Three of us are picking fish toward the end of a clear, breezy day in 1995. We are fishing the east rip on the flood, just off the mouth of the Kenai River. My deckhand this year is Brannon Ames, a friend and experienced hand who usually spends his summer working at his job for an oil company on the north slope of Alaska. Brannon has a jones for fishing, though, and this year arranged to have most of July off so he can crew for me as he considers buying in. I've used him as a third hand on big days in past seasons, so he knows the boat. He's well-connected to the guys in Frank Mullen's group, a few of whom fish fast 'Bobby Boats', made of aluminum by another mutual fishing friend, Bobby Correia. These boats are easy to spot if you know what to look for, and Brannon has fished with Frank, who owns one, so he's tuned in to them on a level I'm not. Frank's group is made of several good fishermen, so when Brannon notices Bobby Boats all running the same direction, we join the chase. It pays off more than once. We aren't as fast as their boats, but the difference doesn't amount to much if we're five minutes behind them and get on the fish while they're still hitting.

I have my nine-year-old son Dylan on board to help pitch fish when we get busy, and the three of us are in a good mood as the day winds down. Unlike Kessler, Dylan loves fishing. We have a decent catch in the hold, and this close to the river, we'll be one of the first boats to deliver. I hear the group radio crackle as Chris comes on. "Anybody hear from Pat lately? He's been quiet for a while."

The last of the net comes on board. I'm already heading into the cabin while the two of them clear the deck. The wind has blown the cabin door closed, and as I approach it, I see puffs of gray smoke curl out the jamb. "Shit! There's smoke coming out of the door!" I hesitate, unsure of whether or not to open it and feed oxygen to a fire.

"Well, open it!" Brannon shouts. He's right. I have to see what's happening. I grab the handle and pull it open to a rush of smoke billowing out at me. Through the haze I see flames a foot high just below the diesel stove by the doorway. "Fire extinguisher!" I yell and I slam the door closed again. One of the extinguishers is inside the cabin in the fo'c'sle and out of reach. The other hangs behind the door on the outside of the cabin, covered by spare rain gear. I furiously start ripping rain gear off the hooks above the extinguisher and throwing them on deck. "What a stupid fucking place to put the fucking extinguisher!" I swear. The wind catches Brannon's jacket as I toss it behind me, and I see it out of the corner of my eye as it's swept off the boat into the sea.

"Get the boathook!" Brannon yells to Dylan as I continue to curse and dig out the extinguisher. Dylan grabs it from its perch in the stern and he and Brannon fish the jacket out of the water while I douse the flames from the doorway. As soon as I'm sure they're out, I duck into the cabin and grab the microphone to our group radio. "Yeah, this is Pat," I bark. "We've got a fire here. I'm just outside the river mouth a few miles." I take a breath, but the mixture of smoke and toxic emissions from the extinguisher catches in my throat. I can't breathe this for long. "I think I've got it out. I'll let you know."

I drop the microphone and rush back out into fresh air, coughing and gasping for breath. I look up to see the bow of a boat I don't recognize just feet from me. The skipper is on the bridge, looking down at me. His deckhand is next to the cabin, fire extinguisher in hand. "You need another extinguisher?" the skipper asks. "He looks at Dylan in the stern, then back at me. "Or we can take you all if you need to get off."

"I think we got it," I cough at him. "Would you mind standing by until I'm sure?"

"Absolutely," he says. "We'll be right here."

"Thanks," I say. I look at Brannon. Smoke is still billowing out the door. "We need to get the windows open so the smoke clears out. It's hard to breathe in there. Take a deep breath. You do starboard, I'll do port." I look at Dylan. "You okay?" He nods at me with a question in his eyes. "We'll be all right. Stay in the stern for now."

Brannon and I both inhale deeply and dash into the cabin. The smoke stings our eyes, but we get the windows open and check the stove for more flames. The teak cabinet that was burning is still smoking, but the fire seems to be out for now. Brannon pours coffee over the smoldering wood. I step back out on deck and wave at my good Samaritan. "I think we're good now. We're heading in. Thanks a lot for being here." He waves back and wishes me good luck, then turns his boat and peels away. There's still an hour before closing. I notice two other boats standing by on the other side start to move off as well.

Cook Inlet doesn't have a Coast Guard presence. The nearest station is in Kodiak, 250 miles away. For the most part, medical emergencies being the exception, the drift fleet is on its own. Our unspoken creed is to stop what we're doing and help a boat in distress. It's true for minor breakdowns as well. If someone knows you and sees you dead in the water, they'll sometimes stop to assist if they can. If you're lucky, your fishing group will give you a spare part or a tow at the end of the period. But if it's a serious affair like a fire, everyone stops to help, whether they know you or not. Because, after all, you could be the guy needing help tomorrow.

What we don't know as we run in is that the fire was the result of leaving the small, quiet stove fan on for three days. The fan is used to push diesel smoke out the stove stack on days when the wind tries to blow it back into the cabin. The wire from the fan to the circuit breaker wasn't installed correctly when the stove was first put in, so when it overheated, the breaker didn't blow. Instead, the wire got so hot that it melted away all the insulation. When it melted off near the fuel hose, the hot wire burnt a hole in the hose, then ignited the diesel dripping onto the teak cabinet below the stove.

What we also don't know is that the other end of the wire melted a pinhole in the hard plastic hose holding the oil that powers our controls. Called hynautics, the throttle and controls are powered by fluid pressure in a closed system. When the boat is put in gear, fluid pushes through the hose and moves a control arm on the engine to forward. When taken out of gear, the fluid moves the opposite way, putting the engine in neutral. With a hole in the system, when I put the boat in gear to head to the river, a small amount of oil leaks out. Once in the river, navigating to the dock from the bridge, I slow the boat down and put her in neutral, causing more fluid to escape. I notice the controls are sluggish, but I don't know why. I'm trying to dock alongside the *Akatez*, run by a guy I only know as Doc, who is out on deck talking with his deckhand and drinking from a coffee cup. "Hey Doc!" I yell over the engine. "I've got a problem! I'm losing my controls here!" He sees me heading in a little too fast, and drops his cup.

When single-propellor boats maneuver to a dock in a river, an experienced skipper will use the current to help the vessel slide into a space by putting the engine into neutral until the boat is barely moving forward while steering at an angle into the current so the river pushes the vessel sideways. If the boat is going too slow, they will put the engine into forward for a brief moment to hold against the current so they don't turn too far and get swept away. I am in the middle of this maneuver when my controls stop responding. I'm helpless to do anything. Unless Doc and my crew can stop me, I'll be out of control in a matter of seconds, with a line of boats twenty feet behind me.

What Doc does is difficult at best, made even more so without adequate warning. "Rig up a spring line!" he yells to his deckhand, and moves alongside his cabin to fend us off as we come in hard against his boat. He lifts a buoy bumper between us at the last second. We bounce harmlessly off the buoy and swing alongside the *Akatez* where his crew loops a bight on our midship cleat with the line he's already wrapped around the *Akatez's*. We slide to a stop so smoothly it looks like we planned it.

"Jesus Doc," I breathe, "That saved our ass. Thank you."

"Yeah," he says, picking up his cup. "Occasionally you win one."

Two hours later the fish hold is empty and a cannery power skiff takes us to the Travelift to get hauled out. The beach gang puts the *Veronika K* on barrels near the launch, and Bill Wegner, the Port Engineer, meets us there with his toolbox. Bill is a hard worker with a ton of boat knowledge and a ready wit. We've had a few drinks together at preseason gatherings around the yard, and I already like him a lot.

"A fire?" he says by way of greeting. "What the fuck, Pat?"

"That's my line," I shoot back. "I have no idea what happened."

"Well let's get you put back together so you can go fishing tomorrow," he smiles. "You know you're open, right?"

I didn't. It's already almost 9:00 pm. I ask Brannon to take Dylan back to the house and let Veronica know I might not be home tonight. He agrees to meet me at 6:00 am back here and they take off. I climb the ladder and join Bill in the cabin. "Here's your problem," he says. "Someone didn't wire this right." He shows me the bare wire coming off the stove fan, melted red insulation hardened to it in fat drips. "That's what started your fire. Look here. The diesel feeder hose is burnt through. The hot wire probably ignited the fuel once it started leaking."

"Shit. I have some spare hose under the bunk. I'll replace that. What about the controls? Any idea what happened there?"

"Not yet. I'll look around while you find that hose."

By the time I come out of the fo'c'sle with the hose, Bill has discovered a bigger problem. The overheated wire was threaded up a PVC tube filled with other wires, and melted them all together. "There's no integrity between any of them. We're going to have to cut and splice them all."

"Jesus. We're going to be here all night." I say, suddenly feeling weary.

"I am," Bill says. "Not you. Replace that hose for me, then head home and get some sleep. I'll fix this up and have the boat waiting in the sling by six. Just wake up some of the beach gang and they'll drop you in the river."

243

Half an hour later the hose is changed. I thank Bill and head out. As I climb down the ladder, I make a mental note to find out what his favorite whiskey is so I can buy him a bottle. It's almost midnight, and I've been up since 2:00 am. I am fried. I'm looking forward to a shower and a few hours in my own bed curled next to Veronica's warm body.

The Veronika K in the sling, 1995.

As I turn to walk to my truck, two women approach me on the boardwalk. I know one of them. She's cute in a rough, edgy way, a deckhand for one of the fishermen in Thor's group. I don't know the other one. They're both a bit wobbly, laughing and passing a bottle back and forth. "Hi Pat!" the one I know smiles at me, tossing her long dark hair over her shoulder. Want a drink?"

"I could use one, that's for sure." I take the bottle and swallow a solid gulp of tequila. The warmth fills my chest. I pass the bottle back to her. "Thanks. I needed that."

She hands the bottle to her friend, grabs my arm and pulls me aside, under the bow of the *Veronika K.* "I wanna talk to you a sec," she says as she fumbles with a pack of cigarettes. She lights one up and gives me a look. "I really wanna fuck you, Pat."

My mind short-circuits. I'm sure my jaw drops open. In a classic example of doing the wrong thing, I laugh and shake my head. "What?" She doesn't get it, and I realize my mistake. "I'm sorry. I don't mean to laugh. We had a boat fire today, and to tell you the truth, I just want to go home and get some sleep."

She doesn't react. Maybe she's too drunk to register that I just laughed at her. "Some other time, maybe," is all she says as she staggers back to her friend and grabs the bottle. I watch them weave down the boardwalk, then head for my truck thanking the Fish Gods I have a wife to go home to.

Chapter Thirty-Eight: Disillusion

The last few years of my fishing career are a mixed bag. I enjoy the group I'm in, and on Thor's deckhand recommendation of "If you don't hire him, I will," I pick up a crew in '96 who turns out to be one of the very best: Rob Seitz. He's the grandson of Larry Lancashire, the homesteader who built 'Larry's Club' bar in Kenai, and who fished for years for Columbia Wards. Rob's brother James joins our group, fishing their Grandpa's old boat, the *Snug Two*. I start tying off with them to a buoy upriver from the cannery rather than getting pinned in at the dock if I have to move the boat. Rob has years of experience, fishing knowledge, and we both appreciate each other's juvenile humor. He's an avid reader, smart and wicked witty. We quickly form a friendship that extends beyond fishing. Veronica and I have Rob and his wife Tiffani over for barbecues several times that season and the next. Unlike so many couples we know, we enjoy them both. They have two sons almost the same age as our boys, and we take them out to help pick on slow days.

Like Don and Dean used to do, Rob occasionally gets me in trouble. We're fishing near the line in the corridor one very slow day, when I decide to try something different. There aren't many boats in our immediate area, and those that are there are all nosed up to the line, towing lightly against the current pushing them back. I find an open spot and set north-and-south, down the line instead of perpendicular to it. As we're laying out the last shackle, a new boat starts setting toward us from our port side. He's obviously in a hurry, trying to beat us to the spot. I goose the engine a little and we win the race at the last moment. Rob lets the last of the net peel off the reel and turns to look as the guy in the other boat stops setting because we're in the way. The other skipper is on his bridge yelling at us. "Hey! That's MY spot! You can't set there! You asshole!"

"I didn't see your name here," I yell back at him, but he's not having it. "You saw me coming!" he yells. "Godammit!"

I turn to Rob and raise my hands, palms up, signaling my *What the fuck?* moment to him nonverbally. He looks at me and starts to chuckle. Then he smiles his biggest smile at the other skipper and flips him off.

The guy comes completely unglued. He's only twenty feet from us, so I can see the veins in his neck pop out as his face turns beet red. He screams and spits curses at us, threatens to come find me on land and kick my ass, threatens to find me on the Inlet and cork ME off. I'm towing a little, so we're moving past him, but when he takes a breath, all I can think of to say is, "Dude. You're gonna give yourself a stroke. Ease up, man. There aren't many fish here anyway."

He stops for a split-second, then launches into his rant all over again. Before I turn away, I see his deckhand, a young kid, watching us from his back deck with a pained expression on his face. I feel bad for the day he's going to have. In my stern, Rob is still laughing.

"Thanks a lot, asshole," I tell him with a smile.

"Seemed like the thing to do," he grins back.

Rob and Pat on Rob's boat, the South Bay, 2015. Photo by VK.

In the 90's fishing becomes more contentious, both between the skippers on the Inlet and politically, between user groups. As our time and areas become more and more restricted by Fish and Game, incidents like the one with the screaming skipper become common. Guys are more in debt as the fleet upgrades and modernizes, so each fish caught becomes more important. Sometimes it can get downright ugly. Unfortunately, I have my moments too.

Stuck in the corridor again, Rich puts out a fish call on a flat calm sunny day. Rob and Dylan are on board, and when we make the run to Rich, Dylan falls asleep at the galley table. We start to set out just north enough of Rich to have room to catch any fish scooting across the line. Just as we begin, a tin boat roars by, setting its gear at full speed south of us not 50 feet away from our net, taking away any chance we have of catching fish. Now it's my turn to be pissed. We only have a half-shackle in the water, so I put the boat in neutral and yell to Rob, "Pick it up!"

He looks over his shoulder at me. "Pick it up?"

"Yep. We're going to set on the other side of that prick."

Rob rolls the net back on and we move to the other side of the interloper's net, maybe 20 feet from his gear. "Throw it out!"

"You sure?"

"Oh, yeah, I'm sure." All I can think about is teaching this guy a lesson.

We take our time, lacing him cork-for-cork, close enough that any fish heading his way will hit our net first. By the time our boats get close, he's screaming at me. "What the actual fuck?" he yells.

I turn and face him. "Remember me?"

"What?"

"I said, do you remember me?" He looks at me like I've lost my mind, and he's mostly right. "I'm the same guy you just

248

did this to five minutes ago." I lean toward him. "How's it fucking feel?"

He starts yelling and swearing again. I ignore him and start towing the boat away. When I glance back at Rob, I see Dylan staring at me from the hatch covers. He's ten years old. I'm immediately embarrassed by my actions.

There's a lot of stress surrounding fishing that contributes to my making bad, even aggressive decisions on the water. When I started fishing, it seemed the drifters and setnetters bickered about fishing time, but the Kenai River had yet to be discovered by sports fishermen. When the oil pipeline was built in the 1970's, Alaska and its politics changed drastically with the influx of thousands of oil workers and their families from Texas and Oklahoma. Republicans took control of state politics, and Anchorage grew like a gold-rush boom town, only with loads of sportsmen – hunters and fishers with money to burn instead of broke gold-panners or homesteaders living on a shoestring.

Unlike most of the other commercial fisheries in Alaska, the Kenai run is accessible by road. When the Anchorage residents discovered red salmon running up the Kenai River by the millions each summer, hundreds of sports fishermen began making the three-hour drive to get in on the action. They were quick to notice that when the commercial fishermen's nets were in the water, the fishing would dry up in the river. They couldn't catch their limits, and they began taking political action. They formed sport fishing associations that lobbied the state legislature for more time; they campaigned for representatives partial to their cause at local and state levels; they wrote opinion letters to the local newspapers in Anchorage and Kenai; and they pumped money into publicly attacking the commercial fishermen for making a living. By 1996 the governor is in their pocket and he stacks the Alaska Board of Fish with members favoring sports issues. For the first time during the middle of a run, the fleet and beach fishermen are shut down notbecause of biology or escapement concerns, but because the governor requests it due to pressure from the sports fishing lobby. Because of politics.

We are furious. I write letters to the Board of Fish. UCIDA, the United Cook Inlet Drift Association, the region's fisherman's union, organizes a protest at the local Fish and Game office. We even stamp our money with red ink stamps proclaiming 'Commercial Fishing Dollar'. All to no avail. We are losing this battle and we know it. Added to this, the legislature passes a law that requires Fish and Game to prioritize a new 'personal use' dipnet fishery at the mouth of the Kenai River. Hundreds, then thousands of people descend upon the peninsula to harvest six red salmon per person per day. It isn't long before the fishery is out of control, with dipnetters taking more than their limits, storing their fish in coolers and freezers in their RV's and selling them once they return to Anchorage or out-of-state. Enforcement of the limits is negligible, and one more piece of the Cook Inlet pie is cut away from the commercial fishery.

A lot of us feel the way one fisherman at the dock puts it during mug-up. "Hell, if they're getting away with this shit, we've already lost." It's like watching our fishery die in slow motion. No wonder we're more willing to bark at our fellow fishermen.

Veronica and I are already thinking of leaving Alaska. Teaching has taken its toll on me, and I'm looking at retiring as soon as I'm eligible. The kids are adolescents now, and Kessler is obviously unhappy here. He's got his sights set anywhere but in a small, conservative-minded town like Kenai, and we can't blame him. Our politics are far left of the mainstream on the peninsula, and we feel it every time we support a sparsely-attended fundraiser for Planned Parenthood. We attend a meeting for the local Democratic Party to support a friend running for the state legislature, and twenty people show up. She wins, but we feel – and are – outnumbered. Veronica's mantra each September becomes, "I don't think I can take another winter here." The problem is that, just as we knew we wanted to come to Kenai all those years ago, we don't have a clue where to go from here.

Derelict skiff on the beach, Halibut Cove, Alaska.

Fat City in Four Directions
(for Jeannie Ouren)

North

We thought we'd all be highliners:
  Each trip out we had visions of plugging the boat.
  We would sink the gear, and tie floats to the cork line
  so we could get the net back on board
  after it filled with sockeye.
  We'd call a tender to off-load us
  while fresh flurries of hits frothed the water's surface.
  We'd roundhaul the final set, deck loaded and the boat so low
  we'd toss the last of the catch into the cabin
  or put 'em in net bags and drag 'em to the bow
  to balance the load.
  We'd fly a broom from the rigging as we came in the river.

  We were on course to Fat City.

252

South

On the way, we bucked into stiff winds and big tides.
    We ran over each other's gear in the glare of the sun
    on steel gray waves,
    and ended up dead in the water with web in the wheel.
    Engine alarms blared as we blew alternators
    and threw fan belts.
    We spent frantic hours jerry-rigging spare parts
    so we could stay on the grounds.
    We swore at our misfortune as reports of big catches
    and fresh hits spat frustration out of tinny deck speakers;
    and we turned off the radio before it described
    any more fish calls we couldn't get to.

We stood adrift in the stern, watching
    even as the best catches of the season moved into the river.
    The rip sucked us into the sticks or the kelp,
    and a faulty solenoid or water in the fuel had us catching a line
    from the tender that would tow us home empty.

East

Some days we'd just flat-out not find 'em:
    move east when they showed on the west side
    stop running a mile short of where they'd pop up,
    or set a net length too far from the rip.
    Worse, they wouldn't be there at all:
    we'd spend the day scratch fishing
    while radio fish filled imaginary nets
    and the hits weren't the bunches we expected,
    just singles, or only a surface show.

The talk would turn to escapement policies of Fish and Game
    and how the biologists, politicians and guides were killing us.
    The only fish on board were headed for the freezer at home.

253

West

Some of us
   still weather low prices and fewer fish:
   In the cold morning dawn silhouettes of boats
   still glide past closed canneries and derelict docks.
   On board, skippers still hold a coffee mug in one hand
   and steer the boat down a darkened river with the other.
   Deckhands still coil lines in the stern and scan
   the sea for jumpers.

But some of us put the boat on barrels and sold the permit.
   Cleaned out our lockers, packed the trailers
   and pulled away in a cloud of dust.
   No more waves to lift us.
   Instead, we steer through the changing currents
   of foreign seas: oceans of commerce and business.
   We ride the ebb and swell of the job market,
   negotiating interviews like we used to quarter the boat
   through heavy weather.
   We still run hard, looking for jumpers.

We still search for Fat City.

Chapter Thirty-Nine: Dylan's in the Bunk

The 1997 season is a battle: either no fish but lots of fishing time, or lots of fish and we are ordered by Fish and Game to stay at the dock. It's a common frustration in the fishing world. If Murphy were a fisherman, this is how he'd write it up. This, and the fact that any time we're put inside a line along the east beach, the fish are always outside it.

But this day has nothing to do with that. 6:00 am has us running hard out of the mouth of the river, with Rob making coffee on the stove while I plow through a three-foot chop looking to get to Humpy Point before opening, some 10 miles south. Dylan is asleep in the bunk, his usual pattern after we get settled on the boat. It could be a form of seasickness, but I think his insatiable desire for sleep when he's aboard is more about the drone of the engine and the rocking motion of the boat in the waves. The fact that we get up to go at around 2:00 or 3:00 am might have a little something to do with it. In any case, once he goes to the bunk, he is a bear to wake up again, and unless we catch a good jag of fish today, I imagine he'll be in the sack for most of it.

The seas settle down a bit after we clear the river mouth, and I open her up. The *Veronika K's* 3208 Caterpillar engine hums nicely, and once she's up on step, we skim the top of the waves, smacking each one as we go by. It's a bit bumpier this way, but the tide is flooding, and I want to have the gear in the water at opening, an hour from now. Rob hands me a cup of coffee, and settles in at the table with yesterday's newspaper. I take a sip and wrap a hand around the warm cup. The end of the season is in the morning air, and the cool humidity at sea level has chilled me more than I realize. There's a steady breeze from the south, and though it doesn't feel menacing, it feels familiar. It feels like fall.

A few boats are running south with us, dark spots on a gray sea, and I listen to Rich and Chris talk sleepily on the radio about where they're headed, the weather, and the price of fish. I'm reaching for the microphone to add my two cents when the background roar of the engine is pierced by a high-pitched alarm. Rob looks up, startled from his paper. I check the gauges and the water temperature is in the red. "We're overheating!" I yell over the alarm and engine. "I'm shutting her down!" I back the throttle off, put the engine in neutral and turn the key. The engine suddenly quiets, but the alarm continues to blare, filling the cabin with an ear-splitting scream. I unscrew the fuse cover in the dash and the alarm stops. The silence is deafening.

Rob and I blink at each other for a moment, trying to sort out what to do. I glance at Dylan in the bunk, and he hasn't moved. Slept through it all. I shake my head. "Unbelievable," I say to Rob who nods his agreement. "I better call someone and let them know what we're up to here."

"I'll take a look below," Rob bends down to pull back the carpeting covering the floorboards. "Probably blew a fan belt."

I pick up the microphone and look at our GPS coordinates. We are three miles from the river mouth, and I watch the last of the boats leaving the river steam by us as we finally stop our forward momentum. The wind and current swing us around in the trough. It's not too lumpy or dangerous, but the boat is rolling steadily as I finish letting our group know our location and that we're broken down. For safety's sake I call the cannery on the VHF and let them know our predicament as well. They want to know if we need a skiff sent out to tie alongside and tow us back in, but I don't want to put anyone through that ride. The river mouth is rolling with the incoming tide, and an open skiff could get in trouble there in a hurry. I decline the offer. "We should be okay," I say, looking at Rob holding up pieces of shredded rubber. "It's just a blown fan belt."

The fan belt in question, however, is on the inside of the pulley at the front of the engine. Powering the heat exchange pump, it sits behind belts for the alternator, hydraulics and washdown. In order to replace it, we have to remove three other belts, which means loosening each one, removing it, then replacing all of them in order again. I slip into the fo'c'sle and root around under the bunks until I find the proper replacement. I set it on the table and proceed to hand Rob the wrenches and other tools he needs as he removes the other belts. As I wait, I casually look around and listen to the radio as other boats make the morning set and report what they see. Distracted, I gaze out the starboard window toward the river mouth, then suddenly realize I am looking at waves breaking less than 100 yards from us. The tide and wind have been pushing us toward shore much faster than I realized. "We're getting a little close to shore here," I put on my coat. "I'm going to drop the anchor." Unconcerned, Rob nods and continues his work.

The *Veronika K* is rolling healthily as I step out on deck. The wind is steady at 15 or 20 knots. I can hear the breakers roar while I move alongside the cabin toward the front of the boat. I have a good handrail all the way forward, so I feel relatively safe until I get to the bow, where I have to sit down and slide along the trunk cabin to the anchor. The anchor is lashed to two teak rails with eighth-inch line, and rests on top of 20 feet of chain and 200 feet of 5/8-inch nylon line. The lashing is square-knotted, which I proceed to quickly untie.

The sound of the sea is changing in my ears as I work. Instead of the wind and the slap of the waves against the boat, I notice I'm hearing the swish of foaming waves as they approach from the port side. The roar to starboard is getting louder, but I know I don't have time to look. Nor do I want to. The lashings fall free, and now I have to lift a 44-pound Danforth anchor over the side of a very small, wildly pitching bow without getting tangled up in the line once the anchor is over. I scootch on my butt to the edge of the trunk cabin and lift myself up to heft the anchor onto the port edge of the bow. Squatting to keep my center of gravity low and stable, I wait for the roll of the sea to drop the port side. I let the anchor go, minding my feet as the chain unravels with a clatter. The boat rolls again, and I fall backwards onto the trunk cabin, sitting hard next to the anchor line as it races overboard. As I watch, a loop of the line comes tight with the tension of the anchor plummeting to the bottom and coils around most of the rest of the line. The entire wad slides over the side and into the water. What the disappearing line reveals sends a cold stab of fear through me.

A normal procedure for boats of our size that carry anchors on the bow but don't have winches is to lash the anchor down so it won't go over or fly through the windshield in a rough sea. Still, lashings are known to fail, and a crew that doesn't want to lose an anchor will attach the end of the anchor line to the bow cleat when under way. In port, though, that line is removed from the cleat so a tie-up line can be secured there. It's important to remember to re-attach the anchor line to the bow cleat once you cast off and head to sea again. A crew's job, skipper and deckhand alike, is to remove the tie-up line when casting off and to put the anchor line back on the cleat. It's something Rob and I have done hundreds of times; something we always do; something that is so automatic that we never need to remind each other to do it. Except today. As the mass of rope that is the bulk of my anchor line slides into the sea with a splash, I find myself looking at twenty feet of line left on the boat and a bare bow cleat.

For a split-second, time stretches. The fast-disappearing line slows to a crawl. I hear the first breaker slap against the port side, hear the waves crash on the rocks to starboard, and I think with icy clarity, *Dylan is asleep in the bunk!*

The thought spurs me to action. Suddenly the remaining line is in my hands and I take a figure-eight wrap around the cleat. I have a foot to spare, so I can't tie it off. I pull it tight and hold on. The line tightens, but my grip on it holds it fast to the cleat. The anchor bites on the bottom, and the bow lurches and dives, swinging violently to port. The boat comes around with a

258

deep roll. I use the anchor line like a rodeo rider uses a bull rope to keep my balance. The boat re-aligns itself on the anchor and settles down. I stand there for a moment, and notice foam on the waves around us. I kneel down and push with my foot on the section of line going off the bow to create slack. The bow dips, and I gain enough extra line to tie off to the cleat. I scramble on all fours back to the handrail above the cabin windows, where I hang on and watch for a minute to be sure we aren't going anywhere. The boat bobs lightly on the waves, anchor line stretched tight. We are 20 yards from the rocks. Convinced it's hooked, I make my way back into the cabin as fast as I can. Rob looks up at me. "Everything ok?" he asks.

"It is now," I answer, heart still pounding, legs shaking. I head to the bunks. "Dylan?" I put my hand on his shoulder. "I need you to get up, bud."

Chapter Forty: Selling Out

The thought of how close we came to disaster that day leaves me shaken. Somehow, I deluded myself into thinking that a new boat would reduce the risk to everyone on board, and it does, but the danger of working on the water is still real. Veronica and I have long discussions about whether fishing with family is worth the risk, and I'm leaning hard toward selling out when the unexpected happens.

1997 is my last year teaching. I pull the plug before going fishing in June, with the expectation of living on my retirement and fishing income, her salary managing a bookstore in town, and any income I can generate with my photography during the winter months. I spend part of my summer each year golfing with one of my good friends, Mark Burgener, brother to Michael, my deckhand from 1981. As a retirement gift, I ask Mark and two other close friends and golfers, Marc Berezin and Dave Forbes to come with me before fishing begins on a 'golf-til-you-puke' trip somewhere together. They agree, and we settle on Olympia, Washington as a destination, where Michael now lives with his wife Barbara. We golf for nine straight days, and I fall in love with the area. I'm also very intrigued by The Evergreen State College located there. It has a refreshing, progressive philosophy toward higher education. I've always liked teaching adults, and I've spent several winters teaching classes at the local community college in Kenai. I'd love to teach at Evergreen, or so I think.

By October, I'm developing a retirement routine. I drive the kids to school, head to the gym for an hour, then grab coffee and spend an hour writing at Veronica's Coffee shop (not my wife's) on the bluff overlooking the Inlet and mouth of the Kenai River. In an ironic twist of fate, a letter arrives unexpectedly from Barbara, who has never written me. In the envelope is a short note and a newspaper clipping. The note simply says, 'I never look at the Seattle Times, and I never look at Want Ads. But I found myself gazing at this today.Think of the possibilities.' The clipping is an advertisement tornout of the paper that reads, 'Interim photography instructor wanted for second semester, 1998. Contact The Evergreen State College HR Department,' along with a number to call.

By Thanksgiving I have a new job and we spend the next month selling, packing and loading our lives into a semi-trailer container van parked down the street from our house, the closest they can get it to us with all the snow and ice on our neighborhood roads. On December 31st, 1997, I drive our car to the movers to be loaded into the van. Everything we own is inside the container that will follow us south on a barge. A friend is driving our family, the dogs and our luggage to the airport to start our new lives. As I walk out of the movers into a snowstorm, I hear a croaking behind and above me. I turn to look and see a raven, feathers fluffed against the cold, looking down at me from the peak of the roof. He bobs once and caws again, in a tone that sounds like an accusation. Alaska has become home. *How can I leave?* I shrug. "I know," I say to him. "I know."

The transition to life in Olympia is rocky. We're so focused on getting out of Kenai, we never consider how deep our roots there go. I love teaching at Evergreen, but dislike the politics and unspoken agendas of academia. One of my teaching colleagues actively sabotages my efforts, and we have a confrontation over it that gets ugly when she sees I have three pages of documented incidents of her duplicities. The stress of it all has me depressed and ready to head north again.

Dylan struggles with being the 'new kid' in school, missing the friends he grew up with and his old life in Alaska. Veronica has difficulty finding a job for the first few months, and the two of us bicker constantly. When our fights escalate, I end up leaving and drive around, wishing I had never left

Alaska. Kessler is the only one of us who is glad we moved. As a fifteen-year-old, he is happy to redefine himself in a new environment. "I feel guilty about liking it here," he confesses one particularly hard night at dinner.

"Don't," we tell him. "You're the one bright spot the rest of us can cling to as we work this out."

The fuel tank in the *Veronika K* developed a leak during the last season we fished, so I'm staring at a large repair bill to start 1998, and will most likely have to leave as soon as school is out for weeks of boat work to fix it. I don't want to leave for two months a year to fish in Alaska. Veronica and I are struggling enough, and my being gone that long won't help keep us together, and leaving her with two teenaged boys would make things even worse. After weeks of soul-searching, we decide to sell the boat and permit. Though it feels right for the family, it feels wrong to me on many levels. After the sale goes through, I realize I have violated all the advice about retirement I've heard at seminars over the past year. "You're retiring," the facilitator would begin. "That's enough stress to introduce into your life. Don't move too. And certainly don't make any other big life-changes on top of that." Yeah. I've moved from a place I loved, I've changed what I do for my winter job, and by selling out of fishing, I've taken away the last bit of self-identity I had. I'm not Alaskan any more. I'm not a teacher. Now I'm not a fisherman. *Who*, I think in my worst moments, *am I?* Most days I try to answer that question by writing about it – unsuccessfully – in my journal.

I occasionally call Frank Mullen, who's moved just up the road to Gig Harbor, to vent about how lost I feel. I never expected to sell out, and for both Veronica and me, the hardest thing to wrap our heads and hearts around is the loss of what we saw as an adventurous life.

Frank hands me a huge gift when he invites me to my first FisherPoets Gathering event in Astoria, Oregon the next winter. Started by a commercial setnetter from Bristol Bay who

262

lives and teaches nearby, the Gathering is a celebration of commercial fishing in poetry, storytelling and song. Frank and I sip beers and join the audience in the Wet Dog Saloon at the end of February, 1999. The stories, the people telling them, the audience, hell, even the rough-edged bar resonate deep within me. I am instantly and completely hooked. *Here*, I think, *is the community I've been missing.* I read one of my pieces at open mic, and the next year I'm invited back as a featured reader. It's the beginning of healing for me, and the start of a new chapter in my life that continues today, almost 23 years later.

I've been back to Alaska several times since moving away, mostly to read fisherpoetry at events in Kenai, Homer and Kodiak. Each time, I take a drive down to the abandoned cannery and walk the grounds, reminiscing. A part of my heart will always be fishing Cook Inlet. Even though I've now lived in Olympia as long as I did in Kenai, I still call Alaska home. I still watch the commercial fishing boats work off the coast of Oregon and Washington. I still stop and look each time I hear a raven.

Mending Holes
~ for Lee

I touched the past
    even as it disappeared before me.
    I placed my hands upon the backs of hours
    loaded heavy with gear,
    and pushed them down an elevated boardwalk
        toward oblivion.

I mended holes in the days
    with a needle and twine;
    swatted mosquitoes like seconds
    as summers sped beneath me.
    I painted coats of the present
    upon planks of history,
    then years later spent months of chainsaws
    cutting them into pieces
    bulldozing them onto the beach
    where I lit the match that burnt them to ashes.
        I even hoisted a beer in their honor.

I've seen compasses lose direction,
    watched a fleet of seasons sink over the horizon;
    seen sail give way to power,
    wood give way to 'glass;
    species disappear under thick coats of oil,
        and lifestyles vanish beneath politicians' dark coats.

I pulled decades of tradition onto shore,
    put them on barrels
    and walked away, leaving them to decay.
    Winter storms weakened them.
    Summer sun bleached them,

and I returned years later
to feel them crumble between my fingers.

What my eyes have forgotten
　　my hands remember:
　　cool, wet cotton gloves,
　　stiff, rough, manila line
　　and the heavy chains of anchors
　　　　covered in generations of mud.

§

I lean into the cool plastic of this buoy:
　　like seconds into hours
　　it gives before resisting,
　　and reminds me
　　that ebbing times,
　　with all the gear,
　　　　work,
　　　　　　and fish,
　　are like a boat on a set in a strong tide:
　　from on board all we see is the set;
　　but from anywhere else,
　　the boat and net grow smaller
　　　　as they drift into the distance.

Chapter Forty-One: A Lot to Hold

I got an email from a good friend in Kenai who said she'd gone down to the old Columbia Wards' Cannery – and the warehouse where I'd spent so much of my time during my fishing career, where my locker was, where I stored supplies and used the little green electric crane to haul shackles of gear up and down to and from the loft; where I'd driven forklifts, where fishermen for decades hung their nets, and where I'd walked hundreds of times with my camera – was no longer there. Gone were the enormous rafters in the egg house, where cannery workers of all nationalities scrawled their names and the years they worked in the plant, some of them as far back as the 1920's when the cannery was rebuilt after the fire. But now those rafters were no more. The entrepreneur who bought the cannery after Wards' Cove shuttered it two years after I left decided it was a bad investment and sold the warehouse for its lumber. Work crews tore down the structure, hauling the pieces away while fishermen who used to dock there tied their boats to buoys downriver, and like all good fishermen paid more attention to the fish, the winds and the tides than to a piece of their history sinking in their wake.

I visit that cannery every time I return to Kenai since moving away in 1998. Far more than Indiana where I spent my childhood, it is where I grew up, and it is a second home to me. Except for the one spring when they remodeled right after the sale – putting in a restaurant and making hotel rooms out of the old fishermen bunkhouses – once it stopped being a cannery it felt like a ghost town. As I walked the yard during those visits, I swear I could hear fishermen long gone still laughing on the boardwalk, forklift backup alarms beeping in the distance as they moved fish totes into the freezer plant from the dock, boats starting up still tied to a float that wasn't there with the throaty roar only a Jimmy can make. Except that the distance between me and those events wasn't measured in knots, miles, feet or fathoms. It was measured in time. I was hearing echoes from a past my footsteps could no longer walk.

I thought about what to write in tribute to this passing, and decided I needed to revisit the following piece. It's about a warehouse that's fortunate to be still standing across the Inlet. Some fishermen (not entrepreneurs) bought it a few years ago. They're trying to keep it alive and working – not as a cannery, but as a lodge. They haven't changed it much, from what I've been told. They're mostly trying to keep it from going further into disrepair. They 'get' what it is that they purchased:

Snug Harbor Cannery
Chisik Island, Alaska

Deck slippers sound muffled on wood. The thick plank floor of the cannery warehouse, worn smooth by decades of footsteps, transmits the noise of my passing with little more than a whisper. I walk back in time. My eyes adjust to dim light filtered yellow by ancient, discolored windows. I pick my way through strewn manila line and coiled electrical cords. The warehouse whispers silently in my head with years of engine repairs and assembly-line canning of salmon. Rusted saws and axes still lean against rough-hewn plank walls and stout support beams. Palette after palette of diesel boat engines wait silently in a row, bound by dust-covered plastic. Nets wrapped in torn and ragged burlap bags sit piled high in dark, forgotten corners like fat men in a steam bath. Nested sheets of faded green corrugated fiberglass roofing lean against a wall beneath broken windows.

Below my feet I can hear small waves of the incoming tide roll the gravel of this remote Alaskan beach. The warehouse sits on pilings above the tide line of Tuxedni Bay on the west side of Cook Inlet, accessible only by boat or float plane. It is my first year as a deckhand, and my skipper has brought us here for groceries, ice for the cooler, and a shower. Wandering off, I have found an unexpected surprise of history in this warehouse.

Under its spell I drift up the stairs to the web loft, where I find wooden floors worn smooth with years of dragging nets and line to racks for mending or hooks for hanging. Outboard motors sit on racks of their own under a ceiling of huge, latticed wooden rafters. The immensity and design of this massive building reminds me of a cathedral. The rafters are old-growth Douglas Fir with deep, rough grooves in their sides and white and yellow words and numbers scrawled on them in chalk. 'Gebenini,' 'Mohr,' 'Humbolt,' 'Showalter,' '63,64,65,' '58, 59, 60.' 'Tanaka, 34.'

Over the years, countless cannery workers, tendermen and fishermen crawled high among these rafters to write their names. After their names they put the dates of the summers they spent here: from as recently as last year to well before I was born. Filipino names, Japanese names, Italian, Norwegian, Native Alaskan. Some with only one date after them, others with repeated, sequential numbers, testifying to summer after summer spent working fish.

The gear locker doors below the beams display more names written in black marker. Names crossed out, one after another, in a legacy of the owners of the lockers' contents, until only one is left uncrossed: 'Hoyt'; 'Johansen'; 'Clark'; 'Hansen'. Behind the mute locker wire wait stores of gear: buoys, line, nets, propellers. I find a piece of chalk on the floor near one locker door and bend down and pick it up. I look up, and for a moment consider writing my name too. But I'm a green deckhand at the start of my first season, and I think I haven't yet earned the privilege. Maybe another year, if I survive. I put the chalk down with a reverence I rarely feel and walk away.

Ten years later, after two seasons fishing as a crew and eight as a skipper, after finally learning ropes I hadn't even realized were there to learn, figuring out how to catch fish, fix boats and survive rough weather, I return, this time looking for chalk.

Dylan in the warehouse loft, Snug Harbor cannery, 1997.

Ten years after that I find myself back again, this time with my eleven-year-old son. Together we climb the old stairs to the loft. I show him my name on a beam near the windows, and the years that are written next to it. There are some more to add today. It is his third season with me, and neither of us know it's to be our last. I ask him if he wants to put his name up there too, next to mine. Together we find half a piece of chalk on a table filled with old mending twine and needles. As I had done alone so many years ago, we climb steep steps up to the planks that lay through the center of the latticed rafters. We lie down and stretch, one at a time, to reach the beams waiting for us, his just above mine. They are above the window that looks out on the bay. Looks out on Snug Harbor. I add my years to the space beyond my name, then hand him the chalk. "Hang on a minute," I say. I go down the stairs, and after he writes his name above mine, I take his photograph.

Once the film is developed, back at home later that month we see the photograph together: the picture is dim and

269

slightly blurred, but he is there forever, more in my mind's eye than on the emulsion, writing his name upon the rafters of our history, of our past, of our lives.

In her note about the Kenai warehouse, my friend said, "I was blown away by the size of the hole that building left behind." That's true in more ways than one. After all, it was a commercial fishing warehouse. It had a lot to hold.

Warehouse, Wards Cove Fisheries (formerly CWF), Kenai, Alaska.

Chalk signatures on the beams, WCF warehouse, 1993.

270

Warehouse, Snug Harbor cannery, Chisik Island, Alaska, 1984.

271

Flash in the Distance

I am from gillnetters: from the *Skookum Too* and *Veronika K.*
I am boats floating a night sea, raindrops on the back of a wave.

I am from salmon slime, flake ice, scales and gurry.

I am hissing stick rips, glassy seas,
wild-horse, white-maned wave stampedes.

I am *waterhaul* and *roundhaul,* radio fish
and sunken nets; clatters, splashers,
nudgers, jerkers, *nothing much*
and *better get over here right away.*

I am from beer on the back deck,
baseball caps, flotation vests and rubber boots.

I am Grundens, XtraTufs, Vickies, and Stormy Seas.

I am where sunrise ignites the sea,
volcanoes vent over the island,
belugas rise to greet stars.

I am needles of rain on my cheeks,
salt spray on the windshield,
the shuddering slam of the hull.

I am a fire in the cabin, a blown fan belt,
oil in the bilge, catching a line from a tender for a tow.

I am a flash in the distance, whitecaps in the rip,
bow slicing an ocean swell, foam in my wake.

Skookum Too, 1980-1987

Veronika K, 1988-1997

Epilogue

I recently had a conversation with my oldest son, Kessler, who is now co-owner of the Red House bar and restaurant in Renton, Washington. He surprised me by saying how he'd really like to visit, maybe even live in Alaska again. I often think about that very thing. I ache for the life we built up there. But then I remember: that life has disappeared like a rapidly ebbing tide.

Most of the fishermen I knew up there are gone: Emery, Cliff and Ray all passed away over the past twenty years. Of the folks I'm still in touch with, Rich left for Prince William Sound. Rob Seitz is fishing shrimp and crab out of Warrenton, Oregon. His wife Tiffani runs a very successful restaurant in Astoria, the South Bay Wild Fish House, which I try to dine at as often as I can. I still see Dean and Don on a regular basis. They both live here in western Washington. We try to connect on someone's birthday or on a camping trip. Michael Burgener and I live two miles away from each other. We get together every few weeks, grab a breakfast croissant and drive to the Port of Olympia, where my youngest son Dylan is the Marina Office Manager, and we eat, laugh and talk as we look out at the water and the Olympic mountains in the distance. Tom Burck and I still exchange the occasional message. He and his wife Liz still live in Alaska, in the same house in Kasilof where we spent several Thanksgivings together. My niece, Sharon moved to Homer, Alaska, and built a wonderful life there. She's co-owner of the Two Sisters bakery and restaurant, and she helped start the Homer Farmers' Market years ago. She's turned into an outstanding person, and we dearly love and enjoy her and all her family.

So many people – so many friends –in the twenty years I fished were instrumental in teaching me and helping me become a fisherman that I can't help but think how fortunate I was. My fishing life was a collaboration, and more than anything, I am far more complete because of the folks who were at my back, alongside, or pulling me through by my bow cleat.

I still follow Cook Inlet fishing each summer. Lately, the news hasn't been good. Over the past few years, the warming waters have forced the sockeye to swim deeper, under the nets of the fleet. But even more disturbing are the politics that now manage the fishery. Because the state wouldn't create a plan for the management of the fishery, last year the National Marine Fisheries Service proposed an amendment to the Fishery Management Plan to prohibit commercial salmon fishing in the federally managed waters that include almost half of the Cook Inlet Central District, effectively killing the Upper Cook Inlet drift fishery. The proposed action would not close any salmon fishing in the waters to the north, as those are managed by the state. The United Cook Inlet Drift Association (the drift fishing union) has gone to court to fight this turn of events, but as of this writing no decision has been reached.

Over the past few decades, the number of Alaskans dipnet harvesting Kenai River sockeye has grown exponentially, and the biologists have shifted their focus to give that 'personal use fishery' preferential treatment. This past year (2021) ADF&G put the drift boats into a five-mile corridor along the east side of the Inlet for the peak of the season (after July 8), severely hindering the fleet's ability to put together a decent season.

The setnetters had it worse. They were shut down entirely before the run developed. The dipnetters were given the bulk of fishing the run, but couldn't harvest all the excess fish. The number of fish escaping into the rivers totaled more than the commercial drift fleet's total harvest. When too many fish get upriver to spawn, they can damage the size of the run four years later. Biology predicts this will happen. Politics doesn't care.

The forecast for the future of the commercial fishing industry in Cook Inlet is grim, as evidenced by the fact that younger fishermen like Thor Evenson's son Taylor, have moved to Bristol Bay, where they can actually still make good money harvesting salmon. The few fishermen sticking it out in the Inlet seem to be doing so because they love being on the water. Plus, there's the occasional clatter in the net that gets the adrenaline rushing. I agree with what John Noble told me after we'd both sold out. He said, "You know what I miss? The action!" The problem is, the action's moved on. We started fishing just as the Inlet hit its peak years, not only for production, but for sheer enjoyment of the fishing life. I think of the old saying, *the darkest hour is just before the dawn.* My twenty years fishing Cook Inlet proved the opposite: it was more like *the golden hour always comes just before sunset.*

I don't want to end on a pessimistic note, though. The future isn't written in stone. Cook Inlet's commercial fishery could survive, just in a different version no one's thought of yet. I hope that's true.

Note to the Reader: If you enjoyed this book, please help it reach others who may also like it. Whether or not you bought this book on Amazon, please go there and leave a review. More reviews on Amazon make this book more visible. And thank YOU for buying it in the first place.

~ Patrick Dixon

GLOSSARY

Cook Inlet

Tides:
A long, narrow and relatively shallow body of water, Cook Inlet has the second-highest tidal exchange from low to high tide in the world. Tides are created by the relative positions of the sun, moon and earth. When they line up properly, Cook Inlet's tidal exchange can exceed thirty feet. The tidal water that moves in Cook Inlet may travel as fast as seven to eight knots.

Rips
Rips are currents that form in a larger body of water. They are created and influenced by tides. The three most common rips that form in Cook Inlet are the east, middle and west rip. They can appear as a line of foam in thewater, be muddy on one side and clear on the other, or be a swath of dancing ripples (hence the name "rip") as wide as afreeway.

During a storm, the tidal action and currents of a rip can contribute to the creation of very rough, steep seas. Rips attract debris floating in the water, such as loose kelp, sticks, and even full-grown trees and logs. Rips also attract salmon. The two sides of a rip can vary in temperature as much as 1.5 degrees F. Salmon often congregate on the warm side.

Salmon

The different species of salmon that swim through Cook Inlet are:

Chinook (King): The largest, averaging 30-50 pounds, King salmon can grow to over 100 pounds. They favor shallow water, and are prized by all fishermen. They are the scarcest of all the species in Cook Inlet, and command the highest price on the commercial market. They return to the river where they were born anywhere between three to seven years of age.

Sockeye (Red): Averaging six to seven pounds, Reds are the most plentiful salmon in Cook Inlet, returning to the two major river systems in the Central District: the Kenai and smaller Kasilof river. The commercial harvest averages roughly 2.5 million per year. Reds fetch the second highest price commercially. They return to the river four years after hatching.

Coho (Silver): Averaging seven to eleven pounds, the Coho salmon harvest in recent years has been managed for an equal balance of sport and commercial fishing, with each user group taking 150,000-200,000 fish. On the commercial market they average around 1/2 to 2/3 the price of sockeye. They return to spawn after one to three years at sea.

Chum (Dog/Keta): Chums are the second largest salmon in Cook Inlet, usually weighing around ten to fifteen pounds. The average harvest over the past ten years has been around 175,000 fish. Pound for pound, Chum salmon get the lowest price on the commercial market, except for Pinks. On average they spend four years at sea, but may spend as many as seven.

Humpback (Pink or Humpy): Pink salmon are the smallest and bring the lowest price of all the species of salmon returning to Cook Inlet, averaging three to five pounds. Their life cycle is two years, all spent at sea.

Salmon Biology

Escapement:
The amount of a particular species of salmon that 'escapes' the fishing fleet and enters the river system where it hatched to spawn and die.

Spawning:
When salmon return to the river, the females dig out a 'redd', or depression in the gravel bottom to lay their eggs. Males fertilize the eggs. Over the next several days or weeks, the adults then weaken and die.

Fishing/Gillnetting Terms

Backlash:
When the net is spooling off the reel as it is set, the web can catch or 'hang up' on a cork or small imperfection in the lines or a snag on the boat and get caught as the reel is turning, tearing a large hole in the net.

Boat Hook:
An approximately
ten-foot-long pole
with a hook at one
end, used to pick
up gear or lines
floating inthe
water.

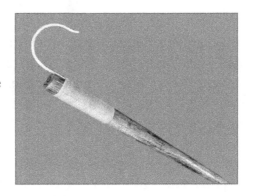

Brailer:
A plastic or canvas bag lowered into a drift gillnet boat's
fish hold into which salmon are tossed by hand. Brailers
hold approximately 100 Cook Inlet sockeye salmon.

Corked/Corked Off:
When a particular fishing boat places its net in such a
manner that it intercepts the fish swimming toward another
nearby boat's net, that boat is said to have corked the other
one off. This is often looked at as picking the pocket of
another fisherman, and is often the source of arguments.

Dip Net:
A six-to-eight-foot pole with a basket of web at one end,
used to catch fish as they fall from the net while coming on
board, or to scoop fish out of the water.

Drift Gillnets:
Designed to hook salmon by the gills when they swim into
the webbing, gillnets are composed of a cork line, which is a
length of rope with Styrofoam, cork or wooden floats
threaded onto it and tied in place with twine; webbing, made
of multiple strands of nylon thread woven into a diamond

pattern with holes large enough to allow a salmon's head to push through, but not the body, catching them by the gills; and a leadline, which consists of a webbing of rope wrapped around a core of lead, which stretches the net downward as it hangs in the water. The corks keep the top of the net visible on the surface.

The web in Cook Inlet is restricted to no more than approximately twenty feet deep and 100 yards long, a far cry from the five-mile-long high seas driftnets that ravage the Pacific by South Korean boats. Cook Inlet nets are easily towed and retrieved. Fishermen will often buy different sized web to target different species of salmon, and will try and match the color of web to the water they intend to fish. The end of a drift gillnet is marked by a bright orange or pink buoy attached to it with a length of line. The buoy is required by law to be marked with the name and registration number of the vessel fishing it.

Shackles:
In the Cook Inlet fishery, a length of web and lines 100 yards long. During the time period described in this book, Alaska regulations limited the number of shackles on a Cook Inlet drift boat to three. Since then, new regulations allow a fourth shackle to be fished with a second fishing permit on board.

Fish Pick
A small tool for peeling web off a fish, made of wood or plastic, with a bent, sharpened nail sticking out of it.

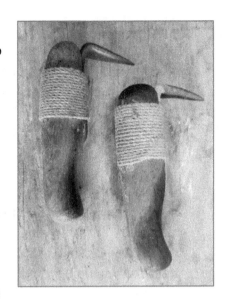

Hydraulics:
A closed system of a pump and oil pushed through valves to power machinery on a boat. On a gillnetter, hydraulics commonly power the reel that holds the net and pulls it aboard.

Oilskins/Rain Gear/Bibs:
Heavy waterproof bib overalls covered by a jacket provide a tough, weather resistant outer covering when working in wet conditions.

Pike Pole:
A pole with a hook and sharp point at one end. Similar in length to a boathook.

Roundhaul:

To wrap fish and net on the reel rather than pick the fish out of the net as they come aboard. This is commonly done to remove the net from the water quickly at the end of a fishing period, or to avoid trouble. Round- hauling damages the fish that are wrapped on the reel, and isn't encouraged unless there's a good reason.

Setnets:

Setnets are similar in size to a drift gillnet shackle and work essentially the same way, except that they are anchored on both ends near shore. Rather than drifting with the tide, setnets are stationary, requiring the fish to swim to them. A setnet permit allows a fisherman to fish three nets (shackles) at a particular location along the shore. Setnets are set and removed from the water with large, stout skiffs powered by outboard motors. Crews of two to four will pull the net by hand across the skiff and pick out the fish. If a net is close enough to shore to reach at low tide, a tractor can drag it onto the beach for picking.

Tender:

A boat that buys and loads fish, transporting them to a fish processing plant where they are bought, cleaned, and processed. Tenders are contracted by canneries to perform several functions: they can take fish from fishing vessels, haul fish to the processing plant, set buoys for the cannery, and deliver goods and equipment to and from destinations. They act as supply, support and rescue vessels for their cannery's fishing fleet, supplying fuel, parts and even groceries to fishing boats, or towing them to port.

Waterhaul:
A gillnet set that catches no fish.

Xtra Tufs:
A popular brand of waterproof boot worn by commercial fishermen.

Halibut Fishing Terms

Ganyons
Pieces of heavy twine a couple of feet long, similar to leaders with a snap on one end and a hook on the other.

Groundline/Longline:
Strong rope used to catch fish on the sea bottom. The line is stretched between two anchors, and baited hooks are attached to it every six feet. The *Inga E* carried ten miles of groundline while fishing halibut.

Halibut:
Halibut are flatfish, symmetrical at birth with one eye on each side of the head. At about six months of age, one eye migrates to the other side of the head. At the same time, the stationary-eyed side of the body darkens to become the top side, while the bottom of the fish remains white. This color scheme camouflages halibut from above and below. Halibut can grow to 500-plus pounds in size.

Power block:
A specialized mechanical winch used to haul nets and lines on commercial fishing boats.

Skate:
A length of groundline stretched between two anchors and baited with hooks to catch halibut. On the *Inga E*, the skates were 1,800 feet long.

Nautical Terms:

Bight:
A bend or a curve in a coastline, river, or other geographical feature. Also, a loop in a rope.

Caulking/Corking:
The cotton or oakum batting hammered into the seam between planks of a wooden boat. Also, the act of sealing the seams with batting.

Cutlass Bearing:
A cutlass bearing, also known as a shaft bearing, is used to control and smooth out the motion of a rotating propeller shaft.

Dory:
A small open boat with a pointed bow and stern.

Fair Leads:
A pair of rollers set vertically on the transom or gunwale of a boat to guide the net on 'fairly'.

Fathom:
A fathom is a unit of length equal to six feet.

Forecastle/Fo'c'sle:
The forward part of a ship below the deck, traditionally used as the crew's living quarters.

Flying Bridge/Bridge:
That area of a boat that is often topmost, where the vessel can be steered and controlled with the greatest visibility.

Galley:
The boat's kitchen, where food is stored and prepared, and where meals are eaten.

Garboard Plank:
The first plank laid next to the keel on a wooden boat.

GPS (Global Positioning System)
GPS is a satellite-based radio navigation system owned by the U.S. government. A low-cost receiver can use the signal from any of several satellites to determine location and time. GPS is currently the most popular navigation system in commercial and pleasure boats.

Gunwale (pronounced gun'nel):
The upper edge of the side of a boat.

Knot:
The knot is a unit of speed equal to one nautical mile per hour, or approximately 1.15 mph.

Loran/Loran-C
A navigation system for sea-going vessels used in the 1970s and 1980s. It was replaced by the much more reliable GPS system in the 1990s.

Picking Well:
The area where fishermen stand to pick fish out of the net, commonly at the stern of the vessel with a lower deck than the hatch covers over the fish hold.

Port:
The left side of a boat as you face forward.

Scuppers:
Holes in the side of a boat just above the decks that allow water to drain out.

Skiff:
Usually, a small, open boat with a pointed bow and square stern. Setnet and seine skiffs are long and wide, powered by strong motors.

Stabilizer 'Fish":
Heavy metal objects with flat 'wings' hung from poles that lower on either side of the vessel to resist roll in a choppy sea.

Starboard:
The right side of a boat as you face forward.

Stuffing Box:
A type of seal wrapped around the propeller shaft of a boat, preventing water from entering the bilge. Consisting of small, oiled rings and batting, the box is tightened just enough to allow a small amount of water to drip, lubricating the shaft.

Transom:
The reinforcement, typically above the waterline, of the stern of a vessel.

Trunk Cabin:
The raised upper portion of the forward fo'c'sle of a boat, projecting above the deck.

Value Added:
Enhancing the quality of a commodity item, i.e., making salmon portions from a full filet, or adding favorite recipes to a memoir.

VALUE ADDED

Favorite recipes for preparing salmon
from some of the characters in *Waiting to Deliver*

Tip: The easiest way to see if your salmon has finished cooking
is to **gently press down on the top of the fillet with a fork or
your finger**. If the flesh flakes—meaning, it separates easily
along the white lines that run across the fillet (strips of fish
fat)—it's finished cooking.

Pat Dixon: Grilled Pesto Salmon
My favorite way to prepare sockeye is to buy a jar of Costco
pesto and smear it on the fileted fish (skin on), then grill it on
the BBQ on medium heat for 5-8 minutes, skin side down. Have
a spray bottle of water handy to douse the flames when the oil
from the pesto flares up.

Michael Burgener: Grilled Salmon
1. Pre-heat <u>grill</u> on high. Clean off grates.
2. Reduce grill heat to medium-high heat.
3. Generously coat your wild salmon (whole sockeye salmon or individual wild sockeye salmon portions) in butter on both sides.
4. Sprinkle wild sockeye salmon with lemon pepper.
5. Start grilling wild Alaskan sockeye salmon *skin side down* for 3-5 minutes. You will see the sides of the fish start to cook.
6. Flip and cook another 3-4 minutes until done. FDA recommends a safe internal cooking temperature of 145° for fish such as wild Alaska sockeye (note: it is always best to check FDA for any updates).
Note: *Do not close the cover while grilling.*

Dylan Dixon: Red Salmon Curry
Prep: 20 minutes
Cook: 20 minutes
Total: 40 minutes

1 - 2 filets fresh salmon depending on size
1 - 4-6oz Red curry paste
2 - 14oz cans unsweetened coconut milk
1 - 16oz bag frozen stir fry vegetables (substitute for fresh vegetables if desired*)
1 - 8oz can bamboo shoot strips (drained)
1 - 8oz can baby corn (drained)
2 tbsp vegetable oil
1 tbsp garlic chili sauce (optional)
1 tbsp garlic powder
1 tsp salt
1 tsp ground black pepper
1 tbsp sugar

Instructions:
1. Rinse salmon filet(s) with cold water. Remove skin and any visible bones. Cut into 1–2-inch cubes. Set aside.
2. In a large pot add vegetable oil on medium heat. Add curry paste and sauté for 2-3 minutes* until it breaks apart, stirring frequently. (Note: The longer it's sautéed the spicier the curry will be.)
3. Add half of the coconut milk to the pot. Stir until incorporated and smooth. Bring up to a boil.
4. Add all vegetables, seasonings, and 1/2 cup of water. Stir well, reduce heat to low, and simmer 5-7 minutes. *
5. Add salmon cubes to curry, mix gently, simmer for 3-5 minutes or until salmon is cooked. Serve over white rice.
Notes:
*If curry is too spicy, add more coconut milk.
*If using fresh vegetables adjust simmering time to 10-15 minutes.

Thor (Nedra) Evenson: Homestead BBQ Salmon
Nedra and Jim both 'crossed the bar' in 2021. In talking to Thor, he recalled Nedra's recipe:

1. Preheat the oven to 350 degrees or so.
2. Mix Sauce ¼ A-1 to ¾ Ketchup.
3. Place a salmon filet on tin foil and slather with sauce.
4. Cover with tin foil and bake for 7-8 min. or until done.

Harold Holten: Bourbon-Basted Salmon
Start with a 1 ½ pound sockeye salmon filet, skin on.

Marinade: combine and mix:
¼ cup brown sugar
3 Tbsp bourbon
1 Tbsp chopped green onion

2 Tbsp soy sauce
2 Tbsp vegetable oil
Pour over the salmon and marinate for 1 hour minimum.

Place salmon on foil-lined baking dish.
Bake at 400 degrees for approximately 20 minutes.
Baste with remaining marinade a few times while baking.

Serve hot or at room temperature.

Veronica Kessler: Honey Mango Salmon
Preheat oven to 400 degrees
Ingredients:
2 wild salmon filets (about 6 oz)
1/2 mango chopped (or use mango salsa)
Olive oil

For the glaze, combine:
2 TB Honey
2 TB Lime Juice
3 TB Orange Juice
Tom Douglas fish spice blend (or mild jerk spice blend)
Pat salmon filets dry with paper towels. Season with fish spice
blend. Rub olive oil on filets to coat.

Heat a heavy oven-safe skillet with 1 1/2 TB of olive oil over
medium heat. Add salmon to the hot pan, skin side up. Cook for
not more than 3 min. Turn filets over, pour the citrus glaze over
fish, add the chopped mango.
Put pan in preheated oven.
Cook for no more than 7 minutes. Fish is done when it can flake
easily. Don't overcook your fish!

Marcia King: Wild Salmon Filet
1. Place on foil on cookie sheet.
2. Mix up some Mayo, Grey Poupon mustard and dill to taste.
3. Drop mixture on to filet, spread with spatula to cover complete filet. Don't be shy! Make it a little thick so you'll have extra to dip your bites in!!
4. Cover with another sheet of foil and roll all 4 edges together to create tent for steaming.
5. Place on outdoor grill (or oven) and cook at 350 or so, and open foil after 7 or 8 minutes to check doneness.

Frank Mullen: Frank's Favorite Salmon Marinade
We lost Frank a few years ago, but his daughter Ashley remembered and shared his favorite marinade. She comments: "Frank would say that his favorite salmon for this would be sockeye, but he also loved King and would go for silvers as well. Definitely would NOT have marinated a humpy or dog. ;)"

Ingredients:
1 cup soy sauce
1/2 cup olive oil
1/8 cup sesame oil
ample crushed garlic
small bit of grated ginger
a few shakes of sesame seeds
optional: honey, orange juice, or maple syrup

Put all into a gallon plastic bag, add your portions of salmon, and marinate in the fridge for up to an hour
Grill on a hot grill, flesh side first.

Dean Pugh: Smoked Salmon with Brine Cure
Brine: 3 quarts water, 1 cup brown sugar, 1 cup white granulated sugar, ½ cup kosher salt.
Dissolve to solution. Chill.

Cut skin-on salmon to desired portion size
Brine in refrigeration for 12 hours
Remove, rinse, pat dry with paper towel.
Air dry on rack for 1 hour.
Smoke at 120 degrees for 8 hours using cherry wood.
Use a water pan to hydrate chamber.
If using a Traeger, set to "Smoke" (don't cover w/blanket).

Don Pugh: Boat Salmon
Filet and skin a sockeye.
Cut into 1" x 3" strips.
Dip salmon strips in Krusteaz pancake batter.
Pan fry in oil until golden brown.
Season with salt, pepper and lemon.

Sharon Roufa: Gravlox

The equipment needed to make gravlox is variable. You will be curing the salmon under refrigeration, which generates a surprising amount of liquid that needs to be drained, preferably not all over your fridge. The first time I saw Pat's deckhand Rob Ernst make it, he had the large filets pressed between spruce boughs and two pieces of plywood, lying on the floor of his arctic entryway as a makeshift refrigerator, draining (mostly) onto a tray. It frankly looked disgusting, but he was extremely proud of his ingenuity.

My Swedish friend Lotta just wrapped hers loosely in plastic wrap and placed it in a baking dish with a plate on top. Very tidy.

I have two containers that nest, and I lay the filets between spruce twigs in one container and place the other container on top with some weights to press extra water out of the fish. Whatever method you choose, make sure you can pour off the extra liquid and flip the fish occasionally while it is curing.

Ingredients:
2 salmon filets, skin on.
1 cup brown sugar
1/2 cup kosher salt
1/2 cup chopped fresh dill or 1/4 cup dried dill

Use a pair of pliers or fancy-ass fish deboner to remove pin bones from both filets. This is optional; you can also pick out the tiny bones later, when you slice and serve.

Coat the flesh side of the filets with the dill. Mix the sugar and salt together and coat both filets on top of the dill. Sandwich the filets together with the skin facing out and place in your chosen container, with a light weight on top, in the refrigerator.

Cure for 36 to 48 hours, turning the fish 2-3 times and pouring off extra liquid.

Before serving, scrape off the excess dill and slice on the diagonal, separating each slice from the skin. Serve with lemon slices, capers, red onion, and a dill garnish.

Rob (Tiffani) Seitz: Baked Salmon with Cream Sauce
Tiff first learned this recipe from Joanne Leech, a wonderful chef and good friend who lives in Chinook, WA. This recipe is often served at the participant dinner of the FisherPoets Gathering in Astoria each February, and is a huge hit.

1. Place a two-pound skin-on salmon filet on a cookie sheet lined with aluminum foil.
2. Rub down both sides of the fish with $\frac{1}{3}$ cup of olive oil.
3. Sprinkle with salt, pepper, fresh garlic and $\frac{1}{4}$ cup capers.
4. Slice & separate 1 small onion into rings & lay on fish along with 8 lemon slices.
5. Cover with tin foil and bake at 400 degrees for 20 minutes for each inch of thickness of the salmon.
6. Remove onion & lemon slices to portion the fish.
7. Serve hot or cold.

Cream sauce:
Combine and mix $\frac{1}{3}$ cup sour cream, $\frac{1}{3}$ cup mayo, 3 finely-chopped green onions, 1 tsp lemon juice, 1 tsp horseradish, 1 tsp fresh dill and $\frac{1}{2}$ tsp freshly chopped garlic.

Layer sauce onto salmon and enjoy!

Patrick Dixon, 1987 photo by Veronica Kessler

Patrick Dixon grew up in Logansport, Indiana. After graduating from Indiana University, he moved to Alaska in 1975. He spent twenty-three years on the Kenai Peninsula, teaching Special Education, Journalism, English, Photography, Yearbook and Drama in the winter. He commercial drift-fished Cook Inlet for salmon each summer.

Patrick is now retired from both teaching and fishing. He devotes most of his time to writing and photography (but mostly writing in recent years).

Patrick's works have been published in *Cirque Literary Journal, Panoplyzine, Raven Chronicles, National Fisherman* magazine, *The Smithsonian* and the anthologies *FISH* 2015 and *WA129*. He is the poetry editor of *National Fisherman*magazine's quarterly, *North Pacific Focus*. He serves on the Board of Directors of the Olympia Poetry Network. Patrick received an Artist Trust Grant for Artists to edit *Anchored in Deep Water: The FisherPoets Anthology* published in 2014. His poetry chapbook *Arc of Visibility* won the 2015 Alabama State Poetry Morris Memorial Award.

Patrick and his wife Veronica live in Olympia, Washington with their 18-year-old tuxedo cat, KitKat, and their seven-year-old Golden Retriever, Chinook. Their son Kessler lives in Seattle with his partner Marina Gonzales, and their dog Roux. Their other son Dylan lives in Olympia with his wife Brandy Geyer, their children AnnaBelle, Ella and Harlan, and a brailer bag of cats and dogs.